The Black Book

A Northern Monastic Estate in 1379 with
Additional Documents, c.1113-1536

Translated and edited by

Richard Britnell, Claire Etty

and Andy King

HEXHAM LOCAL HISTORY SOCIETY

2011

Hexham Local History Society

Hexham, Northumberland

First published 2011

© The authors and Hexham Local History Society, 2011.

All rights reserved

ISBN: 978-0-9565078-3-9

Cover illustration: "De monacho avaro", manuscript illustration, collated by William Bowyer, *Heroica Eulogia,* (1567), San Marino, California, The Huntington Library, ms. HM 160, fol. 136, reproduced by permission

Printed by Lightning Source UK, Milton Keynes, MK11 3LW

CONTENTS

List of tables and illustrations	iv
Foreword	v
Preface	vii
Abbreviations	viii
1. Introduction: The Priory and its Estates in 1379	1
2. The Black Book: Manuscript, Text and Translation	25
3. The Black Book of Hexham	35
4. A Calendar of Additional Documents	149
5. Properties of Hexham Priory Acquired by 1379	239
6. Glossary of English Words in the Black Book	271
7. Gazetteer of the Black Book	275
Maps of Properties Listed in the Black Book	283
Index	286

LIST OF TABLES AND ILLUSTRATIONS

Table 1: Hexham Priory's mills recorded in the Black Book — 16

Figure 1: Location of the Properties of Hexham Priory — 283

Figure 2: West Tynedale detail — 284

Figure 3: East Tynedale detail — 285

Richard Britnell is Emeritus Professor, University of Durham. He edited *Records of the Borough of Crossgate, Durham, 1312-1531*, Surtees Society 212 (2008). Other recent publications include *Britain and Ireland 1050-1530: Economy and Society* (2004), and, with John Mullan, *Land and Family: Trends and Local Variations in the Peasant Land Market on the Winchester Bishopric Estates, 1263-1415* (2010).

Dr. Claire Etty is Senior Assistant Researcher for the Oxford English Dictionary. She is the author of 'Neighbours from Hell? Living with Tynedale and Redesdale, 1489-1547', in *Liberties and Identities in the Medieval British Isles*, ed. M. Prestwich (2007).

Dr. Andy King is Research Fellow in the Department of History at the University of Southampton, and the editor of *Sir Thomas Gray: Scalacronica (1272-1363)*, Surtees Society 209 (2005), and, with Michael Penman, *England and Scotland in the Fourteenth-Century: New Perspectives* (2007).

Dr Etty and Dr King are jointly preparing *England and Scotland, 1286-1603*, to be published by Palgrave Macmillan.

FOREWORD

The translation of the 'Black Book' of Hexham Priory into English for the first time was originally proposed by Jim Hedley, one of our members, as a Millenium project for the Hexham Local History Society. It was later taken forward by David Jennings, our then chairman. Without David's enthusiasm and persistence in finding and briefing a translator, Dr. Andy King, through the good offices of Dr. Margaret Harvey at the University of Durham, our plans would have gone nowhere. David also secured financial support for the project from the Sir James Knott Trust, for which support the Society is very grateful. Andy, assisted by Dr. Claire Etty, undertook the initial Black Book translation. We are aware that he did so amidst various other research programme commitments, but was still able to add translations of a variety of additional documents which throw further light on the development of the Priory's estates. We greatly appreciate the additional dimension this brings to the current work and Andy and Claire's efforts on our behalf.

They provided the foundation for the completion of the work by Emeritus Professor Richard Britnell of the University of Durham. In bringing to bear his great knowledge of the medieval English economy and society and his experience with the difficult source material of the period he has made a major contribution to the finished work. We are particularly grateful to him. The Society of Antiquaries of Newcastle-upon-Tyne kindly gave permission for us to obtain copies of Reverend Hodgson's own manuscript transcriptions from the original Black Book. This enabled Professor Britnell to improve the confidence with which Raine's transcription can now be used in a full English translation for the first time, to the great benefit of readers today and – we believe- long into the future.

The project was seen through to publication in the past three years by our treasurer, Dr. Greg Finch, with technical assistance from Peter Rodger in the latter stages. Our programmes officer, Liz Sobell, found the delightful image of a medieval monk carefully measuring his land, which graces the book's cover, and we are grateful to The Huntington Library for granting permission for us to reproduce it here.

J. B .Jonas
Chairman, Hexham Local History Society
September 2011

PREFACE

The preparation of this volume has been the direct result of the enterprise of Hexham Local History Society in commissioning the work and helping it on its way. It has taken longer than we expected to come to fruition, but the Society has shown exemplary patience. We are particularly grateful to Greg Finch for his help and support at each step of the way. The volume has been greatly improved by the addition of the three maps, which we owe to the skill and generosity of my brother William Britnell.

Although nothing can supersede Raine's edition of the Black Book until the manuscript is rediscovered, we have aimed to produce a necessary companion to his work by annotating the text and identifying the principal places to which it relates. The translation is as reliable as we can make it, so that readers not wanting to engage with Raine's Latin text can nevertheless obtain a satisfactory knowledge and understanding of the Black Book's content and significance. The supplementary documentation we have added, which is partly dependent on sources that Raine gathered together, should make it easier than it has been hitherto to relate the Black Book to the earlier development of the Hexham Priory estate.

Richard Britnell

ABBREVIATIONS

Abstract. (F.) M(adden) and (?J. G.) N(ichols), 'Abstract of a Fragment of a Cartulary of Hexham Abbey, Northumberland', in *Collectanea Topographica et Genealogica*, 6 vols (London, 1840), VI, pp. 38-46.

CChR. *Calendar of Charter Rolls Preserved in the Public Record Office*, 6 vols (London, 1903-27)

CIPM. *Calendar of Inquisitions Post Mortem*, in progress (London, 1904-present)

CPR. *Calendar of Patent Rolls Preserved in the Public Record Office*, in progress (London, 1891-present)

Charters of David I. *The Charters of David I*, ed. G. W. S. Barrow (Woodbridge, 1999)

Chronicon de Lanercost. *Chronicon de Lanercost, MCCI - MCCCXLVI*, ed. J. Stevenson, Bannatyne Club (Edinburgh, 1839)

DNB. *Oxford Dictionary of National Biography*, ed. H. C. G. Matthew and B. Harrison, 60 vols (Oxford, 2005)

EYC. *Early Yorkshire Charters*, ed. W. Farrer and C. T. Clay, 12 vols (Carnforth, 1914-16, vols 1-3; Yorkshire Archaeological Society Record Series, extra series, 1935-65, vols 4-12)

Episcopal Acta Durham 1153-95. *English Episcopal Acta, 24: Durham 1153-1195*, ed. M. G. Snape (Oxford, 2002)

Episcopal Acta 1241-83. English *Episcopal Acta, 29. Durham, 1241-1283*, ed. P. M. Hoskin, (Oxford, 2005)

Feet of Fines, Northumberland and Durham. *Feet of Fines, Northumberland and Durham*, ed. P. Oliver, Newcastle upon Tyne Records Committee (Newcastle-upon-Tyne, 1931)

Gray's Register. *Archbishop Gray's Register: The Register, or Rolls, of Walter Gray, Lord Archbishop of York*, ed. J. Raine, Surtees Society 56 (Durham, 1872)

Handbook of British Chronology. E. B. Fryde, D. E. Greenway, S. Porter and I Roy, *Handbook of British Chronology*

Heads of Religious Houses 940-1216. D. Knowles, C. N. L. Brooke and V. London, *Heads of Religious Houses, England and Wales: 940-1216* (Cambridge, 1972)

Heads of Religious Houses 1216-1377. D. M. Smith and V. London, *Heads of Religious Houses, England and Wales, II: 1216-1377* (Cambridge, 2001)

Hedley. W. P. Hedley, *Northumberland Families*, 2 vols (Newcastle upon Tyne, 1968-70)

HHN. J. Hodgson, *A History of Northumberland in Three Parts*, 7 vols (Newcastle-upon-Tyne, 1820-58)

Knowles and Hadcock. D. Knowles and R. N. Hadcock, *Medieval Religious Houses of England and Wales* (London, 1971)

Lanercost Cartulary. *The Lanercost Cartulary*, ed. J. M. Todd, Surtees Society 203 (Durham, 1997)

Mawer. A. Mawer, *The Place-Names of Northumberland and Durham* (Cambridge, 1920)

Monasticon Anglicanum. *Monasticon Anglicanum*, ed. W. Dugdale and R. Dodsworth, re-edited and augmented by J. Caley, H. Ellis and B. Bandinel, 6 vols in 8 (London, 1817-30)

NCH. Northumberland County History Committee, *A History of Northumberland*, 15 vols (Newcastle-upon-Tyne, 1893-1940)

Northumberland Lay Subsidy Roll. *Northumberland Lay Subsidy Roll of 1296*, ed. C. M. Fraser (Newcastle-upon-Tyne, 1968)

PH. *The Priory of Hexham*, ed. J. Raine, 2 vols, Surtees Society 44 and 46 (Durham, 1864-5)

PQW. *Placita de Quo Warranto*, ed. W. Illingworth, Record Commission (London, 1818)

RRS I. *Regesta Regum Scotorum, I. The Acts of Malcolm IV*, ed. G.W.S. Barrow (Edinburgh, 1960)

RRS II. *Regesta Regum Scotorum, II. The Acts of William I, 1165-1215*, ed. G.W.S. Barrow (Edinburgh, 1971)

Sanders. I. J. Sanders, *English Baronies: a Study of their Origin and Descent, 1086-1327* (Oxford, 1960)

SANT. Manuscript extracts from the Black Book, taken by Revd J. Hodgson c.1841: Northumberland Record Office, Society of Antiquaries of Newcastle-upon-Tyne bequest, SANT/BEQ/18/5/16

Taxatio. *Taxatio Ecclesiastica Angliae et Walliae Auctoritate Nichilai IV Circa A.D. 1291*, Record Commission (London, 1802)

Three Early Assize Rolls. *Three Early Assize Rolls for the County of Northumberland*, ed. W. Page, Surtees Society 88 (Durham, 1891)

Watts. V. Watts, *The Cambridge Dictionary of English Place-Names* (Cambridge, 2004)

1. INTRODUCTION

THE PRIORY AND ITS ESTATES IN 1379

Hexham Abbey, founded in 1113, was a house of Augustinian canons. It was of middling wealth, with an income (net of pensions and chaplains' salaries paid by the priory) of about £251 18s. 2d. a year at the time of its dissolution in 1536.[1] Its local base was the town of Hexham, its largest block of properties being in the town itself and nearby at Bingfield, Anick, Sandhoe, Dotland, and other smaller places in the Liberty of Hexham. The Liberty, otherwise called Hexhamshire, stretched from Bingfield and Cocklaw north of the Roman wall southwards to Whitley and Allendale, with the Liberty of Tynedale bordering it to the west and Devil's Water to the east.[2] The word 'shire' in this context was a particular type of lordly estate sometimes known as a multiple estate because it had a central point — in this case Hexham — and numerous appendages all under the jurisdiction of a single lord. Originally some of these appendages would have been townships, others would have been grain farms, or special units for sheep or cows. The lord of Hexhamshire was not the priory, however, but the archbishop of York, and the priory was obliged to the archbishops for their endowment here.[3] The archbishop had jurisdiction over the Liberty, with the right to exclude the king's officers, but allowed the priory a subordinate role. The Black Book reports that within Hexhamshire the prior and convent had soke and sake and other liberties, namely enforcement of the assize of bread and ale, and their servants bearing the rod to make distraints, summons and attachments, and correction of all trespasses of all their tenants in the prior's court'.[4] This represents in fact a fairly ordinary level of lordly jurisdiction.

---

[1] Document 4. Knowles and Hadcock adopt a figure of £266: Knowles and Hadcock, pp. 140, 160.
[2] There is a useful map in R. A. Lomas, *County of Conflict: Northumberland from Conquest to Civil War* (East Linton, 1996), pp. 84-5.
[3] Documents 1A, 1B, 2, 9-17.
[4] Black Book 5, and see document 3 (item 2).

Only about 29 per cent of the priory's income was from Hexhamshire in 1536, at the time of the abbey's dissolution by Henry VIII. The Black Book shows that by 1379 it had acquired property scattered in over a hundred different towns and townships across the northern counties, of which the manor of Kirkheaton and Coldstrother in Northumberland and the prebend of Salton in North Yorkshire were the most lucrative.[5] In some instances the priory had isolated, individual smallholdings, such as the messuage and four acres at Benwell, or the acre of land and four acres of peat moor at Ouston.[6] Even when the priory owned a whole township, this need not mean very much in terms of land or income. They are said, for example to own the township of Knarsdale, but it seems to be mostly an area of wild pasture, and no tenants are mentioned.[7] The Black Book is nevertheless an informative source about the characteristic rural institutions of the northern counties, and repays close attention to detail.

Townships and their lands

The word *villa,* which occurs frequently in the Latin of the Black Book and the priory charters, was generally rendered 'town' in medieval English, but has been translated as 'township' in the translation of the Black Book and in the calendared documents. It is true that 'a township should no more mean a little town than a fellowship should mean a little fellow'.[8] Nevertheless, it is a useful term for describing medieval communities in the northern countryside, most of which were far too small to be called towns but had institutional characteristics not adequately represented by the words village or hamlet. In particular, townships usually had definite territories, with boundaries that were distinct from parish boundaries because northern parishes usually contained a number of separate townships.[9] Though township boundaries might be more

---

[5] Black Book 41, 74, 75.
[6] Black Book 59, 65.
[7] Black Book 12.
[8] F. W. Maitland, *Township and Borough* (Cambridge, 1898), p. 9.
[9] *Lanercost Cartulary*, ed. Todd, pp. 23-5; B. Dodds, *Peasants and Production in the Medieval North-East: The Evidence from Tithes, 1270-*

indefinite on the edges of extensive moorland than in more densely settled regions, they were important for defining the rights of families farming in each community, as well as for various administrative duties such as the collecting of ecclesiastical tithes or royal taxes. Townships were frequently units of lordship, in which case the words *villa* and *manerium* ('manor') could be used interchangeably.[10]

The residents of northern townships were commonly settled in homes around a green. These homes occur as two main types. The domestic plots of 'husbands' or 'bondmen', the principal customary tenants of each lordship, generally comprised a toft and a croft. The toft was a small plot facing the green, on which a house was built, usually of the type known as a long house, with a timber frame filled with wattle and daub on a low stone foundation wall. Behind the toft was a croft, a larger plot, typically ½ an acre to 1½ acres in size, and enclosed by a bank, a hedge, or a wall. Some peasant households had an additional garden. These enclosed plots around peasant households were used for growing fruit and vegetables, and flax and hemp, and also for keeping animals such as hens, pigs, ducks and bees. The second main type of home was the cottage. Villages often had a number of cottages grouped together, which might or might not have crofts or gardens attached.[11]

Each township required communal pasture for feeding sheep, cows, and plough oxen. The Black Book reports the right of the priory and its tenants to common with a stipulated number of animals throughout Alston Moor.[12] Wherever numbers are defined in this way, it is obvious that the canons did not treat the pasture in question as private property, and had to share their right with others. At Wardoughan their common pasture was limited to 80

1535 (Woodbridge, 2007), p. 166; Lomas, *County of Conflict*, pp. 108-10; Winchester, *Landscape and Society in Medieval Cumbria* (Edinburgh, 1987), pp. 22-3, 27-9.
[10] J. E. A. Jolliffe, 'Northumbrian Institutions', *English Historical Review*, CLXI (1926), p. 5; A. J. L. Winchester, *Landscape and Society*, pp. 27-33.
[11] Lomas, *County of Conflict*, p. 72. For northern settlement plans, see especially B. K. Roberts, *Landscapes, Documents and Maps: Villages in Northern England and Beyond, AD 900-1250* (Oxford, 2008).
[12] Black Book 15.

plough-horses and 80 mares, at Hayden to 30 plough horses and 120 sheep with their lambs, at Walwick to 240 sheep, 16 oxen and 10 cows, at Slaley to 300 sheep, at Steel to a further 300 sheep, at Cowden to 100 oxen and cows, at Colwell to 400 sheep, 30 oxen, 10 cows and a bull, at Little Bavington to 60 sheep, 15 oxen and 2 horses, at Whalton to 360 sheep, and at Kimblesworth to 360 sheep and 8 oxen.[13] In some places, however, there was no such restriction, especially where common pasture was shared by several townships. No limit is stated to the priory's rights on *Craklaw Moor*, or on 'the common pasture lying between Eachwick and Whitchester'.[14] Yet these commons were not Nomansland; even where pasture land was not assigned to a single township, rights over it were vested in one of the great lordships and could be so defined. [15] The priory, for example, had common pasture rights 'through the whole lordship of Featherstonehaugh, and also in the former Lucy lands lying beyond the [township] boundaries of Byres, Ulpham and *Langedene*'.[16]

In addition to common pastures, mostly on uncultivated moorland, each township also had ploughlands in private ownership that were subject to common grazing at certain times of the year when they were not under crops. It was a characteristic of township lands that the holdings of different tenants were interspersed. The arable land attached to a township, and shared by its inhabitants, was organized into 'flats' that varied considerably in size, depending on the landscape.[17] These corresponded to the furlongs of the Midland open-field system.[18] Each flat was in turn subdivided into

---

[13] Black Book 11, 21, 26, 27, 37, 40, 42, 45, 70.
[14] Black Book 51, 54.
[15] Jolliffe, 'Northumbrian Institutions', pp. 12-14; A. J. L. Winchester, *The Harvest of the Hills: Rural Life in Northern England and the Scottish Borders, 1400-1700* (Edinburgh, 2000), pp. 27-33. Winchester, *Landscape and Society*, pp. 81-96.
[16] Black Book 19.
[17] For the use of 'flats' as a generic term, see, for example, Black Book 74 (Little Broughton): 'And they have also various *flattes*', and later, 'There are also various *flattes* '. The word is Latinized as *flatta* in the account of Bingfield: Black Book 4. See, too, *Oxford English Dictionary*, under flat, sb^3 7.
[18] The word furlong in this sense occurs in field names: *Halffurlang* at Bingfield, *the Furlanges* at Temple Thornton, *Halfforlang* at Dalton,

Introduction

long, narrow strips, or selions, known as rigs.[19] Rigs in Northumberland and Durham usually contained less than half an acre of land, though they could be larger.[20] At Bingfield, the canons held 16 rigs 'on the Schellez' containing 11½ acres, and a further 25 rigs there containing 12½ acres, which works out at an average of 0.6 acres per rig.[21] The rig was the basic unit of land ownership, and an individual holding would be made up of a number of separate rigs scattered across the township's different flats. These arrangements ensured that holdings had a mixture of different soils and drainage conditions, and so helped to spread the risks associated with an uncertain climate. A number of tenants were likely to own rigs in the same flat. This is implied by numerous pieces of township land said to be in various places on particular flats, or in the middle of them.[22] Individual husbandlands are rarely described in detail in the Black Book, though their dispersed character is evident from the recorded details of two husbandlands at Slaley,[23] two husbandlands at Gunnerton,[24] a single husbandland at Stannington,[25] and five bovates of husbandland at Flaxton.[26] Four husbandlands were probably dispersed amongst others at Silksworth, though the relevant text is unfortunately confused.[27] At Chollerton Hugh Colstane's tenure comprised an unspecified number of dispersed husbandlands, and Alan Hoghird's virtually identical holding there was probably husbandland as well.[28] In no instance are the various flats and other parcels of arable said to be

---

Blafurlang, Halffurlang,, Blalangfurlang and *Crosfurlang* at Heugh, *Mildilfurlange* at Great Stainton, and *Wesebek furlang* at Kirkby in Cleveland (Black Book 4, 44, 55, 56, 71, 77).

[19] 'And there are there 16 selions (*selliones*), called *rigges* in English': Black Book 4.

[20] R. A. Butlin, 'Field Systems of Northumberland and Durham', in A. R. H. Baker and R. A. Butlin, eds, *Studies of Field System in the British Isles* (Cambridge, 1973), pp. 131-2.

[21] Black Book 4.

[22] E.g. at Great Broughton: Black Book 75.

[23] Black Book 27.

[24] Black Book 34.

[25] Black Book 47.

[26] Black Book 84.

[27] Black Book 73.

[28] Black Book 32.

divided between two, three or four fields, as in the classic midland system.[29]

Many of the priory's demesne lands - lands not subject to the customary rights of tenants - were similarly dispersed amongst the township lands. At Little Broughton the demesne lands included various flats 'lying between husbandlands'.[30] The Black Book's detailed descriptions of such lands show that the canons of Hexham often had control of whole flats. At Sandhoe, they held the *Cotesflatte*, containing 4 acres, a flat called *Baxstansyde*, containing 30 acres, and one called *Hormescheles*, containing 8 acres.[31] Some such lands, even though apparently lying in or by the township field, were free of common pasture rights during the open season, as at Little Broughton.[32] Elsewhere, however, priory lands in the town field might be just as fragmented as those of any tenants, as at Temple Thornton, Eachwick, Heugh, Great Stainton, Great Broughton or Kirkby in Cleveland.[33] At Stannington the priory's land is described as a husbandland in the township field, its lands lying adjacent to those of another husbandland called Raysland; it had perhaps been a customary tenure before it was given to the priory in the twelfth century, though it is possible that in this case the word husbandland was being used as a measure equivalent to two bovates.[34] It may reasonably be assumed, in the absence of any counter indication, that such lands were subject to common rights. In its account of Cheeseburn the Black Book distinguishes between the lands of the Grange which were not subject to common rights and other lands in the township field that were.[35]

Each township also had a smaller area of meadow land, typically lying beside a stream or river, that was similarly parcelled

---

[29] H. L. Gray, *English Field Systems* (Cambridge, Mass., 1915), pp. 215-18. Gray did not appreciate that the Black Book dates from 1379, not 1479.
[30] Black Book 74.
[31] Black Book 3.
[32] Black Book 74. There is no indication, in these instances, that the lands in question were part of a separated demesne area of the township.
[33] Black Book 44, 54, 56, 71, 75, 77.
[34] Black Book 47; document 3 (item 52).
[35] Black Book 60.

Introduction 7

out amongst the different holdings. This was grass reserved to make hay for feeding to oxen during the winter months. In the Black Book arable and meadow are often taken together, so that there is no independent statement of its area. There was an exceptionally large supply of meadow on the demesne at Anick, assessed as 50 acres in nine or ten different blocks, and lesser but still large resources of 23¼ acres in four blocks at Matfen, 20½ acres at Salton, 16¾ acres in six blocks at Bingfield, 14 acres in at least six blocks at Dalton, and 13 acres ' dispersed among the meadows of that township around the *karre*' at West Herrington.[36] The frequent references to meadow as a normal component of both demesne and peasant holdings confirm the importance of livestock husbandry in the economy of the priory estate.

Tenants

There were four principal categories of tenant recorded in the Black Book: hereditary freeholders, lessees, 'husbands' (or bondmen) and cottagers. The first two categories, which are not always easily distinguishable, occupied properties of very different sizes, but the holdings of the latter two classifications were more predictable.

The category of freeholders is most clearly represented by the tenants of feudal tenures. All the priory's property at Whitlow was in the hands of William of Whitlow 'by homage and fealty'. Whitfield was similarly held by Mathew Whitfield, Stocksfield by William Ayrike and Stelden by John of Middleton.[37] Other freeholders occur as occupying a portion of one of the priory's properties, as at Slaley, where John Forister of Corbridge held a property called Dalton Place by fealty.[38] At Kirkheaton with Coldstrother, John of Stirling, knight, Thomas of Horsley, John Kemp, John of *Marlaye*, Thomas of *Beckeburne*, John of Dalton and Thomas of Ilderton, knight, all held lands 'by homage and

---

[36] Black Book 2, 4, 55, 57, 78.
[37] Black Book 13, 14, 28, 38.
[38] Black Book 27.

fealty'.[39] The obligations of such tenants varied greatly. They were fixed by old agreements or tradition, and were often very slight, as it seems in the case of those at Kirkheaton and Coldstrother, though they owed suit to the prior's court there.

The obligations of lessees, by contrast, were subject to renegotiation every time a lease fell in. These were lands that the priory could if it wished, cultivate directly for its own profit, as at the *Merehak* in Hexham itself,[40] though by 1379 it was becoming more usual for landlords like the priory to pass the risks on to lessees who would pay an annual rent. The Black Book is not systematic in recording such tenures, and even where it records leases it more often than not omits to note the length of the term. Nevertheless, there are a number of explicit instances. Bingfield Grange, for example, was leased for twelve years by a consortium of three tenants, and Thomas Henreson held Grottington for three years.[41] The Black Book sometimes signals leases by a marginal annotation *dimissio*, as at Healeyfield, which Sir John of Stirling and his wife leased for the life of whichever of the two survived longest.[42] However, this usage of *dimissio* (and the verb *dimittere*) is not to be depended on since at Colwell a hereditary tenure is recorded as a *dimissio*.[43] At Eachwick the demesne meadows were 'demised' to tenants at the lord's will.[44] In most cases of 'demise' the terms of tenure are unstated, and it can only be a matter of supposition that they were formally leased.

The holding of a husband or bondsman was recorded in the Black Book as a *terra husband*, which translates naturally as 'husbandland', or as a *bondagium*, here translated as 'bondland'. The latter terminology occurs on the Yorkshire estates. In either case, a husbandland or bondland traditionally comprised two bovates in northern England.[45] Husbandlands under cultivation by

---

[39] Black Book 41.
[40] Black Book 1.
[41] Black Book 4.
[42] Black Book 67.
[43] Black Book 40.
[44] Black Book 54.
[45] G. Lapsley, 'Boldon Book', in *Victoria History of the County of Durham*, I (London, 1905), pp. 295-6; T. Lomas, 'South-East Durham:

hereditary tenants occur at Anick, Sandhoe, Bingfield, Dotland, Yarridge, Rowley, and Dalton in Hexhamshire, at Slaley, Kirkheaton, Stannington, Eachwick, Dalton, and Nesbit in Northumberland, at Priorsdale by Alston in Cumbria, at Silksworth in Durham, and at Little Broughton in Yorkshire. These tenures were for the most part, at least notionally, of standard size in each community.[46] At Anick, for example there were 12 husbandlands each containing 16 acres of arable land and pasture, at Sandhoe 13 husbandlands each containing 24 acres, and at Bingfield 12 husbandlands again each containing 24 acres, which was the commonest size for such holdings in Northumberland. The smallest husbandlands on the estate were of 15 acres at Dotland, and the largest were of 34 acres at Coldstrother and Eachwick.[47] The duties owed from bondlands recorded on the Yorkshire properties were assessed on bovate (or oxgang) units, which also varied in size from place to place; they were mostly of 8 acres at Little Broughton, of 9 acres at Salton and Brawby, and of 15 acres at Flaxton.[48] Eight bovates made up a carucate (or ploughland), which also varied in size from place to place but was sometimes used as a measure for larger properties.[49] It is impossible now, and probably always was, to give any systematic explanation for variations in the size of bovates and carucates, or to analyse what their implications were. The acres in which their area is sometimes stated were customary units that also differed from place to place. It may be, too, that land was more valuable in some places than others, and that the size of husbandlands was modified accordingly. Alternatively, customary units may have been larger in some townships than in others

---

Late Fourteenth and Fifteenth Centuries', in P. D. A. Harvey, ed., *The Peasant Land Market in Medieval* England' (Oxford, 1984), p. 270; Winchester, *Landscape and* Society, p. 65. Cf. 'They also hold ... two bovates, called 1 *husbandland*': Black Book 17.

[46] For husbandlands and bondlands in northern England, see too R. A. Lomas, *North-East England in the Middle Ages* (Edinburgh, 1992), pp. 172-5; Lomas, 'South-East Durham', pp. 270-1.

[47] Black Book 2, 3, 4, 5, 41, 54; R. A. Lomas, 'Medieval Bingfield', *Hexham Historian*, 6 (1996), p. 9.

[48] Black Book 78, 79, 84.

[49] In the Black Book at Slaley, Newton in Coquetdale, and Whalton: Black Book 27, 43, 45, and see documents 2 (item 3), 3 (items 13, 21, 26, 36, 38, 40, 51, 58), 5, 19, 38, 41, 49, 62-3, 65, 71 (item 2).

because their size was defined at a time when land was less valuable. This may account for the presence, in some instances, of more than one standard in the same township. At Eachwick there were seven bondlands of 24 acres and five husbandlands of 34 acres, the latter having been acquired by the priory independently of the former, and at Dalton 8 husbandlands had 16 acres and another 11 had 23 acres.[50] The fact that such units were kept unchanged from generation to generation nevertheless implies that the land market had long been controlled by custom. Customary holdings could be sold or otherwise exchanged only through the prior's courts, and by implication custom remained powerful enough to prevent their being split up or amalgamated. We have here evidence of a powerful obstacle to the development of a land market on the priory estate, though there may have been short-term sub-letting of which there is no record.[51]

Although husbandlands were subject to customary control in this way, the 'husbands' or 'bonds' who held them were freer than the villeins of England further south.[52] The Black Book tells us that they owed labour services, though quite light ones, as generally in Northumbria.[53] There is no reference to the week work on the lord's demesne lands that characterized villein tenure in southern and midland counties.[54] The twelve husbands of Anick, for example, had to work one day a year at the mill pond, when necessary, accompanied by a mate; they had to maintain something called the *hegeyard*; they each had to carry millstones to Anick Mill and help

---

[50] Black Book 54, 55.
[51] C. Dyer, *Standards of Living in the Later Middle Ages* (Cambridge, 1989), pp. 120-2; I. Kershaw, *Bolton Priory: The Economy of a Northern Monastery, 1286-1325* (Oxford, 1973), pp. 47-9; Lomas, 'South-East Durham', pp. 293-4; Lomas, 'Medieval Bingfield', p. 11.
[52] P. L. Larson, *Conflict and Compromise in the Late Medieval Countryside: Lords and Peasants in Durham, 1349-1400* (New York, 2006), pp. 62-3; Lomas, *North-East England*, p. 174-5.
[53] Joliffe, 'Northumbrian Institutions', pp. 4-8.
[54] R. H. Hilton, *A Medieval Society: The West Midlands at the End of the Thiirteenh Century*, 2nd edition (Cambridge, 1983), pp. 131-40; E. Miller and J. Hatcher, *Medieval England: Rural Society and Economic Change, 1086-1348* (London, 1978), pp. 121-8; P. Vinogradoff, *Villainage in England: Essays in English Mediaeval History* (Oxford, 1892), pp. 167-9, 278-88.

Introduction

with the upkeep of the mill walls and roof at their own expense; they each owed a day's ploughing every year at Anick Grange, and had to give the priory a cock and a hen at Christmas.[55] The bondmen at Salton had to carry foodstuffs 'everywhere within Yorkshire', carry constructional timber and stone for Salton manorial buildings and the mill, maintain the mill, the mill pond and the mill race, clean a ditch around *Frensholme*, and mill their grain at the lord's mill. They also took responsibility for electing suitable manorial officials.[56] These services were clearly not enough to supply the work that was needed year in and year out on the priory's own lands. Those who leased them had to employ wage-earners to do their ploughing, sowing, weeding, harvesting, carting, threshing, and all the other seasonal tasks that made up the agricultural year.

The medieval husband with his 15 to 34 acres can be considered a subsistence peasant farmer, probably able to maintain his family from his land. However, one of the striking features of medieval rural society, often commented upon by rural historians, is the large number of people below this level of wealth, who must have depended on something other than their own land for subsistence.[57] In the Black Book these families are best represented by the cottagers who occur on quite a number of the priory properties, often alongside husbands, suggesting that village communities had two easily identifiable status groups, the husbands and the cottagers. It seems likely that the latter were often employed as farm labourers either on the priory's own lands or on the lands of their tenants. Cottagers often had smallholdings. At Anick the 12 husbandlands were complemented by 19 cottages, whose occupants mostly had small acreages of land ranging between half an acre and, in one instance, 9 acres. Cottagers in Northumberland often had six acres, as at Bingfield.[58] In some places there are correspondences between the number of husbandlands and the number of cottages that suggest deliberate planning. At Sandhoe 13 husbandlands were matched by 12

---

[55] Black Book 2.
[56] Black Book 78.
[57] R. H. Britnell, *Britain and Ireland, 1050-1530: Economy and Society* (Oxford, 2004), pp. 172-7; Lomas, *County of Conflict*, p. 77.
[58] Lomas, 'Medieval Bingfield', p. 9.

cottages, at Bingfield 12 husbandlands by 12 cottages, at Dotland 10 husbandlands by 10 cottages.[59] These are likely to be the people who did most of the paid farm work in these villages, though some of them may have had other occupations in manufacturing and services. Some of the cottagers at Anick had surnames that indicate what they or their forbears did for a living - there was William Smyth, John Couper, William Oxhyrd, Alice Stobhyrd, Thomas Milnar, and Thomas Schiphird.[60]

The comparative freedom of the majority of priory tenants, both husbandmen and cottagers, distinguished them from a minority who were more strictly bound to their lands and the priory as hereditary neifs. In theory, at least, neifs held their lands at the will of their lord, although in practice, they were usually allowed to inherit lands, on payment of a fine. Most significantly, the status of neif was not attached to the holding of particular lands, but was hereditary. By the 1370s there were very few men left on the priory's estates who were still classed as such.[61] The Black Book refers to only 13 neifs, all in Northumberland: three in Anick, four in Sandhoe, one Bingfield, two in Dotland, two in Kirkheaton, and one in Eachwick. Some of these neifs were clearly related, as in the case of John, William and Robert of Matfen, in Sandhoe, and Marmaduke and William son of Henry in Dotland.[62] Their economic status varied considerably.[63] Some had little on which to subsist, such as William Oxherd and John Roger of Anick, who held cottage plots, or John Alanson of the same township, who held no more than an acre of meadow. On the other hand, another neif, John Sire, held four of the twelve husbandlands at Eachwick, amounting in all to 116 acres of arable and meadow, as well as two cottages, and was perhaps the wealthiest of the priory's tenants there.[64] Most of the other neifs listed in the Black Book held at least 2 husbandlands. Though none are recorded among the tenants on

---

[59] Black Book 2, 3, 4, 5.
[60] Black Book 2.
[61] Lomas, *County of Conflict*, p. 82; idem, *North-East England*, pp. 178-9.
[62] Black Book 2, 3, 4, 5, 41, 54.
[63] J. A. Tuck, ' Tenant Farming and Tenant Farmers: The Northern Borders', in E. Miller, ed., *The Agrarian History of England and Wales, III: 1348-1500* (Cambridge, 1991), p. 591.
[64] Black Book 54.

the Durham, Cumberland and Yorkshire lands of the priory, this does not mean that the status of neif was unknown in those parts of the country. There were still some on the estates of Durham Priory in the fourteenth century and later.[65]

At the other extreme of legal freedom, though not necessarily of economic status, were the inhabitants of the small market towns of the region, whose terms of tenure were designed to be compatible with a life of trade and industry. The Priory had urban rents in Priestpopple and Pudding Row, now Pudding Mews. In Priestpopple they list at least 23 tenants with very little explanation. The list seems to concern houses or cottages with their owners, some of whom had more than one - Thomas Monk occurs three times and Archibald Diksun twice, and there are two John Whyts as well as John Whyt's widow. There was evidently some accumulation of properties here - perhaps for subletting or for accommodating family members.[66] The priory tenements in Priestpopple in Hexham, and Pudding Row are not described as burgages, though they were evidently urban in character. Elsewhere the canons had eleven tenements described as burgages in Corbridge, two in Newbiggin by the Sea, and another seven in Newcastle, though they had lost track of some of them.[67] These more urban holdings, designed for artisans and tradesmen, constituted a very small part of the priory's total assets, but they serve as a reminder that there was active town life in the North as well as the rural economy that is better represented in the Black Book.

Compact holdings and several pastures

The priory's demesne lands, that were free of hereditary tenant rights, and which they could cultivate for their own purposes, came in different forms according to their origin. In some cases, as

---

[65] Larson, *Conflict and Compromise*, pp. 64-6, 103-4, 147; idem, 'Local Law Courts in Late Medieval Durham', ed. C. D. Liddy and R. H. Britnell (Woodbridge, 2005), pp. 105-6; Lomas, *North-East England*, pp. 178-9.
[66] Black Book 1.
[67] Black Book 30, 46, 66.

we have seen, they were scattered in amongst the lands of their tenants over a wide area. Elsewhere, however, their properties were compact blocks of territory. Such holdings were created outside the core fields of townships. Especially during the twelfth and thirteenth centuries, when population was expanding and trade increasing, landlords who had secured rights over the waste were likely to expand their own agricultural activities, or to exercise patronage on behalf of others, by taking in new land from the moors and creating new farms on previously uncultivated land. Rural Northumberland in the Middle Ages, as today, was one of the less densely populated parts of England, and large parts of the region outside the river valleys were without villages of any size, and without large areas of cultivated crops. These more empty landscapes were the sort of country where all over England, but especially in the North, landlords were creating new farms to the advantage of favoured laymen and houses of religion,[68] and we can pick up this tendency in the Black Book in the large number of named properties in which the Abbey had a block of land, detached from the fields of the township in which they were situated, with no community of tenants. The larger of these new farms were often called granges as, on Hexham Priory estate at Bingfield Grange, Milbourne Grange, Cheeseburn Grange, Stelling Grange and Farringdon Grange near Silksworth in County Durham.[69] Anick Grange is not described by reference to fixed boundaries, and was apparently less compact than the others, but even so the Black Book describes one enclosed parcel of demesne containing 40 acres.[70] Some compact holdings were enclosed as parks, as at Dotland, Isell,

---

[68] *Lanercost Cartulary*, ed. Todd, pp. 20-1; H. M. Dunsford and S. J. Harris, 'Colonization of the Wasteland in County Durham, 1100-1400', *Economic History Review*, 56 (2003), pp. 43-8; R. A. Lomas, 'Crookbank, Beckley and Andrew's House and the de Laley Family', *Durham Archaeological Journal*, 13 (1997), pp. 99-102; idem, 'The Durham Landscape and the Battle of Neville's Cross', in D. Rollason and M. Prestwich, eds, *The Battle of Neville's Cross, 1346* (Stamford, 1998), pp. 66-77; idem, *North-East England*, pp. 155-8; R. H. Britnell, 'Fields, Farms and Sun-Division in a Moorland Region, 1100-1400', *Agricultural History Review*, 52 (2004), pp. 33-7.

[69] Black Book 4, 51, 60, 62, 73. Stelling Grange is not so called in the Black Book, but see *Northumberland Lay Subsidy Roll*, no. 92, p. 34.

[70] Black Book 2.

Introduction

Fethreschaue in Sewing Shields park, Byers, and Warden.[71] Not all such moorland farms were granges or parks. The Black Book describes a compact farm hard up against the Roman Wall at Carraw, north of Haydon Bridge. Other examples are at Wardrew in the township of Thirlwall, Byers in the township of Hartleyburn, *Langdene* 'by Ulpham', Owmers and Little Owmers in the township of Allerwash, Beaumont in the township of Chollerton, the *Fenhall* in Greencroft, and *Maydenstanhall* in the township of Lanchester.[72] At Newton in Coquetdale they had a compact ploughland outside the township lands of *Northnewton* and Burradon.[73] In reciting the boundaries of these granges, parks and farms, the Black Book evokes features of the countryside sometimes identifiable at the present day.

Another category of property that implies the private exploitation of tracts of moorland by landlords is that of 'several' pasture, meaning pasture not subject to common rights. They had all the pasture in Knarsdale within defined bounds between the lordship of Gilsland, Maiden Way and Glendue Burn. Most of this land, reaching up to the watershed above Glendue Fell, must have been rough moorland. The Black Book's account of Priorsdale evokes the landscape of the medieval moors like few other records can. It describes a region of several square miles south of Alston and Nenthead on both sides of the South Tyne that was subsequently heavily worked over for lead. Enough of the place names survive - Ash Gill, Burnhope Head, Crook Burn, Crossgill Head, Noonstones Hill and the rivers Tyne and Tees, to be able to plot its dimensions quite closely, and it is unambiguously an area of moorland pasture, rising at Burnhope Head to 2,448 feet above sea level. The line of the watershed described between the head of Ash Gill and Burnhope Head is the county boundary between Cumbria and Durham. This is the most impressive of the priory's wildernesses.

---

[71] Black Book 5, 6, 18, 25.
[72] Black Book 8, 9, 18, 19, 23, 24, 31, 68, 73.
[73] Black Book 43.

Table 1. Hexham Priory's mills recorded in the Black Book

place	rent
Northumberland	
Allerwash	10s.
Anick	£3 13s. 4d.
Bingfield	10s.
Carraw	waste
Dalton	£2 16s. 8d.
Hexham	?
Nafferton	waste
Newbiggin	waste
Whitley	£4 13s. 4d. (paid to the cellarer)
Cumberland	
Plumbland (¼ part)	15s.
Durham	
Silksworth (wind mill)	£1 6s. 8d.
Yorkshire	
Little Broughton	13s. 4d.
Salton	£4 6s. 8d.

Source: Black Book 1, 2, 4, 5, 6, 22, 55, 62, 74, 78.
Note. Other than Silksworth all were watermills.

Mills and suit of mill

The suit of mill included in the obligations of the bondmen of Salton conforms to customary expectations across the estate wherever the priory had a mill, which means particularly in Hexhamshire. One of the first things the Black Book tells us is that tenants in Hexham ground their grain at the priory's mill.[74] A similar obligation of Anick husbands to grind their grain at the priory mill in Anick is implied by the work they had to do to maintain it. At Bingfield the Black Book is explicit that the husbands should their grains at the lord's mill, and at Dotland they

---

[74] Black Book 1.

Introduction

owed suit to Whitley Mill.[75] This right of medieval lords to a monopoly of milling was carefully safeguarded, especially in northern England.[76] It was not necessarily restricted to a lord's own tenants. At Allerwash the priory had nothing but the mill and the mill lands, so no tenants of their own, but the mill had suit of all grain grown in Allerwash and *Allerwasseschelez*.[77] In other contexts - at Thirlwall, Alston, Barrasford, Birtley, Eachwick - the priory's tenants owed suit to the mills of other lords, usually on favourable terms.[78] The Black Book record eight working water mills across the priory estates, together with a quarter share of a mill at Plumbland, near Cockermouth in Cumberland, and a windmill at Silksworth in Durham (Table 1). Three other mills were not in use, for various reasons, and the wording of the Black Book suggests there must once have been another mill, now out of commission, at Brawby.[79] The income of these mills was earned by exacting from each tenant a proportion of the grain ground there as mill toll. The proportion varied from mill to mill - a twentieth for priory tenants at Hexham, a thirteenth for tenants of Allerwash and *Allerwasseschelez*.[80] The rate of toll might vary between different categories of suitor; at Dalton Mill the lessees of the priory demesnes at Cheesburn owed a twentieth, but the customary tenants and cottagers of Nesbit owed a thirteenth.[81] This same social distinction is represented in even more elaborate differentials at Silksworth Mill, where the principal demesne lessees paid a twentieth, while the husbands owed a thirteenth for grain grown on their customary holdings but only a sixteenth for grain grown on land held from the demesne.[82]

---

[75] Black Book 4, 5.
[76] J. Langdon, *Mills in the Medieval Economy: England 1300-1540* (Oxford, 2004), pp. 32-3.
[77] Black Book 22.
[78] Black Book 9, 15, 33, 35, 53, 54.
[79] Black Book 79. Note, too, the reference to a mill close there.
[80] Black Book 1, 22, 73.
[81] Black Book 60, 61.
[82] Black Book 73.

Churches

There were various rights that individuals or institutions might have over churches and chapels in medieval England. They might have the patronal right of advowson, an 'incorporeal' right entitling them to present a priest when a benefice was vacant, though canon law required all nominees to be examined for suitability by the diocesan bishop.[83] Additionally they might have a more obviously financial interest through ownership of a rectory, entitling them to income from tithes and glebe lands, as well as various dues and offerings, though with the obligation to maintain a priest.[84] Long before the fourteenth century, the Church had become intolerant of arrangements allowing the nomination of priests and the ownership of rectories by laymen. In accordance with this pressure, from the eleventh century it was common for laymen to surrender their advowsons and rectories as pious gifts to monasteries.[85] In this way the priory acquired the advowsons of Alston and Stamfordham from lay lords in the earlier thirteenth century.[86] For similar reasons laymen were often inclined to donate their financial interests in rectories as suitable endowments for favoured monasteries. A religious house could in this way become the corporate rector of the parish, entitled to administer all its income. Such a parish would normally be served by a vicar, who would be paid a proportion of the living.[87] Appropriation required the consent of the diocesan bishop, and after 1279, was further restricted by the Statute of Mortmain, requiring royal licence in addition. Securing consent could be a protracted process if there were conflicting interests, as amply illustrated by the case of Stamfordham. This case also illustrates the fact that a monastery

---

[83] F. Pollock and F. W. Maitland, *The History of English Law before the Time of Edward I*, 2nd edition, 1898), vols (Cambridge), II, pp. 136-9; R. N. Swanson, *Church and Society in Late Medieval England* (Oxford, 1989), p. 68.

[84] Swanson, *Church and Society*, pp. 206-7, 210-17.

[85] D. Knowles, *The Monastic Order in England* (Cambridge, 1950), pp. 596-600.

[86] *HHN*, IV [part 2, vol . 3], p. 41; documents 2 (item 3), 3 (item 58), 47.

[87] In 1379, for instance, the parochial chaplain of St John Lee received a stipend of a 13s. 4d. per year: Black Book 3.

might be endowed with the rectorial dues of dependent townships without having possession of the principal church.[88]

Hexham Priory's income from churches is only incidentally recorded in the Black Book, but its importance for their total revenue requires recognition. Figures are lacking for calculating its importance in 1379, but at the time of the Dissolution, if we are to trust the valuation calendared as document 4, spiritual income for tithes and other offerings, after the deduction of chaplains' salaries, pensions and other ecclesiastical dues, amounted about half the priory's net income, £124 17s. 0½d. out of £251 18s. 2d. Some of this income had been acquire relatively shortly before 1379. The priory received a boost to its ecclesiastical endowment in 1378, when granted the advowsons of Ilkley and Ovingham by Henry Percy, in both cases (to judge from the survey of 1536) with an income to support the incumbent.[89] In 1378, too, Alston church was finally appropriated to the priory.[90] These three churches between them contributed £40 15s. 7½d. to the priory's net income in 1536, which suggests that the income from churches was a somewhat lower proportion of the priory's income before 1378 than it afterwards became.

The importance of these 'spiritualities' to the priory's income is not apparent from the Black Book, which is a register of land and tenancies, the 'temporalities'. Glebe lands are mentioned at St John Lee, the church of St Oswald at Heavenfield (near the site of a battle in which the saint triumphed over the king of Gwynedd and his army in 634), at Alwinton and at Isel, but their total contribution to the priory's estate was predictably meagre.[91] The importance of tithe income appears, only when one starts to look for it, in the otherwise inconspicuous tithe barns that occur on so many of the priory's properties, at Bingfield, Acomb, Wall, Keepwick, Hallington, Rowley, Catton and Ninebanks (all in Hexhamshire) and at Haydon, Chollerton, Barrasford, Gunnerton, Chipchase, Little Swinburn and Colwell.[92] These alone, on the

---

[88] Documents 47, 48.
[89] Document 55; document 4A, 4B.
[90] Document 56.
[91] Black Book 3, 5, 6.
[92] Black Book 4, 5, 21, 32, 33, 34, 36, 39, 40.

pages of the Black Book, apart from an exceptional mention of the lease of tithes at Isel,[93] represent the benefits the canons derived from several discrete gifts of tithes, notably of all the those arising within the liberty of Hexham given by Archbishop Thomas II of York (1109-14), the grant of Chollerton church with its dependent chapels of Birtley, Chipchase, Gunnerton, Little Swinburn, Kirkheaton and Colwell given, sometime before 1182, by by Odinel I or Odinel II, barons of Prudhoe, and the grant of Warden church with its chapels at Stonecroft, Haydon and Langley given, sometime before 1232, by Adam de Tindale I or Adam de Tindale II, barons of Langley.[94] The resulting tithe revenues figure more prominently in the survey of 1536, which is the chief justification for including it (anachronistically) in the collection of documents from before 1379.

Beyond the Black Book

Although there is no earlier survey of the Hexham Priory estate to compare with that of 1379, the documents summarised in the Calendar of Additional Documents that follows the translation contain a good deal of information about the past history of the individual properties. In many cases it can be surmised with some confidence that the Black Book describes features that were a century or two older. The charters carry back evidence of many of the northern institutions we have discussed - townships, commons, husbandlands, bovates - as far as it is possible to go with surviving documentation, since little survives from northern archives earlier than the twelfth century, when the Hexham material begins. The Black Book enables us to flesh out some of this earliest evidence. For example, it describes in detail a husbandland at Stannington that corresponds to a gift of two bovates made to the priory sometime before 1188. It would have been too cumbersome to draw attention to these correspondences in annotations to the Black Book or to the Calendar of Documents, but the necessary links are supplied by the list of properties following the latter which gives a summary view of all the priory's possessions in 1379, and notes

---

[93] Black Book 6.
[94] Document 3 (item 2, 8, 14).

where possible how and when it acquired them. From this it is possible to identify numerous instances where the Black Book allows a look back into the past. The distinction between interspersed township lands and the compact holdings beyond them can be shown in this way to have had a long history.

Close examination of the Black Book also demonstrates that, for all its traditional features, many older characteristics of the estate were undergoing transformation. In the absence of more precise information about earlier events it is impossible to explain or date the various features of change that the Black Book describes, but it is likely that some losses of income went back over three generations or more. The Scottish invasions that had caused the priory so much trouble in the late thirteenth century were repeated in the context of ongoing conflict between England and Scotland under the three Edwards, and their adverse effects of the economic stability of the region were compounded by the severe famine of 1315-18, wartime taxation after 1337 and the severe epidemics of 1348-9 and 1361-2. Depopulation is implied in parts of the Black Book by the number of waste tofts - 5 waste tofts out of 7 at Temple Thornton, 3 waste tofts out of 15 at Nesbit.[95] Cottages, too, were being abandoned either directly because of depopulation or indirectly because their former tenants had found superior accommodation - 5 cottages out of 14 were waste at Bingfield, 3 out of 8 at Kirkheaton, 7 out of 11 (so it seems) at East Matfen, 3 out of 5 at Nesbit, and 5 out of 13 at Brawby.[96] Cottages could be described as 'built' (that is, still standing) or unbuilt (that is, derelict or demolished). At Salton there were notionally 39 cottage sites 'of which 17 are built, and 19 not built and demised for herbage; and 3 cottages are completely waste and untenanted'.[97] Parts of the estate also show evidence of patches of formerly cultivated land land that had gone out of cultivation and turned to waste, another widespread feature of the period.[98] Such were the 38

---

[95] Black Book 44, 61.
[96] Black Book 4, 41, 57, 61, 79; Lomas, 'Medieval Bingfield', pp. 10-11.
[97] Black Book 78.
[98] S. J. Harris, 'Wastes, the Margins and the Abandonment of Land: The Bishop of Durham's Estate, 1350-1480', in C. D. Liddy and R. H. Britnell, eds, *North-East England in the Later Middle Ages* (Woodbridge, 2005); idem, 'Changing Land Use in a Moorland Region: Spennymoor in the

acres in two flats at Sandhoe, 33½ acres at Bingfield, the two fields of Morewra and Aldeby at Isel, the 30 acres on the Crosflatte at Dalton.[99] At East Matfen it seems a substantial amount of arable had been taken out of cultivation, since the Black Book notes that if the lords of Fenwick and Matfen should decide to put the waste in the township back into cultivation, the prior and convent would receive a third of all that was so reclaimed.[100]

These changes were probably modest in comparison with those of the following hundred years. Institutional change, in particular, was more rapid after 1379 than before. For thirty years or so after the Black Death, despite depopulation and an accompanying contraction of food production, estate managers were generally successful in maintaining traditional forms of agrarian organization. This was partly because it remained possible to find tenants for many of the holdings that had fallen vacant through crisis mortality, and partly because prices remained sufficiently high relative to wages to encourage landlords to produce for the market.[101] However, a deep recession in the late fourteenth century marked a turning point in their ability to stem the tide of change. At different speeds, different estates found they had to make compromise after compromise, so that the rural institutions of the early sixteenth century were very different from those of the early fourteenth.[102] The fact that the Black Book was compiled in 1379 rather than 1479 is accordingly of more than minor significance. By 1479 the Hexham Priory estate is likely to have looked very different, and it is improbable that it would have been surveyed in the same way. We have here a historical source of major importance for its own period, and - when read with care - it

---

Fourteenth and Fifteenth Centuries', in B. Dodds and R. H. Britnell, eds, *Agriculture and Rural Society after the Black Death: Common Themes and Regional Variations* (Hatfield, 2008), pp. 168-78; Lomas, *North-East England*, pp. 160-2; Winchester, *Landscape and Society*, pp. 6-7, 44-51.
[99] Black Book 3, 4, 6, 55.
[100] Black Book 57.
[101] A. R. Bridbury, 'The Black Death', *Economic History Review*, 2nd series 26 (1973), pp. 577-92.
[102] R.H. Britnell, 'Englsh Agricultural Output and Prices, 1350-1450: National Trends and Regional Divergences', in Dodds and Britnell, eds, *Agriculture and Rurtal Society*, pp. 26-31.

enables us to look backward into the past history of the Hexham estate, but its evidence represents a fleeting moment. Within a few generations it would have appeared archaic in many ways, a relic of a bygone age.

2. THE BLACK BOOK OF HEXHAM:
MANUSCRIPT, TEXT AND TRANSLATION

The Black Book of Hexham is a major source for the social, agrarian and landscape history of the northern counties of medieval England. Its length, and the quality of its detail, is rivalled only by the contemporary Hatfield Survey of the estate of the bishopric of Durham,[103] though for topographical detail the Black Book is more revealing. Its location is currently unknown, though it was until fairly recently in the private possession of Viscount Allendale.[104] In 1841 it was in Hexham. John Hodgson wrote in that year to James Raine, senior, father of the Black Book's editor, that though he was in Hexham and had copied part of the manuscript he had not been able to check his transcript because of ill health: 'doing so hurts my head'.[105] It was still in Hexham, in the archives of W. B. Beaumont, as lord of the manor, when the younger James Raine, from whom most of our knowledge of this record derives, transcribed it for his edition. He describes it as follows: 'The manuscript is a thin folio, twelve inches in length by nine in width, and is neatly written on parchment in a uniform hand, and with a wide margin. There are in it seventy-five folios. The book has sides of thick black leather ... now much faded, and the back is of wood. The sides are lined with coarse canvas. The volume is folded double, and is secured by a leathern flap. It is in a good state of preservation.'[106] Raine does not comment on the date of the manuscript, so it is not clear whether it was contemporary with its contents or a later copy. It was known as the Black Book at least as far back as Elizabeth's reign. Ralph Errington of Bingfield attested as a witness in 1611 that he had been a court official at Hexham in the period 1586-1602, and had seen an old parchment book

---

[103] *Bishop Hatfield's Survey*, ed. W. Greenwell, Surtees Society 32 (Durham, 1857).
[104] G. R. C. Davis, *Medieval Cartularies of Great Britain: A Short Catalogue* (London, 1958), p. 55.
[105] *PH*, II, p. xcvii-xcviii.
[106] *PH*, II, p. 1n.

recording the Hexham Abbey estate 'commonly called the Black Book'.[107]

The title of the volume describes it as a rental of all the lands of Hexham Priory in Hexhamshire, and in the dioceses of Carlisle, Durham and York 'in the first term beginning at Pentecost A.D. 1479'. There are several anomalies to comment on here. First of all, the manuscript makes a serious error over the correct date which, as can be established from internal evidence, is 1379 rather than 1479.[108] The record describes the grange of Bingfield as leased for twelve years starting at Pentecost 1377. A lease of Grottington is similarly recorded for three years from this same date.[109] By 1479, there would have been no point in recording leases that had expired 90 years previously. The fourteenth-century date is confirmed by some of the men who are recorded as the priory's tenants. William of Blenkhowe, Thomas Chapman, John Fayte, John Forester, William Hogg, William Hunter and Robert Hudspeth are all recorded in the Black Book as tenants in Corbridge; they also all appear in deeds relating to Corbridge dating from 1378-81.[110] The references to prominent men such as Sir William Heron, Sir Thomas of Ilderton, Sir Ralph of Eure, Robert of Ogle, Sir Aymer of Athol, Roger of Widdrington and John Lewyn also suggest a late-fourteenth century date. Normally one would expect a rental to relate to a fixed point rather than to 'begin' at a certain point, which sounds more like an account. In fact, the survey had probably been begun before 1379; it mentions lands held by Sir John of Stirling in Kirkheaton, who died in August 1378, so this bit of the survey was probably compiled by then.[111]

There is a further curiosity about the initial description of this record as a rental. This would usually imply a list of tenants and the rents they owed, as in the case, for example, with the almost

---

[107] TNA, E.134/9Jas1/Mich22. We owe this reference to Greg Finch.
[108] That this error is in the manuscript is established from its description in TNA, E.134/9Jas1/Mich22.
[109] Black Book 4.
[110] NCH, X, p. 98 note. The relevant deeds are printed in NCH, X, appendix, nos. 53-5, 93.
[111] Black Book 41.

contemporary rentals of the Bursar of Durham Priory.[112] The Black Book of Hexham is in fact an estate survey, giving extensive details about individual properties, including those that were not rented. For instance, in the township of Throckley, in Northumberland, the priory held '51 acres of land and meadowland, and ½ an acre and ½ a rood'. The land is described as spread across the village field in eighteen separate parcels, including three parcels of meadow, and the location of each parcel is carefully specified. No mention is made of a rent. It may well be that the land was leased, but it was plainly not the prime purpose of the Black Book to record either the fact or the details.[113]

The Black Book was edited by Raine for the Surtees Society in 1865,[114] and, particularly in the absence of the manuscript, we are fortunate to have his version in print. However, this edition is now difficult to find outside academic libraries, and it has two disadvantages — one more serious for the general reader and the other additionally serious for the professional historian. The drawback for the general reader is that the edition reproduces the Latin text with much abbreviation, no translation, and with hardly any assistance for identifying people and places. The additional drawback for the professional historian is that the edition falls way below modern critical standards. Its text is a bare transcript. Raine did not explain his editorial principles and conventions as a modern editor would, and we cannot be sure what editorial licences he allowed himself. He sometimes puts text in square brackets, which may mean that it was omitted in the original, though it could also mean that the document is damaged at that point. Some small items of text he puts in italics without explaining why. In addition, Raine made little attempt to settle the numerous textual problems his transcript presents, some of which could have been better resolved with the manuscript in hand. Lack of adequate revision is implied by his failure to realize that he had transcribed two versions of a

---

[112] *Durham Cathedral Priory Rentals, I: Bursars Rentals*, ed. R.A. Lomas and A. J. Piper, Surtees Society 198 (1989)
[113] Black Book 63.
[114] *PH*, II, pp. 1-82.

lengthy section of the survey of Salton and assigned one of them to Kirkby in Cleveland.[115]

The only other witness to the manuscript is the small set of transcripts of parts of the survey made by John Hodgson, now on deposit by the the Society of Antiquaries of Newcastle upon Tyne in Northumberland Record Office,[116] complemented by numerous citations in his *History of Northumberland*. The Hodgson manuscripts contain complete transcripts of the Black Book material for Elrington, Stonecroft and Settlingstones (Black Book 7), Byers (Black Book 18), Allerwash Mill, Owmers, Little Owmers and Warden (Black Book 22-25), together with substantial extracts from the entries for Carraw (Black Book 8), Thirlwall (Black Book 9) and *Langdene* (Black Book 19). Hodgson also transcribed the 'Liberties of Kirkheaton and Coldstrother' from the account of that manor (Black Book 41). In addition, there are notes, mostly transcribing place-names, relating to *Ryscheles* in Henshaw, Knarsdale, Whitlow, Byers, Temple Thornton and Beaumont. The transcripts give extra information about the distribution of text through the manuscript: the account of Elrington, Stonecroft and Settlingstones began on fo. 14v, Carraw on fo. 15, *Ryscheles* on fo. 16, Thirlwall on fo. 16v, Byers on fo. 20, Ulpham and 'Langdene' on fo. 21, Allerwash Mill and Owmers on fo. 22b, Little Owmers and Warden on fo. 23, Walwick on fo. 24v, Temple Thornton on fo. 34v and Cheeseburn on fo. 46v. The 'Liberties of Kirkheaton and Coldstrother' were on fo. 33v.

Hodgson's transcripts suggest that Raine's principal property headings were in the margin of the manuscript, and that there was less difference between them and the subordinate headings than there is in the printed edition. In his transcript of the accounts of Warden and Walwick, for example, Hodgson represents *Manerium de Wardon* and *Pastura in pasc' de Walwyk* (Raine's principal headings) in the same manner as he does *Le Crossflat, Langacr', Cotag', Batella de Wardon*. Some of Raine's choices in making principal divisions indeed look arbitrary, such as the division between Milbourne Grange and *Byresfeld* of Milbourne, though in the absence of the manuscript we cannot judge what

---

[115] Black Book 78.
[116] *SANT*.

The Black Book: Manuscript, Text and Translation

warrant he had for making it.[117] Doubts about these divisions of the material are a matter of some importance for interpreting the structure of the Hexham estate, since they mean we cannot assume that the properties grouped under Raine's principal headings were in fact administratively connected, or that places with secondary headings were dependencies of the property under whose principal heading they are placed. Under the heading of Dotland, for example, the Black Book includes properties at Rowley, Alwinton, Acomb, Wall, Keepwick, Hallington, Catton and Ninebanks, but nothing in the text, or in the history of these properties, suggests that should all be regarded as dependencies of Dotland.[118] Nor does it make much sense that Chesterhope in Redesdale is grouped with Priorsdale.[119] Raine's principal headings have been retained in this translation, for want of sufficient mandate to reconstruct the original clerk's conventions, even though it is likely that an editor working from the manuscript would want to do things differently. In the few cases where this principle of conservatism has been dropped the problem is indicated in a footnote. These main headings have been numbered in sequence for ease of reference.

There are unfortunately many discrepancies between Hodgson and Raine in the transcription of place-names, and differences, indeed, between Hodgson's own versions. The situation is complicated further by Hodgson's references in his *History* to alternative sources of the text that seem not to have survived. It is puzzling that he should have chosen to record the material for Knarsdale 'from a bad copy', perhaps no more than an earlier transcript of his own. For Priorsdale he used 'an old translation' that includes 'the fountaine of Kekburne wane', a spelling of 'fountain' that looks appreciably earlier than his own.[120] His surviving transcripts are likely to be from the same manuscript that Raine used. They demonstrate, as might be expected, that the anachronistic hyphens that litter Raine's text are editorial, separating the elements of names that were once joined, as when Hodgson has *Stodhirdelogherheuede* and Raine has *Stod-hird-clogher-heuede* in the transcript of the account of Byers. (The

---

[117] Black Book 51, 52.
[118] Black Book 5.
[119] Black Book 17.
[120] *HHN*, IV [part 2, vol. 3], pp. 43-4, 90.

disagreement here about the number of e's in the word is all too frequent.) The hyphens would not be tolerated in a modern edition, and have been abolished in the following translation. Raine was also inclined to extend place-name forms that a modern editor would probably leave. In the transcript of Carraw, for example he has *Corne-strothre* where Hodgson has *Cornestrothr'* and *Thormer-strothre* where Hodgson has *Thormerstrothr'*, though it must be added that Hodgson's own practice is not consistent. Hodgson's transcripts also show that Raine (like Hodgson himself) was inconsistent in his transcription of a consonantal u; he has *Smalburnheued* rather than *Smalburnheved* at Dotland, for example, but has *Seven-acresse* where Hodgson has *Seuenacrosse* at Temple Thornton.[121] The very numerous inconsistencies between Hodgson and Raine in the transcribing of place-names are alarming, but rarely of great significance for purposes of identification. In the translation Raine's readings are adopted unless there is good reason to accept Hodgson's, which is probably balancing on the right side; Raine's palaeographical skills were the greater, to judge from a few passages that Raine succeeded in reading where Hodgson failed. Where Hodgson's reading of a name seem to be of possible significance for identifying the place in question it is recorded in a footnote, together with an indication of whether it is taken from his manuscripts or his printed *History*. However, Hodgson's familiarity with Northumberland topography sometimes gave him a decisive advantage, and in a few cases - maybe too few - his readings have been preferred and incorporated in the translation. In these instances the source of the adopted reading is indicated in a footnote, followed (after a square bracket) by the rejected reading of Raine, and any alternative readings from Hodgson.[122] One one occasion an adopted reading, *Feuenhope,* a lost place-name from near Knarsdale, results from the need to compromise between the two transcribers, but is closer to Hodgson's *ffevenhope* or *Favenhope* than to Raine's *Fenen-hope.*[123]

Despite all misgivings, the present translation necessarily takes Raine's version of the Black Book as its base text, and his

---

[121] Black Book 5, 44.
[122] For example, Hodgson's *Glendeuburn* at Knarsdale is clearly preferable to Raine's *Clenden-burn*.
[123] Black Book 12.

The Black Book: Manuscript, Text and Translation 31

transcriptions of place-names have been adopted throughout, except where indicated. It would have been possible to modernize the minority of place-names that are known to survive, but this would have resulted in a hybrid text. As an alternative to introducing such inconsistency, names for which we have found a modern equivalent on Ordnance Survey maps are marked with an asterisk, and a gazetteer at the end of the translation gives both their modern equivalent and a National Grid reference.[124] Although this decision will cause readers occasional inconveniences, most of the principal fourteenth-century place-names are not so different from their modern forms as to be unrecognizable. It is to be hoped that local knowledge may add to the number of medieval places that can be identified. English words in the original text have been left in the form in which Raine transcribed them, since they supply evidence of northern vocabulary in the fourteenth century. They are given a modern equivalent in the glossary that follows the gazetteer, though most of them hardly need such attention. It should be noted that it is sometimes uncertain whether a word is a proper noun or not, and in a number of instances our translation treats as a noun in English a word that Raine capitalized as a place-name. Our translation 'in the *beengarth*' at Anick, for example, represents Raine's 'in le Beengarth'.[125] The following additional issues have cropped up in the course of translation.

(1) Either the clerk or clerks who compiled the manuscript from which the printed edition was taken, or its transcriber, have had difficulty with one of the numerous qu- abbreviations that frequently precedes *in medio* in the Black Book. Earlier in the text (at Renwick and Scales)[126] it appears as *quae in medio*, but later (at Chesterhope, Temple Thornton, Stannington, Eachwick, Heugh, Matfen, Ouston, Great Broughton, Ingleby and Kirkby)[127] as *quia in medio*. Both these readings are puzzling, but in this translation the difficulty has been resolved by reading *quasi in medio* ('about in the

---

[124] Names are not asterisked when they are covered by a central or marginal capitalized heading - e.g. references to Bingfield under the general heading BYNGFELD or references to Todridge following TODRYGE: Black Book 4.
[125] Black Book 2.
[126] Black Book 6.
[127] Black Book 17, 44, 47, 54, 56, 57, 59, 75, 76, 77.

middle'). At Gunnerton the Black Book has *fere in medio* as an alternative.

(2) The printed text frequently combines a French definite article with an English noun or place-name, as is common in records of this period, and this is consistently translated as 'the'. Sometimes a plural definite article (*lez*) is combined with a singular noun. Rather than suppose that these words or names should be pluralized, the translation assumes that writer of the Black Book was indifferent between *le* and *lez*. There are some instances that justify this assumption, notably *ex parte orientali lez Castell-way, buttando super eandem* at Stannington, *una clausura vocata lez Milnclos* at Salton, *lez Estmore* used with a singular verb, also at Salton, and *una clausura in mora vocata lez Cotgarth* at Brawby.[128]

(3) Some problematic words have been consistently translated in the same way, notably *averia* ('working beasts'), *bracinagium* ('brewing'), *cultura* ('cultivation' or 'ploughed land'), *dimissio* and *dimittere* ('demise', 'to demise'), *Dominus* ('Father', where the man concerned is Sir Priest rather than Sir Knight), *domus* ('building'), *opera* ('labour services'), *placea* ('plot'), *portio* ('piece'), *rivulus* ('burn'), *tenura* ('holding'), *villa* ('township'). *Includere* has been translated as 'to enclose' only where there is mention of a wall, hedge or ditch, where the property is a park, or where no other translation is meaningful; normally, if boundaries are mentioned, it is translated as 'contain within'.

(4) The use of numerals in the printed text has been retained, except for the substitution of Arabic for Roman forms.

It has been necessary to use special devices to indicate particular features of the text. The following conventions have been adopted.

[ ]	square brackets in printed edition
( )	round brackets in printed edition
(Husband)	brackets and italics in printed edition

---

[128] Black Book 47, 78, 79.

\ /	italics in the printed edition
milnfleme	an English word in the Latin text
<*comment*>	an editorial comment
<three>	an editorial insertion or correction (with an explanatory footnote)

3. THE BLACK BOOK OF HEXHAM

A RENTAL OF THE PRIOR AND CONVENT OF HEXTILDESHAME* OF THE FARMS AND RENTS OF ALL THEIR LANDS AND TENEMENTS IN HEXTILDESHAMSCHYRE*, <AND> THE DIOCESES OF CARLISLE, DURHAM AND YORK FOR THE FIRST TERM BEGINNING AT THE FEAST OF PENTECOST, IN THE YEAR OF THE LORD <1379>.[129]

[LIBERTY OF HEXTILDESHAM]

<1 HEXTILDESHAM>

That prior and convent have in Hextildesham various tenements and lands, some demised to various tenants as set out below, and some lands under their own cultivation; and a water mill on the Tyne, with suit of multure from tenants both of the lord archbishop and of the prior and convent themselves in the township of Hextildesham. And they will mill their grains for a toll of one-twentieth. And if any tenant of that township withdraws himself with his grain from that mill for the sake of a mill elsewhere he will on that account forfeit a horse with a saddle to the lord archbishop and a sack of grain to the lord prior.

PRESTPOFYLL.* Thomas Monk holds 1 tenement in Prestpofill and pays 18d. a year. Mariot Wer' holds 1 tenement <and pays> 8d. <Similarly,> John Laverok, Patrick Laverok, Thomas Monk, Thomas Barthelemew, John Greene, John Wanles, Archibald Dikson, Robert Milnar — also from him for a garden, Roger Bischop, John Hurde, le Turpyn's heir, John Lee, William Whytskalez, William Chaumer, Archibald Diksun, John Whyt

---

[129] The manuscript says 1479. See the discussion on p.26.

cobbler, John Whyt, Thomas Monk, John Whyte's widow, John Whytskale, Joan Nuthode.

Joan Huton, Richard Armstrang, Richard Hunter, Thomas Heslihop.

PUDDYNG RAW. Joan Gladow, William Chaumyr, Patrick Laverok, Roland Watsun, John Watsun, officer,[130] John Scot. There is also a waste <tenement> there. John Leschman, Robert Hyn's widow.

William Spavyne, Robert Nicolson, Robert Stokall, John Patonson, Thomas Elysun, John Elysun, Alice Hudson, William Symson, Joan Batsun, Robert Barkar, John Lytill, William Gladow, Thomas Hyrd, Alice Hird. There are also 3 gardens there. William Jonsun.

DEMESNES IN THE TERRITORY OF HEXTILDESHAM. The prior and convent retain under their own cultivation at the Merehak 10 acres; also in the territory of Prestpofle at Wyndmylnstob on either side of the road, 8 acres; also they hold there 1 acre of arable land; also they hold at Harelaw in the same territory, 5 acres; also they hold in the territory of Hencotis*, in the place called Haynyngcrofte*,[131] 2 acres; also they hold in Ovinhousgat, 4 acres; also they hold the Milnflatte with 2 acres of meadow there, containing in all 12 acres; also the cellerar holds by the *milnfleme* a piece of meadow that contains ½ acre; also John of Walworth holds there, by demise of the prior, 2 acres; also they hold between the Hallorchard and Halywelldene, 6 acres of meadow;[132] also they hold a piece of pasture called the Staners between Tyne water and the *milnfleme,* and it contains by estimation 20 acres; also they hold 1 close on the northern side of Tyne water called the Medhop, and it contains by estimation 14

---

[130] *client'*: meaning uncertain.
[131] The site of Haining Croft is clearly indicated on a map of c. 1844, the relevant part of which is reproduced in Greg Finch, ' Another Old Map of Hexham - And a Medieval Boundary', *Hexham Local History Society Newsletter* 57 (2010), p. 3.
[132] These six acres are identifiable from the map of. c.1844 as lying opposite Broomhaugh Island at NY 940644. They are now crossed by the railway line.

The Black Book of Hexham 37

acres, of which 5 acres belong to the township of Aynwyk*; also they hold 2 acres of land at the end of the Tyne mill pond, lying in the Harthornflatte by the *regne*.

<2> AYNWYK*

Also they hold Aynwyk grange, in which stand various buildings, apple trees and dovecotes. They also hold a sheepfold, with 1 garden enclosed with a wall, containing 2 acres, on the eastern side of the grange. Also in this grange they hold 1 garden enclosed to the east with a wall, and it contains 1 acre. In it they also hold 2<4>8½ acres[133] of demesne land under cultivation, and 50 acres of demesne meadow, lying in various places, of which 8 acres are used for the needs of the grange, and 42 are used for Hexham Abbey; also they hold there 40 acres of demesne land that are enclosed with the Medhop;[134] also in the territory of Corbryg* they hold 30 acres of land called the Bisschopprek, and they are joined to the ploughed land at Aynwyk. The total amount of these demesne lands and meadows <amounts to>[135] 363½ acres,[136] which are <here> listed one by one with their metes and bounds.

DETAIL OF THE LANDS.[137] First, on the southern side of the large barn lie 1½ acres and 1 sheepfold, with 1 walled garden containing 2 acres; in the *beengarth*, 4 acres; and in the Cotisflatt, 12 acres; and in the Pingar, 4 acres; in Ho, 8 acres; and in Henresdene with the Toftes, 16 acres; and below Beuanfront* park, 13 acres; and on Claverige, 13 acres; and on Hastrige, 12 acres; and

---

[133] Raine's text has 218½ acres, but the later specification of these lands sums them at 248½ acres. The items in fact add up to 249½ acres.
[134] *includuntur cum le Medhop*. Here *includuntur* is translated as 'enclosed' because of the earlier reference to the Medhop as a close of 14 acres of which 5 belong to Anick. However, the text here is inconsistent with that reference, and should probably read '40 acres of demesne land of which 5 are enclosed within the Medhop'.
[135] The words 'amounts to' are represented by a dash in the printed edition.
[136] This is 5 acres less than the pieces specified, and suggests some further error of transcription,
[137] In the printed edition this heading is placed lower down, before the list of meadows, not before the list of arable lands.

on Colstanflatt, 8 acres; and on Harbugh with <the> [138] Wetlandes, 16 acres; and below the Langsyd, by the Pulmedou, 5 acres; and in the Estelys, 20 acres; and in the Thornebankys, 9[139] acres; and in Scolebrad, where the *connyngarth* was situated, 4 acres; and on the Sevenrigges, 2 acres; and on Edenrigge, 20 acres; and on the Estflores, 20 acres; and on the Westflores, 18 acres; and on Melmirpul, 14 acres; Wlwardethorne, 14 acres; and on the Rede, 10 acres; and on Malabrelande, 4 acres. \The total of that arable land,/ 248½ acres.

And in the territory of this grange there are various acres of meadow, listed below according to their locations, and <the meadows are> demised.[140] First, in the *bengarth*, 5 acres; and in the Holmedow, by the Cottisflatt, 1½ acres; and in Horsmyres, on either side of the burn, 9 acres; and below the Knolles, 2½ acres; and in the Bradmedow, with the Carracacre, 9 acres; and in the Pulmedowe, 13 acres; and in the Mylnmedow, 2½ acres; and in the *medow* below the barn <or the grange>, 6 acres; and in the Countes medow, 1½ acres. \The total acres of meadow,/ 50 acres.

Also they have a road 10 perches wide out of the township of Aynwyk through the middle of the hedged enclosure of Akwod*, from the sheepfold of Aynwyk due north as far as the common pasture beyond Birkburne*.[141]

SEVERAL PASTURE. Also they hold two pastures in severalty, of which one is called the Esteles, and the other is called the Draknese, and <they> contain by estimation about 30 acres.

DEMESNES BELONGING TO THE TOWNSHIP. Also there are 15 acres 3 roods of desmesne there demised to tenants of the township, and they lie between the grange and the township of Aynwyk, and they pay in all 11s. 9¾d. a year.

---

[138] *de* (for *le*).
[139] *viiij*, perhaps in error for *viij*, which would mean that the total of 248½ acres was correct. Alternatively *viiij* has been misread as *viij*.
[140] *per certa loca; et dimissa*. It is difficult to know what to make of this.
[141] See documents 9, 16 (item 18).

The Black Book of Hexham

LABOUR SERVICES AND CUSTOMS OF THE HUSBANDLANDS. Also there are 12 husbandlands there, each of which contains 16 acres of arable land and meadow; and each of those lands will work for 1 day with 1 man in the mill pond when necessary, and will make good all round the *hegeyard*, and will give 1 cock and 1 hen at Christmas, and will carry the millstones of Aynwyk mill, and will make the walls of that mill at his own expense, and will roof the mill at his own expense with the lord's roofing material. And each husbandland will plough with its plough on grange land 1 day each year when asked to do so.

HUSBANDLANDS. John Robinsun, Richard Sourbe, John Reyde, Robert Sourbe, Thomas Robsun, Alan Kell, John Greene, William Sourbe, John Copden, John Stodard, Thomas Robinsun, Roger Robinsun, Isabel Gibsun.

COTTAGES' LABOUR SERVICES. There are 19 cottages there, and each cottage will perform service and labour services at that mill like the husbandlands. COTTAGES. Thomas Stobart holds 1 cottage and ½ acre of land, and pays 21d. a year; he also holds 1 cottage and ½ acre of land, and pays 21d. a year; he also holds 2 cottages and 2½ acres of land, and pays 4s. a year. William Smyth holds 1 cottage and 7 acres of land, and pays 4s. 9d. a year. John Couper holds 1 cottage and 5 acres of land, and pays 6s. 4d. a year. Agnes of Chesburgh* holds 1 cottage and 1 acre of land, and pays 21d. a year. William Oxhyrd, a neif of the lord, holds 1 cottage <and> 3 acres 3 roods of land, and pays 2s. 6d. Simond Clyde holds 1 cottage <and> 1½ acres of land, and pays 2s. 10d a year; he also holds 1 cottage and 3 roods of land, and pays 2s. 6d. a year. Alice Stobard holds 1 cottage and 3 roods of land, and pays 21d. a year. John Sprot holds 1 (cottage) and 2 acres of land, and pays 2s. a year. John Roger, a neif of the lord, holds 1 cottage and 4 roods of land, and pays 2s. 7d. a year. John son of Alan holds 1 cottage and 5 acres of land, and pays 3s. 6d. a year. Alice Stobhyrd holds 1 cottage, and pays 18d. a year. Thomas Milnar holds 1 cottage and 7½ acres of land, and pays 5s. 4d. a year. Thomas Schiphirde holds 1 cottage and 9 acres of land, and pays 6s. a year. John Steele holds 1 cottage and 5 acres of land, and pays 3s. 3d. a year. Thomas Schiphird holds 1 cottage and 1 acre of land, and pays 3s. a year; he also holds 2 acres by the Schepbrig, and pays 12d. a year. Simond Clyd holds 2 acres of land there, and pays 14d. a year. John

Alanson, a neif of the lord, holds 1 acre of meadow called Malabrenndon, and pays 12d. a year. John Sprete holds a parcel of meadow called Petillislaw, <and pays> 12d.

DEMESNE LANDS. Richard Plummar holds 3 acres below Beufront* park, and pays 2s. a year; he also holds 2 acres in the Langesyde, and pays 20d. a year.

BREWING. John Couper holds the common brewery of the township of Aynwyk, and pays 5s. a year.

MILL. Richard Forester of Akome* holds a mill <...>,[142] and pays 73s. 4d. a year.

John Vaus holds 2½ acres <...> of Beaufront*, <and> pays 2s.

PANNAGE. Tenants of Aynwyk will give pannage like tenants of Hexham, and in normal years it is worth 6d.

<3> SANDOW*

Alice Webster holds 1½ acres of land in the Frerrescrofte, and pays 20d. a year. Simon of Sandow holds 1 acre of land, and pays 12d. a year.

DEMESNE LANDS. All the tenants of the township hold the Cotgarth and the Cotesflatte, which contain by estimation 4 acres, and they pay 2s. 6d. a year. And there is 1 *flatte* there between Harelaw on the southern side and Hathornfur on the northern side, with the Derstrete* on the eastern side and the *husbandlandes* on the western side, and this *flatte* is called the Baxstansyde, and contains by estimation 30 acres. And it is waste in the lord's hand. And there is another waste flat on the western side of the *schepcott*, which is called Hormescheles and contains 8 acres.

---

[142] Missing material here, and in the following entry, is represented by three dots in the printed edition.

LABOUR SERVICES AND CUSTOMS. There are 13 husbandlands there, each of which contains 24 acres of arable land and meadow. And each land will perform labour services and customs at Aynwyk* Mill like tenants of that township, and each husbandland will give to the lord 1 cock and a hen at Christmas.

(\Husbandlands/). Simon of Sandow, a neif of the lord, holds 1 husbandland, and pays 8s. 5½d. <and> labour services as above. Adam of the Hall holds 1 land there, and pays 10s. 5d. a year. William of the Hall holds 1 land there, and pays 8s. 5½d. a year. Adam of <the> Hall, William of Wall <and> Adam of the Hill hold 1 land, and pay 8s. 5½d. Adam of the Hill holds 1 land there, <and> pays 8s. 5½d. a year. John of Bywell* holds 1 land there, and pays 8s. 5½d. a year. Simon of Sandow and Thomas Litilskill hold 1 land, 8s. 5½d. John of Matfen*, a neif of the lord, holds 1 land, and pays 8s. 5½d. Thomas Litilskill holds 1 land there, and pays 8s. 5½d. a year. John Whytyngeham holds 1 land there, and pays 8s. 5½d. John Bywell and Simon of Sandow hold 1 land there between them, <and> pay 8s. 5½d. All the tenants of the township hold between them 2 lands there, and pay 12s. 5d. a year. \Total,/ £5 7s. 5d.

COTTAGES' LABOUR SERVICES. There are 12 cottages there, and each cottage will perform labour services at Aynwyk* mill like the husbandlands. The tenants are as follows.

Isabel of Stellyng* holds 1 cottage and three-quarters of an acre[143] of land, and pays 18d. a year, 1 cock and 1 hen and labour services. William of Matfen*, a neif of the lord, holds 1 cottage and 1 acre of land, <and> pays 22d. and 2 hens.[144] John of Whyttingeham* holds 1 cottage and 1 garden, and pays 8d. a year. Simon of Sandow, a neif of the lord, holds 1 cottage, and pays 12d. a year. Alice Webster holds 1 cottage, and pays 13½d. a year. Alice Schiphyrd holds 3 cottages and 3½ roods of land, and pays 10s. 10½d. a year and 2 hens. Robert of Matfen*, a neif of the lord, holds 1 cottage and ½ acre of land, and pays 2s. and 2 hens. Adam

---

[143] *di. acr. di.*

[144] *et ij gall.* The same abbreviation occurs below in the entries for Alice Schiphyrd, Robert of Matfen and John of Matfen. The entry for Adam of the Hall is printed more specifically as *ij gal(l)inas.*

of the Hall holds 1 cottage and ½ acre of land, and pays 8d. a year <and> 2 hens. John of Matfen*, a neif of the lord, holds 1 cottage <and> 3 roods of land and pays 2s. 6d a year <and> 2 hens. Isabel of Stellyng* holds 1 cottage and ½ acre of land, and pays 22½d. a year. Simon of Sandow, a neif of the lord, holds 1 *letch*, and pays 2d. a year; he also holds 1 rood of land by the Hanyarburne, and pays 3d. a year; he also holds 2 *sykes* of meadow, and pays 4d. a year. Adam of the Hyll holds 1 *syk*, and pays 2d. a year.

PANNAGE. And the tenants of the township will give pannage like tenants of Aynwyk*, in normal years 6d.

<WASTE.> There is a waste plot of land in the *lonyng* toward the moor, developed from the lord's waste, and it used to pay 6d. a year.[145]

<GLEBE LANDS.> Also Father Peter of Gonwarton*, chaplain of the parish of Sant John Le*, holds a piece of land there called Kyrkland, being glebe of that church, and it contains 8 acres in severalty throughout the year, and it is allocated to his stipend, 13s. 4d. a year.

They also hold land called Kirkland adjoining the church of St Oswald,[146] and it is glebe of that church, and contains by estimation 3 acres of arable land. And Father Robert of Dissington*, the celebrant there, pays 8d. a year for those 3 acres.

<4> BYNGFELD*[147]

<MANOR AND DEMESNE ARABLE.> They hold 1 manor there, in which stand various buildings and 1 chapel, with three gardens on the eastern side, and 1 garden on the western side,

---

[145] *et solet reddere p. a. vjd.* It would be more natural here to have *solebat*, since it is difficult to interpret the rent as any other than a reference to the period before the plot was waste.

[146] The church of St Oswald in St.John Lee parish, at Heavenfield (NY 937696). .

[147] The Black Book account of Bingfield is examined in detail, with a useful map, in R.A. Lomas, 'Medieval Bingfield', *Hexham Historian*, VI (1996). pp. 3-16.

The Black Book of Hexham   43

containing 2 acres in all by estimation; and there is 1 tithe barn there.

And there are in demesne there 238 acres of arable land and 16 acres 3 roods of meadow, of which, on Crawlaw, on the southern side by Ereanbrig*, lie 30 acres of arable land; and on the western side, by the manor, 24 acres; and on the northern side, by Essewell *medow*, on the Sandilandes, 5 acres; and on the western side of the Linburne*, on the Toftes, 6 acres; and in the Linburnflatt 4 acres; and on the western side of the *schipcote*, on the Leyacre, 12 acres; and on the Cotisflatt and the Cotehill, 30 acres; and on the southern side of Halidenway, on Twystes, 6 acres; and on the Halffurlang, by the Cotelech, 4 acres, of which John Oxhird holds 1 acre with his cottage; and on the eastern side of Linburn*, on the Linburne*, on the Langflatt, and on the 2 Schortbuttes, 24 acres; and on the Brereflatt, toward the northern side, 10 acres; and on Warinlawsyd, toward the west, 3 acres; and by Ereane burn*, 3 acres; and on either side of the road that leads to the township of Riell*, on the Langlyes and the Wallaw, 18 acres; and on the southern side of that road toward the east, on the Langthombesflatt, 6 acres; and on the same side of that road toward the west, on the Goscroft, 3 acres; and by the Bradmedow, on Hollchestirbank, 4 acres; and on the southern side of Cammedow, on Cammislaw, 12 acres; and on the same side toward the east, on Halywelflatte, between the township of Bingfeld and Todrige*, 15 acres; and on the eastern side of that township, by the Bradmedow, 15 acres. \Total acres of arable land,/ 238 acres.

DEMESNE MEADOWS. And a piece of meadow called Whitwelmedow abuts on Craulaw, <and> contains 7 acres; and in the Coltmedow, near that meadow, 2 acres; and below the Toftes, in the Holemedow, 2½ acres; and on the eastern side of the Linburne*, in the Fulmedow, 2 acres 1 rood; and in the Bradmedow, 3 acres, of which 2 acres lie on the western side, <and 1> on the eastern side. \Total acres of meadow (blank)./ [148]

SEVERAL PASTURE. And there are 16 acres of several pasture between Eryane and Craulaw on the northern and southern sides, and the Derestret* on the western side, and the Graystanes on

---

[148] The total is 16 acres, 3 roods, as stated previously.

the eastern side, between that pasture[149] and pasture of Roger of Widryngton*. \Total acres of pasture,/ 16 acres.

TODRYGE*. And there is a piece of arable land there lying between Grotyngton* and territory of the township of Byngfelde, formerly called Litil Grotington, now called Todrige, and it is the lord's several demesne throughout the year; and it is contained within these bounds: that is, within the Blakedyke on the eastern side; and then, descending along the Oppots and Todrygeburn to the Halywell on the northern side; and from there on the western side ascending eastward along the Grenelech on the southern side, between territory of Boclyve* and Todrygefeld as far as the Blakdyk first mentioned.

DEMISE OF BYNGFELD GRANGE. Robert Colstan, William of Ledome and William Taylor of Eryngton* hold between them, jointly and severally, all Byngfeld grange, with all the lands, meadows, pastures and profits listed above, for the term of 12[150] years, paying for the first three years £6 a year, and for the next three years £7 6s. 8d. a year, and for the 6 following years £8 a year, the first term of payment beginning at the feast of Pentecost in the year of the Lord 1377.[151]

Also there is a piece of waste land there which is called the Greencame, and it lies between the *husbandlandes* on the western side, and Donnismore* on in the southern side, and the *fote* of the Sweteleche, abutting on Wyneacrebank, on the eastern side, and the *husbandlandes* on the northern side, and it contains by estimation 4 acres; and there is there 1 flat of waste land on the Gryndstanlaw*, and it lies between Donnismore* on the western side, and the Sweteleche on the southern side, and the Grensyde on the northern side, and the *husbandlandes* on the eastern side, and contains by estimation 18 acres; and there are there 16 selions, called *rigges* in English, lying on the Schellez*, by the Solpark on the southern side, and they contain by estimation 11½ acres.

---

[149] It is unclear what is referred here to by 'that pasture'.
[150] *xiij* for *xij*.
[151] 17 May, 1377.

The Black Book of Hexham

And there are there, on the said Schellis*, 25 selions, of which 4 selions lie on the northern side of the Schellawe* and 21 on the southern side of the Schellawe*, and they contain by estimation 12½ acres; and there is there 1 flat by Halydenway, and it abuts on Eriane burn* on the northern side, and abuts on Warinlausyde on the southern side, between the *husbandlandes* there, and contains by estimation 7 acres, and they are demised to William Bewmonde for £8.

Also there is there 1 sheepfold with 1 garden containing 4 acres, and it lies on the Eryane burn* toward the west, from which sheepfold of Byngfeld the prior and convent have free entry and exit through the territory of the township of Colwell* to the common pasture of the township of Colwell*, commoning all over that pasture, throughout the year, up to four hundred <*i.e. 480*> sheep[152], thirty oxen and 10 cows, with 1 bull, as expressly specified in charters.

LABOUR SERVICES AND CUSTOMARY SERVICE.[153] And there are 12 husbandlands there, each of which contains 24 acres of arable land and meadow, and each land will carry its share of timber and millstones, and will maintain the walls and roof of the mill at its <tenant's> own expense except on the *louthre*; and they will clean the pool and lead water to the mill whenever necessary; and they will mill their grain at the lord's mill. The tenants are as follows:

William of Ledom holds 1 husbandland and pays 11s. 6d. a year, of which 12d. is for multure. John Lam holds 2 husbandlands, one of which is without multure, and pays 33s. 10½d., 6d. for multure. John, son of John Thomsun, holds 1 land with multure, and pays 16s. 10½d. a year, 2s. 6d. for multure. William Leene holds 1 land with multure, and pays 16s. 10½d. a year, 2s. 6d. for multure. Adam Kempe holds 1 land without multure, and pays 14s. 4d. a year. Walter of Sandow*, a neif of the lord, holds 2 lands, one without multure, and pays 34s. 6d., 12d. for multure. William, son

---

[152] For an indication that in ennumerating sheep 'one hundred' meant the long hundred of 120, see the entries for Slaley and Steel, where 300 is rendered as '15 score'.

[153] The printed edition places this heading above the list of cottagers.

of Richard of <the> Hall, holds 1 land without multure, and pays 17s. a year, 2s. 6d. for multure.[154] John Oxehird and William Trout hold 2 lands without multure <and> pay 22s. 6d. a year. John Thomson holds 1 land, and pays 16s. a year, 12d. for multure.

There are there 12[155] cottages, and each cottage performs service at the mill like the husbandlands. The tenants are as follows:

William, son of Richard of the Hall, holds 1 waste cottage and pays 12d. a year; he also holds 1 waste garden and pays 2d. a year. John Lame holds 1 cottage and 6 acres of land with multure, 4s. 7½d. Marjorie of Law holds 1 cottage and 6 acres of land with multure, and pays 4s. 7½d. a year. John, son of John Thomson, holds 1 cottage and 6 acres of land, and pays 4s. 7½d. a year. William of Rokehope* holds 1 cottage and 6 acres of land with multure, <and> pays 4s. 7½d. a year. John Thomson, *lang*,[156] holds 1 cottage and 6 acres of land with multure, <and> pays 4s. 7½d. a year. Adam Kemp holds 1 cottage and 6 acres of land with multure, <and> pays 2s. a year; he also holds 2 roods of land, and pays 3d. a year. William Colstane holds 1 cottage and 6 acres of land with multure, <and> pays 4s. 7½d. a year. John Oxhyrd holds 1 cottage and 6 acres of land with multure, <and> pays 4s. 7½d. a year. William Amokson holds 1 cottage and 6 acres of land with multure, <and> pays 4s. 7½d. a year. John, son of John Thomson, holds 1 waste cottage with 1 rood of land, <and> pays 2d. a year. Walter of Sandow* holds 1 acre of land, and pays 10d. a year. Robert Colstane holds 1 waste cottage, <and> pays 1d. a year. John, son of John Thomson, holds 1 waste cottage, <and> pays 1d. Adam Kempe holds 1 waste cottage, and pays 1d. a year.

THE TOWNSHIP'S BREWING. Robert Colstane holds the township's brewery at the lord's pleasure, 2s.

MILL. John Oxhird of Byngfeld holds a water mill, <and> pays 10s.

---

[154] There seems to be an error in the text here.
[155] The following list has 14 cottages, 5 of them waste.
[156] The meaning of *lang* here is here uncertain.

THE SEVERAL TENURE OF GROTYNGTON*. Also they hold Grotyngton, which is contained within these bounds: that is, between the Pont burn* on the southern side and the Derestrete* on the eastern side, the *lonyng* of Boclive* and the Graystanes, lying between Grotyngton and Codlawmore, on the northern side, and an old ditch between Grotyngton and that same moor on the western side. And Thomas Henreson holds all Grotington with all its profits for a term of three years, paying 40s. the first year, and no more that year because he will newly build there at his own expense; and for the two following years 50s. each year, the first term of payment <dating from> the feast of Pentecost in the year of the Lord 1377.

<5> DOTLAND*

<DOTLAND PARK.> They also hold Dotland park, as enclosed within the circuit of the its walls, with all the liberties and rights pertaining to a park, with 27 acres and 1 rood enclosed within it.[157]

CUSTOMS. There are 10 husbandlands there, each of which contains 15 acres of arable land and meadow, and each land will give 1 cock and 1 hen at Christmas; and they will mill their corn at Whytley mill* for a toll of one thirteenth.

Marmaduke son of Henry, a neif of the lord, holds 3 lands, <and> pays 15s. John son of Robert holds 2 lands there, <and> pays 10s. a year and customs. John son of David holds 3 lands there, and pays 15s. a year. William son of Henry of Dotland, a neif of the lord, holds 2 lands, <and> pays 10s.

There are 10 cottages there, and each will give 1 hen at Christmas. The tenants are as follows.

John son of David holds 1 cottage and 3 acres of land, and pays 2s. a year; he also holds 1 cottage and 1½ acres of land, and pays 18d. a year; he also holds 1 cottage and 1 acre of land, and pays 16d. a year. Walter Chamebreleyn holds 1 built cottage and 1

---

[157] See documents 16 (item 10), 17 (item 3).

acre of land, and pays 12d. a year <and> a hen. John son of Robert holds 1 built cottage with 1 garden containing ½ acre of land, <and> pays 18d. <and> a hen. William Breuster holds 1 built cottage and 3 acres of land, and pays 2s. a year. Walter Chambreleyn holds 1 cottage with 1 garden containing half a rood of land, <and> pays 6d. <and> a hen. William son of Henry, a neif of the lord, holds 1 built cottage and four acres of land, <and> pays 3s. Walter Chambreleyn holds 1 built cottage and ½ acre of land, and pays 6d. a year; he also holds 1 built cottage and 4½ acres of land, and pays 2s. 1d. a year.

DOTLAND DEENE. There is 1 wooded place there, called Dotlande *deene* in which no tenant will cut any greenwood without the lord's licence and the reeve's supervision.

There is also 1 field between Dotlandfeld and Dipden* to the west in which a hamlet once stood <...>.[158] There is also 1 place in Knytlech in which there used to be a sheepfold with 1 garden containing by estimation 4 acres. There is also there 1 place called Randalphsrydyng, and it lies between the *croftes* of Dotland on the northern side and common pastures there, and it contains 15½ acres, and used to pay[159] 2s. a year. There is also 1 field there below Dotland toward the south containing within it 90 acres of exchequer land,[160] and it lies between Doteland field on the western side and Henry Hunter's field on the eastern side. There is also 1 field below Dotland toward the east containing within it 60 acres of exchequer land, arable and meadow, which they hold for the repair of Whitlye mill*, and it lies between Robert of Wollon's field on the eastern side,[161] and so along a burn called Smalburn, ascending along the northern side as far as Smalburnheued, to Dotland field. There is there in that field a parcel of land containing 34 acres of exchequer

---

[158] *in quo constructus erat quondam hamelectus de eodem modo. De eodem modo* is here untranslated; it is perhaps a misreading.

[159] *sol. r.*, which could be 'is accustomed to pay'.

[160] Exchequer land was land for which the rent was collected directly by officials of the archepiscopal exchequer (the archbishop's accounting office), rather than by local manorial bailiffs.

[161] The western and southern boundaries are omitted. Moreover, the switch from block to linear boundary descriptions is unusual, and perhaps implies some disturbnce of the text here.

land between that burn on the southern side and the road that leads from Ewardlaw, between that land and Dotland *park*, to the common pasture of Dotland *more*.

YAROWRYGE.* There are 6 husbandlands there, each of which contains <...>[162] acres of arable land and meadow.

HUSBANDLANDS. William Culgath holds 1 husbandland, and pays 6s. a year. Henry son of Thomas holds 2 lands, and pays 12s. a year. William of the *Abbay* holds 1 land, and pays 6s. a year. John of Culgath holds 1 land, and pays 6s. a year. All the tenants of the township hold 1 land between them, and pay 6s. a year.

TWO ACRES OF MEADOW. They also hold 2 acres of meadow lying by Nobbokscheles* for laying and drying peats there.

They also hold 2 water mills in Neulandes,[163] that is Neubigyng* mill and Whytlye mill*, with the whole suit of multure of all the tenants in Neulandes, of which 1 is waste, and the other is demised to Robert of Wollone by lease, for which he pays 7 marks a year <to the> cellarer.[164]

They also hold 1 plot by Whytlye mill* for leading water to the mill, and it is called the Milnels, and it begins below the mill on the eastern side, ascending northward beside the *smythous* as far as the *hegegarth* of Daltonfeld*; and then westward along the *hegegarth* as far as Simon Swye's former holding; and then descending southward as far as the *mylnfleme*, and from the *mylnefleme* straight to Roulyburn*; and then eastward along that burn as far as the mill. And it is demised at lease to John Haumond, and he pays 6d. a year.

---

[162] Raine represents the missing figure with a dash.

[163] Greg Finch informed us that 'by the early modern period the land we now regard as Hexhamshire south of the town was commonly defined as the Newlands and Rowley Ward of Hexham Manor. Newlands was the land to the south of Rawgreen - the Lillswood area - which would leave Rowley to be the land immediately to its north but south of Dotland'.

[164] Raine represents the missing words with a dash.

ROULYE*. Robert of Ogle* holds 1 husbandland in Roulye, and pays 4s. a year.[165]

<COCELYE*.> Memorandum that the lord of Cocelye should pay the prior and convent 4 marks annually for licence to have a mill in his demesne of Cocelye or Lanhope*, and for suit of multure of that demesne.

<ALWENTON*.> They also hold the site of one building in the township of Alwenton near the church on the eastern side, with 1 garden and 1 croft containing half an acre of land, and it is glebe of that church, and is allocated to the stipend of the chaplain celebrating there, 6s. 8d. a year.

AKOME*. They also hold 1 tithe barn in the township of Akome with 1 garden, and it contains in all 1 rood of land, and Father Peter of Gonwarton* holds that garden and pays 12d. a year.

WALL*. They also hold in the township of Wall 1 tithe barn with 1 adjoining garden, and it contains in all 1 rood of land, and pays 6d. a year.

KEPEWYK*. They also hold 1 tithe barn in the township of Kepewyk with 1 adjoining garden containing 1 rood of land. And Roger Underhill holds the herbage of that garden, <and> pays 6d.

HALIDEN*. They also hold 1 tithe barn in the township of Halidene with 1 adjoining garden containing 1 rood of land and more. And John Lorimer holds the herbage of that garden and will maintain its walls, and he pays 6d. a year.

ROULY*. They also hold 1 tithe barn in the township of Rouly with 1 garden, and it lies on the eastern side of the township, and <is> waste.

CADDEN*. They also hold 1 tithe barn in the township of Cadden with 1 garden and waste.[166]

---

[165] In 1362, the inquest *post mortem* on Robert of Ogle (father of the Robert named in the Black Book), recorded that he held the manor of Rowley, in the liberty of Hexham, of the archbishop of York: *CIPM*, XI, no. 401, p. 317.

NYNBENKYS*. They also hold 1 plot in Nynbenkes for 1 tithe barn containing in all 1 rood, and it lies at the end of the township toward the west, between the township and the mill. And John Bales holds that plot, and pays 4d. a year.

LIBERTIES WITHIN HEXHAMSHYRE*. They also have within Hextildeshamschyre soke and sake and other liberties; that is, the correction of <offences against> the assize of bread and ale; and their servants carrying a rod <of office> for making distraints, summonses and attachments; and the correction of all trespasses of all their tenants in the prior's court.

[LANDS ETC. IN CUMBRIA]

<6 RAVENWYKE*, SCALES*, ISALL*, ALNEBURGH*, CARLISLE>

RAVENWYKE.* They hold there the site of the rectory[167] in which there are two buildings, with 3 surrounding gardens, and 1 building called the Presthous together with a small garden within that site. And 6 acres of arable land called the Kyrkcrofte by Wlthwaytefeld toward the north; and 1 acre on Godrikhow by a ditch that leads to the moor on the southern side of the *lonyng*; and 3 roods, about in the middle of Braythwate *flatte*; and 5 roods of land on Havirberghe; and 1 acre on the Langlandes by the *thorne*, on the western side of the field; and 1 acre on Mouresflat by the mill; and 2 roods on Petemirhalfacre toward the south; and 1 acre on Donaldcrofte toward the north; and 2 roods on Johnshonshousbank; and 1 acre of meadow in Kilngille; and 2 roods of meadow in Avenames.[168]

---

[166] *cum j gardino et vasto.* The should perhaps be 'with one garden and <it is> waste', as at Rowley.

[167] *situm rectoris*, probably in error for *situm rectorie*.

[168] A map that locates some of these lands is provided by A. J. L. Winchester, *Landscape and Society in Medieval Cumbria* (Edinburgh, 1987), p. 73.

SCALES.* ARABLE LANDS. And they hold 5 acres there by the *redcrosse*, of which 2 lie toward the east, and 3 on the northern side near the *crosse*; and 1 toft and croft containing 1 acre of land about in the middle of the township; and 1 acre on Scharlow on the northern side; and 4 acres in various places there, of which one piece lies in the middle of Derhow *flatte*, and another piece on the Monktoftes, and another piece at Kilngilheuede. And those buildings and lands are demised at lease to Adam Thomson of Ravenwyk* for the term of 6 years, and he pays 10s. a year.

ISALL.* THE CHURCH'S GLEBE WITH COTTAGES. They also hold the site of the rectory there, and it is entirely waste; and 2½ acres of arable land of the church's glebe. And the vicar there holds at lease 1 tenement in the township together with those 2½ acres, and pays 3s. 6d. a year. William Hudson holds 1 tenement there and ½ acre of land, and pays 12d. a year. Agnes Mason holds 1 tenement and 3 acres of land, and pays 3s. a year. John Henreson holds 1 tenement and 3 acres of land, and pays 18d. a year. John Thomson holds there 1 tenement and 6 acres 1 rood of land, and pays 4s. 4d. a year. Henry Morland holds 1 acre of land called Hoggiscrofte, and pays 9s.; he also holds 1 field called the Priorfeld at the eastern end of the township on the northern side of Derwent water,* bounded by a ditch, in which there are two buildings, and he pays 10s. a year.

And there is 1 wooded *bank* there, called the Priorbank on the same side of that water, between that field[169] and the township, in which no tenant will cut greenwood without[170] licence of the warden there.

And there is 1 field lying between the Priorfeld and the road that leads to Sundreland,* and it is called the Morewra, and is waste.

They also have common pasture in all wastes and pastures there outside Isale park, <which is> newly enclosed.

---

[169] Presumably Priorfeld.
[170] *sive* in the printed text should be *sine*.

They also have a turbary and peatery there for themselves and their tenants there to meet all their needs, either to be enclosed with a ditch,[171] or for maintaining the common brewing there, as pertains to the prior's free tenement there.

And there is also 1 field there at the eastern end of the township on the northern side of that road that leads to Sondreland*, and it extends as far as the lord's new park of Isale and is called Aldeby, and is entirely waste.

They also hold a quarter share of Plumland* mill with the suit of multure belonging to that share, and in normal years it is worth 15s.

<ALNEBURGH.*> They also have in the township of Alneburgh 1 waste toft with an adjoining croft, containing by estimation 1 acre of land in all, and it lies at the eastern end of the township on its southern side by Thomas Spilgild's toft. In the field of that township they also have 20 acres by estimation of arable land and meadow, of which 1 acre of arable and meadow lies at the eastern end of a *flatte* called the Ganell; and at the *stanbrig*, 2 acres of arable land and meadow; and on the Gresseflatte, on the eastern side, by Wilkenbusk, 1 acre 1 rood of arable land; and on the Midilholme by Matwra, 1½ acres of arable land and meadow; and on Midilholme on the *northwest* side of the Hassockis, 1 acre; and on the northern side of the Matwra, 1 acre of meadow; and on Hexhamcrofte with the Olysyk, 3 acres; and on the Seeflatte with an adjoining piece of meadow between that *flatt* and the Alne burn,* 4 acres by estimation, and it pays 6s. 8d. a year.

<ISALE* TITHES.> And John of Fausyd (and) William Parcar of Isale hold the garb tithes of Isale parish, with all those lands and tenements of Isale, Plumbland* and Alneburgh*, and this year they pay for everything 22 marks, of which £10 to the cellarer of the kitchen.

---

[171] *ad fossatum claudendum,* perhaps for *ad fossato claudendum,* as translated. This is still problematic, but the phrase as printed (literally 'for closing the ditch') is even more so.

<CARLISLE.> And they hold 1 tenement with 1 croft in the city of Karleon* in Caldwelgat on the southern side, by the burn called Donsbett.[172] And it is demised at lease to Robert Goldsmyth of Karleol* for the term of 20 years, and he pays 18d. a year, and no more because he put a new building on that tenement at his own expense; it used to pay 4s. a year. Robert also pays a yearly rent for one tenement there, by that other tenement, for which he used to pay 4s. a year; now he pays 2s. 6d., on account of decay and waste.

THE LIBERTY OF TYNDALE* WITH PRESDALE* AND ALDENNESTONMORE*

<7 ELLERYNGTON*, STANCROFT*, SADLYNGSTANES>

<ELLERYNGTON.*> They also have an annual rent of 13s. 4d. issuing annually from Elleryngton mill, by gift of the late Nicholas de Vieuxpont.[173] The lord of that mill, whoever it may be at the time, should pay this rent at the usual terms.

<STANCROFT.*> They also hold 1 toft in the township of Stancroft and the 20 acres of land nearer that toft toward the *southest*, and they are contained within these bounds: that is, begin<ning> on the western side of the cross standing in Karlelgate called Doddiscross; and so directly northward along a boundary between that land and Doddisfeld as far as Stancroftburn; and so, descending eastward along that *burne* as far as the Nonnesfeld; and then southward along a boundary between that land and the Nonnesfeld as far as Karlelgat; and then, following the Green Way, as far as the western <side> of that cross. And John Thomson holds that land at lease and pays 8s. a year.

---

[172] The two places here seem to be Caldewgate and Dowbeck (perhaps *Doubecc'*):cf. national grid references NY 392554 and 372545. The location of the property was where the beck met the road, probably about NY 394549.

[173] The *inspeximus* charter of 1298 records the donor as Ivo de Vieuxpont: document 3 (item 7).

<SADLYNGSTANES.*> They also hold 1 toft at Sadlyngstanes at the western end and on the northern side, and 1½ acres of arable land next to that toft on the northern side; and 3 acres of meadow by Fenkilleslaw on the northern side, and to the east of the 2 acres, which the same (\sic/) almoner once had; and pasture for 4 cows and 20 sheep. And they are demised at lease, as is set out below.

They also hold 1 toft there, near the already mentioned toft on its eastern side; and 20 acres of arable land there, of which 6 acres lie by that toft on the northern side, and 4 acres lie by Heppeleche to the east, and 5 acres in Hoddesflatte, and 5 acres by Berecrofte to the north; and 4 acres of meadow, of which 1 acre in Haudensyde in the middle, and 1 acre lies on the western side of the stone called Sadlyngstane, and 1 acre lies to the west of the Heppeleche, and 1 acre lies on the southern side of Hoddesflatte; and they have pasture there for a hundred <i.e. 120> sheep and 30 working beasts and 4 horses. And John Forestar of Neuburgh* holds those tenements and lands at lease, and pays 10s. a year in all.

<8> CARRAW*[174]

<FETHRESCHAUE.> Robert of Ogle*[175] holds at lease from the prior and convent a parcel of the pasture of Carraw called Fethreschaue, enclosed within the eastern side of Sewyngshelez* park; and it extends from the wall of the park on that side as far as Cornestrothre spring; and northward along the burn issuing from that spring as far as the Crokidburne; and southward from that spring along 1 siket as far as Sewynscheles* *moss*; and then eastward, following the *moss*, as far as the park wall situated in Fethresschawsyd, first mentioned; and he pays 8d. a year.

---

[174] The entry for Carraw is twice transcribed in *SANT*, (a) up to the lease of Thomas Hoggerson and his associates, (b) up to the reference to mining in the pasture of Carraw, where it breaks off in mid-sentence. There are therefore in some instances two different readings from this source. The passage is translated up to the sub-entry for ' Aldescheles' in *HHN*, IV [part 2, vol. 3], p. 397.
[175] See, too, the entry for Rowley, with Black Book 5.

<TOWNSHIP OF CARRAW.> They also hold the whole township of Carraw, and it is several throughout the year, through all the township field on the southern side of the wall of the Romans, within these metes and bounds: beginning from the eastern side, as the spring flows away from that wall in Thormerstrothre,[176] and westward from the burn isssuing from that spring, along a ditch between the Graysyd and Carraw field; and then toward the *southwest*, following that ditch between Stancrofte moor and the Syde as far as the Langstrothre; and from there along the boundary stones placed in the Langstrothre as far as Grensyde ditch; and from there westward along the burn, <and then> northward along the boundary stones[177] called *mers* placed between Carraw field and Houden moor, as far as the already mentioned wall; and so eastward along the wall as far as the spring first mentioned.

They also hold the pasture of Carraw, and it is a severalty of the township, except for 80 animals of Tepermore*. And the mining of coals and digging of turfs, in that pasture belongs exclusively to the prior and convent. And it is contained within these bounds: that is, within Driden on the eastern side, and the Crokeburne on the northern side, and Sewyngscheles *park* on the western side, and the wall of the Romans on the southern side. And Thomas Hoggerson, John Couper, Richard of Gofden*[178], Adam Proktorman[179] <and> William Jonson hold all that township at lease, and pay £4 a year.

Item, there used to be a water mill there, and it is altogether waste for want of a flow of water.

They also have common pasture all through the pasture of Syde for all animals coming from Carraw throughout the year.

---

[176] *Thormerstrothr'* or *Thornestrother, SANT; Thormerstrother, HHN.*

[177] *et exinde per rivulum occidentaliter versus bor. per lapideas metas.* This reading is evidently corrupt. It seems to be confirmed by *SANT*, though Hodgson had difficulties with the word *occidentaliter*, which he (twice) saw as *occidentlez*. The proposed translation accommodates the change in the character of the boundary that the text implies.

[178] *Gofden, HHN] Gosden, PH.*

[179] *Pktourman, SANT; Pictourman, HHN.*

The Black Book of Hexham

<ALDESCHELES> They have 1 yearly rent issuing from the land of Aldescheles by Teket by gift of Sir Henry Graham, of whom Sir William Heron is the heir, and he should pay that rent, which is 8s., annually, and it is 40 years in arrears.

<TEKET*.> They also hold 1 toft and croft in Teket and ten acres land in a piece of ploughed land called Postulon, and it lies between these bounds: that is, beginning at a ditch ascending southward from Fenwykburne* between Postolon and Nicholas of Ridle's field called Kinrenhowe as far as Aldscheles *bog*; and from there along that *bogg* as far as a siket; and then northward along that siket descending between Postolon and Ald Teket into Fenwikburn; and then, following that burn, as far as the *fote* of the ditch first mentioned.

<GRENDON*.> They also hold 1 rood of land in a demesne toft in Grendon on the western side, and it is demised at lease.

<HENNISHALGH*.> They also hold in the territory of Hennishalgh, at the western end of the township there, a parcel of land called Hamyside lying between Hamyburn on the eastern side, and the Templereyne on the western side, and it contains 9½ acres of arable land, with 1 acre of meadow, and they are joined to the tenure of Rischeles.

RYSCHELES.[180] Item, they hold all the lands and tenements of Rischeles within the territory of Hennishalghe, which are contained within these bounds: that is, beginning at the eastern side of the *ludyet*[181] between Ryschels and Holmishalhraw*[182]; and from there southward to the *crossstandanestan* <; and then> toward

---

[180] The entry for 'Ryscheles' is both summarised and fully transcribed in *SANT* and translated in *HHN*, IV [part 2, vol. 3], p. 326. *SANT* notes that 'Reshiel estate .. is situated between Henshaugh on the East and Melkrige on the West and extended as here(?) mentioned <to> Karlegate, or as it was more lately called the Causey'.

[181] *Ludyet* and *lidyete* are here interpreted as 'lidgate'. Hodgson, however, thought that this was the name of 'the laid or made road, which was the highway between Haydon-bridge and Haltwhistle': *HHN*, IV [part 2, vol. 3], p. 326.

[182] *Holrinshalh raw*, *SANT* (twice); *Holrinshalh-raw*, *HHN*.

the *southest*[183] along an old ditch as far as the Morehak that stands between Thomas Hardor's field and Rischeles; and then straight westward from the *hac* as far as the *strothre* <; and so westward> as far as the Bondrydyng;[184] and from the Bondridyng northward as far as the *stanegate* called Karlelgate;[185] and so westward along that road as far as Milkrigeburn*; and so, ascending northward by the *burne* as far as the *heuedyarde* of Rischeles; and so eastward along the *heuedyard* as far as the eastern side of the *lidyete* first mentioned.

DEMISES OF HENNESHALGH* AND RYSCHELEZ. And Robert Pikryng holds a parcel of those lands, and pays 13s. 4d. a year. William Nicolson of Haltwesyle* holds another parcel of those lands, and pays 6s. a year. Adam Smythmaugh holds a third parcel of the same, and pays 7s. 8d. a year.

<9> THRILWALL*

They hold some lands and tenements there called Wardrew*[186] with 1 close called Orbelawschawe,[187] and they are contained within these bounds: that is southward, as the *syk* to the Frerislawheuede descends, as far as the Burreclough; and from there as far as the Temelhope;* and then westward, following the *dike* of the Temelhope*, as far as Yrthin water;* and then northward, following that water, as far as the Oviryardclough; and

---

[183] *et exinde usque austr. ad le Cross-standane-stan usque le south-est.* The transcripts in *SANT* similarly has *usque*. 'Usque' should probably be 'versus' in both instances.

[184] *et sic a la Hac directe usque le strothre versus occid. usque le Bondrydyng.* The version in *SANT* is the same. The translation assumes that the MS text accidentally omits the words '*et sic versus orientem*' following '*le strothre versus occidentem*'.

[185] *Karlegate, SANT* and *HHN. Karlelgate* is the road to Carlisle. This, Hodgson says, was the Roman Road between Little Chesters and Carvoran: *HHN*, IV [part 2, vol. 3], p. 326.

[186] 'Wardrew is situated on the left bank of the Irthing and the western confines of the county': *HHN*, IV [part 2, vol. 3], pp. 143, 147. The entry relating to Wardrew is transcribed in *SANT*.

[187] *Orlelawschawe, SANT*; *Orlewawschaw, HHN*, IV [part 2, vol. 3], p. 143.

from there as far as the *hegeyard*; and from there eastward as far as Wardrewhous; and from there as far as the *sic* at the Frereleheuede first mentioned.

CRAKDALE MEADOW. They also hold there 1 piece of meadow between Alexander Jonson's field and the field of Wardesnakcolfe called Crakdale, and it contains by estimation 1 acre. And John Clerk and John Mabson his brother hold those lands and they pay 15s. a year. (See the charters <or charter> for other lands not specified here.[188])

Philip Badkok holds Wyrchsnakecolfe as it is enclosed by old ditching there; and he also holds 1 parcel of meadow lying at the *northest syd* of Werthmaybe, and it contains by estimation 3 roods and more, and he pays 5s. a year.

Thomas Jonson of Thrilwall holds Wyrthkeryne by homage and fealty, and he owes suit to the court of Aynwyk* twice a year, and he pays 4s. a year.

John of Thrilwall holds a parcel of land there called the Priorbank lying on the northern side, near Thrilwall *castel*, by homage and fealty, and he pays 3s. a year.

They have also by charters <the right> that the prior's tenants in Thrilwall will mill their grain at Thrilwall mill without multure or any customs and demands, as in the charters.

They also hold 1 place called the Welhouse in which there is 1 newly constructed building with 1 garden on its northern side and 1 croft on its eastern side, and it contains by estimation half an acre; and 1 acre on the northern side of that building called the Swynlandes; and 1 waste acre by that acre toward the west; and 1 rood lying in the Crowkes by Wardogheelgarth. And Thomas Bourdale holds that building and land <and> pays 18d.

They also hold a tenement called Croymagh or Coomhoue in which there are 2 buildings, and some lands there. And they are all contained within these bounds: that is, beginning at the *salgh*

---

[188] Raine records that this bracketed note is in the margin of the manuscript.

standing in the *hegegarth* on the western side of that building; then eastward, descending westward along the *hegegarth*, as far as the *syk* on the western side <of land> of Adam of London; and then straight northward as far as the wall of the Romans; and from there westward, along that wall, as far as a *syk* between Craymokhill and the lands of Croymagh; and then southward, along that *syke*, as far as the *salgh* first mentioned.

<10> FLAGANCLOUGH[189]

There also hold 1½ acres of arable at the foot of Flaghonburne which runs down on the southern side of the common pasture of that holding, and it lies on either side of the *burne*. And John Mody holds those lands and tenements for the term of his life, and pays 6s. 8d. a year.

<11> WARDOGHALL*

They also hold a quarter share of Wardoghall with a built toft and a croft, <with appurtenant rights> in woods, open lands, wastes and assarts, meadows, pastures, moors and marshes; and all the quarter share of Clesket belonging to that toft's quarter share, with all the arable lands, as it is divided among the tenants there within the bounds of Wardoghall.[190] One piece of the lands of this quarter share, the croft, lies on the northern side of the building on that toft and contains 1 acre in total; and another piece lies on the western side by the grange, half an acre; and a third part lies on the western side of the part just mentioned; and another part lies on the southern side <of> the *Wall* in various places on the Crokehilles; and another part in the Bergholme, 1 acre; and another part lies on the Bankes in two places, 1 acre; and another part lies in the Holedall, 3 roods; and another piece lies below the Schaw, ½ acre;

---

[189] Neither the property nor the burn have been identified. To judge from its positioning in the Black Book *Flaganclough* was in the vicinity of Thirlwall, perhaps near Greenhead and Blenkinsopp Castle, where several 'cleughs' (from Old English clōh, 'a ravine') run down to Tipalt Burn.

[190] The Latin construction of this sentence is not very convincing, and there may be some error in the text.

and another part lies in the Bradedale, 1 piece, ½ acre; and in Wardoghalschaw* toward the east, one piece in two places, ½ acre; and, on the western side of that *schaw*, one piece; and on Cowgarth, one piece of waste land; and 1 acre of meadow lies on the eastern side of Wardoghhall by the *hegegarth* there; and another piece of meadow lies below the Schawe, by Poltreskburn*. And William Henreson holds all those lands and tenements <and pays> 13s. 4d. a year.

PASTURE. They also have common pasture within the whole fee of Thirlwall for 80 working beasts, the same number of mares, 80 pigs, and up to 40 goats, with one year's offspring of both pigs and goats. If there should be a smaller number of mares the number may be made up by other animals with their offspring of <up to> two and a half years.

<12> LAND WITH PASTURE IN KNARESDALE*[191]

They also hold all the land with the pasture in the township of Knaresdale within these bounds: that is, beginning from the boundary of the lordship of Gillisland* as far as the Lanerdsete, following the watershed that divides Feuenhope[192] and Glendeu*[193]; and so from Lanerdfote descending as far as the Maydengate*[194] at its nearest point; and northward from the Maydengate* as far as Glendeuburn*[195]; and so, ascending along that burn, as far as the boundaries of the march of Gillisland* first mentioned.

---

[191] Hodgson paraphrases this entry concerning Knarsdale 'from a bad copy': *HHN*, IV [part 2, vol. 3], p. 90. However, he also supplies a 'more exact translation' on p. 352.

[192] *Feuenhope*] *ffevenhope, SANT; Favenhope, HHN; Fenen-hope* PH. This name occurs as *Fefnehope* in a charter of the late twelfth or early thirteenth centuries: *HHN*, IV [part 2, vol. 3], pp. 89-90.

[193] *Glendeu, SANT* and *HHN*] *Glenden, PH*.

[194] *Maydenegate* is the Roman road of Maiden Way, which ran from Kirkby Thore, near Appleby, to the fort of Carvoran on Hadrian's Wall, and is so marked on Ordnance Survey maps.

[195] *Glendeuburn, SANT Glendue burn, HHN; Clenden-burn, PH*.

<13> WHYTLAW*

William of Whytlaw holds the whole of Whytlaw[196] by homage and fealty; and he will perform suit at the prior's court at Aynwyke, that is at two head courts annually, and he pays 4s. a year.

<14> WHYTFELD*

Matthew Whytfeld holds the whole of Whytfeld by homage and fealty; and he will perform suit at the prior's court at Aynwyk annually, and he pays 16s. 8d. a year, of which 3s. 4d. a year to the sacrist's office, and 13s. 4d. to the office of the cellarer of the kitchen.

<15> ALDENESTON*

They also hold some lands and tenements in the township of Aldeneston, on the eastern side of Tyne water, by these bounds: that is, as Natresgille* burn falls southward into the Tyne; and then, descending on the western side, as far as the old bridge, or the site of the old bridge; and from there, ascending along an old ditch, as far as St John's land on the northern side; and due eastward along that land as far as the long ditch; and then, following the long ditch, as far as Natresgill* burn first mentioned.[197]

DEMISE: <...>[198]

They also hold in the same township certain lands and tenements on the western side of the Tyne, within these bounds: that is, beginning at the western head of the old bridge, or site of the old bridge there; and then, rising along the highway and ditch as far as a burn called Foulesyk that runs down on the southern side of

---

[196] The identity of *Whytlaw* as 'a hamlet, the antient enclosed grounds of which are situated in the angle formed by the left bank of Gildurdale burn and the Tyne', is established by *HHN*, IV [part 2, vol. 3], p. 69.

[197] These bounds recite those in Ivo de Vieuxpont's charter of 1223-32: document 28.

[198] Dashes in the printed edition imply that the two entries relating to demises are left blank.

Crosseland; and then, descending along that burn, to Tyne water; and then, descending along the Tyne, as far as the site of the old bridge first mentioned. And it is tenanted.

DEMISE: <...>

PASTURE: They also have there common pasture throughout Aldestonmore for themselves and their tenants for 40 cows, 10 mares and a hundred <*i.e.120*> sheep, all with their offspring of two years, by reason of the demesne lands there. They also have pasture throughout Aldestonmore for themselves and their tenants there for 24 cows and 60 ewes, with their offspring of three years, by reason of the cottages <*or* cottage>. And all the prior's tenants there will mill at the mill of the lord of Aldenston there without <paying> multure.

<16> GERARDGILL*

They also hold in Gerardgill one toft called Thruswell, and pasture there for 10 cows and 2 mares with with all their offspring of two years.

<17> PRESDALE*[199]

They also hold the whole of Presdale, and it is several throughout the year; and, if anyone grazes within the bounds of the pastures at Predale with any beasts at any time, then he should be attached to the prior's court there and be brought to justice. And it is contained within these bounds: starting below Esgylheued*, following the watershed as far as Edestan*; and from there as far as Burnhopheuyde*; <and then> along Hardrode, following the watershed, as far as Brounspotlane[200]; and from there as far as the Crokytburnheued*; and along Crokitburn* as far as Tees water; and then from where the Crokitburne* enters the Tees ascending as far as the top of Fendesfell; and from there straight as far as

---

[199] The first paragraph of this entry is translated in *HHN*, IV [part 2, vol 3], pp. 43-4. He uses 'an old translation'. He observes that 'all the names in this description are still well known excepting Cokeley Fell'.

[200] *Burnpot Lane, HHN.*

Wakstaneghe; and from there as far as Kexburwane spring[201]; and from there as far as Crosgilheued*[202]; and from there eastward across the moss as far as Ninistanes*[203]; and from there as far as Cokeleyfell; and from there, descending along Ellirburne, as far as Tyne water; and so along the Tyne as far as Eskgilfote*; and from there, ascending along Eskgille*, as far as Eskgillheuede* first mentioned.

They also have free entry, passage and exit to Presdale throughout the fee of Aldestone* without anyone impeding them, both for the prior and convent's men and for their animals of every kind; they may not be challenged nor harassed in Aldenestone* pasture, outside those stated bounds of Presdale, whether returning, passing through or tarrying with their working beasts, either by day or night. And the prior and convent may common at their pleasure throughout the whole pasture of Aldenestonmore*, with all their animals going out of Priesdale, every day from sunrise to sunset without anyone's gainsaying.

LIBERTIES AND EASMENTS AT PRESDALE IN ALDENESTONMORE*: The prior and convent and their men dwelling in the township of Aldneston also have estovers in Aldneston woods for building and maintaining their buildings and fences and for all other necessities as they have occasion, without any anyone's gainsaying.

<CHESTREHOPE IN REDESDALE.> They also hold 2 tofts and 2 crofts in the township of Chestrehope* in Redesdale*. These crofts with the tofts lie together about in the middle of the township, on the southern side of the *ford*, on the *peth* that leads to the common pasture, lying on the northern side of that *peth*; and two bovates, called 1 *husbandland*, containing the same number of acres[204] as the other husbandlands in that township, that is 24 acres. And they lay waste for almost 40 years; and they are <now> all

---

[201] *the fountaine of Kekburne wane*, HHN.
[202] *Crosgilheued*] *Grosgilheued*, PH; *Crossgill head*, HHN.
[203] *Nunstanes*, HHN.
[204] *cont. di. acr.* (literally 'containing half an acre'). This is obviously wrong; the translation assumes that the intended reading was or meant *continentem tot acras*.

demised together for the term of 10 years, paying annually 10s. And each year during the term of those 10 years, 6s. 8d of this rent is remitted by the prior to the tenant, Adam of Lee, for his good counsel and service, and so for those years he pays only 3s. 4d.

BARONY OF LANGLYE*

<18> [BYERES*][205]

They hold a tenement called the Byres with lands, woods and pastures, in which there is a park, that enjoys a franchise and all rights just as other parks. And if anyone should graze with his beasts within those lands and pastures at any time of year without the prior's licence he should be attached by the prior's bailiff, and brought to justice for damages in the prior's court there; except that, by concession of the prior and convent <of Hexham>, the prioress and convent of Lamblye* have pasture for their own working beasts coming out from Lamblye* into the pasture at Byres called the *comonpastur*,* that is, on the southern side of Litilblakburn*. However, neither those nuns nor their servants may usurp, take, or remove anything, nor cause damage in the woods of that pasture nor < in?> the park there in any way,[206] nor on the southern side of that *burne*, when they enter with their livestock.[207] And that tenement, with each of its component parts, is contained within these bounds: that is, beginning at Fauenhephed[208] along

---

[205] There are two version of the entry relating to Byers in *SANT*, one as a note and one as a transcript. The entry for Byers is also translated in *HHN*, IV [part 2, vol. 3], pp. 351-2.

[206] *in boscis dictae pasturae, neque quoquo modo parcum ibidem*. This evidently flawed reading is confirmed by *SANT* (transcript). It may be that a word such as 'depascant' has dropped out here, following 'quoquo modo', signifying that the nuns of Lambley were prohibited altogether from grazing in the park and the land south of Litilblakburn.

[207] See documents 32 and 33.

[208] *Fauenhephed*, *SANT* (transcript)] *Fauenhophed*, *SANT* (note); *Favenhopehed*, *HHN*; *Fanen-hemp-hed*, *PH*. See the entry above for land with pasture in Knarsdale.

Glendeuburne*[209] as it descends eastward as far as Maydengate*; and from there northward along the Maydengate* as far as Litilblakburne*; and from there, following the Threpgarth between Lamblye* pasture and the tenement of Byres, as far as Hartelyburne* at the eastern end of Carslye;[210] and from there, following the *heggegarth*, as far as the Midilyate[211] between Kellaw* field and Ulgham* field; and from there, following the *heggegarth*, as far as Stodhirdclogherheuede;[212] and from there southward as far as Foulpote, as it used to run down formerly as far as Mikleblakburne*;[213] and so, following Mikleblakburne*, as far as the *overnoke* of the Coliclose; and from there, following the *park* wall, as far as the Pykitstane; and from there, along the watershed between Gillisland* and the Byres, as far as Fauenhephed[214] first mentioned.[215]

And the prioress of Lamble* pays annually to the prior's chamber one towel suitable for for the prior's table, and holds of the lord prior by fealty.

The prioress also holds at the prior's will a piece of pasture there on the western side of the Maydengate above Litilblakburne* between Maydengate* and a new ditch constructed by the prioress within that pasture, and it contains by estimation 2 acres, and pays 4d.[216] a year.

They also hold a tenement with land and pasture by the Byres called Ulgheham*; it is several throughout the year; and it is contained within these bounds; that is, beginning at the Byreslidyat,

---

[209] *Glendeuburne, SANT* (transcript) altered from *Eldenburne*] Glendeuburne (?), *SANT* (note); *Glenden-burn, HHN*; *Elden-burne, PH*.

[210] *Carslye, SANT* (note); *Carsbye, SANT* (transcript) and *HHN*.

[211] *Midilyate, SANT* (twice) and *HHN*] *Midil-yale, PH*.

[212] *Stodhirdclogherheuede, SANT* (transcript); *Stodhirdcl"gherheuede, SANT* (note); *Hodhirdclogher-hevede, HHN*.

[213] *sicut decurrebat antiquo tempore usque Mikle-blak-burne.* Perhaps this expression implies that the size of Foulpote (or indeed of the 'heggegarth') had been reduced so that it no longer reached the burn.

[214] *Fauenhephed, SANT* (transcript)] *Favenhopehed, SANT* (note); *Favenhophed, HHN*; *Fanen-hemp-hed, PH*.

[215] Cf. the bounds described in document 32.

[216] *3d., SANT* (transcript).

eastward along the *heggegarth* as far as the Midilgarth between Kelloue* field and Ulgheham*; and from there northward along the Mydilgarth[217] as far as Kellauburne*; and then, ascending along that *burne*, as far as the *fote* of the Lanburne where it descends into Kellauburne*; and then westward, following the Lanburne,[218] as far as the *heggegarth* belonging to Langdene*;[219] and then southward, following the *heggegarth*, as far as the Bireslydyete first mentioned.

<19> LANGDENE*[220]

They also hold a tenement, with some lands and pastures that are several throughout the year, by Ulgheham,* and it is called Langdene; and it is contained within these bounds; that is, beginning at the *fote* of the Lanburne where it descends into Kellauburne; and from there northward, following a *syk* between Kellow* field and Langdene field (formerly called Prentkepitsyke, now called Thudeschawesyke), as far as Carlelgate;[221] and then westward from Karlelgate as far as Prentkepitlaw; and from there southward along the *standande stanes* between Gillisland* and Langdene as far as the *heuede* of Stodhirdclughe,[222] which is at the western end of the Byresfeld; and from there eastward, following a *heggegarth*, as far as the *lydyete* of the Byresfeld. And it is tenanted.

And Ulgeham* and Langdene with all appurtenances pay in all 33s. 4d. a year. And when it comes to be built, Langdene is

---

[217] 'from Midilgarth', *SANT* (transcript)

[218] Both *SANT* (transcript) and *HHN* omit 'where it descends into Kellauburne;and then westward, following the Lanburne'.

[219] *usque le hegge-garth tenur' de Langdene*, confirmed by *SANT* (transcript).

[220] There are versions of this entry is transcribed in *SANT* both as a note and as a transcript. It is translated in *HHN*, IV [part 2, vol. 3], p. 352. The name *Langdene* is lost to the Ordnance Survey, but the the description 'by Ulpham' suggests the adjacent dene running down to Hartley Burn.

[221] Though this (and Karlelgate below) seems to be the road to Carlisle it is not easy to envisage which road is meant.

[222] *Stodhirdclughe*, *SANT* (twice)] *Stodhirdcleughe*, *HHN*; *Stod-hirde-highe*, *PH*.

accustomed to pay 42s. a year for four *husband* tenements and 1 cottage.

COMMON PASTURE OF FETH<I>RSTANHALGH*.[223] They also have common pasture throughout the whole fee of Fethirstanhalgh and also in the former Lucy lands[224] lying outside the bounds of the Byres*, Ulgheham* and Langedene, as is specifically contained in charters.

<20> [WHYNETLYE*] [225]

They also hold a built tenement in Whynetle with a croft on the *northest* side of that tenement, on the northern side <of> Ladmannisgate, with some lands and meadows on the southern side of that tenement that are contained within these bounds: that is, beginning at the eastern end of the tenement, where a boundary divides those lands from a piece of land called Perotland[226] that William of Redeschawe holds freely from the prior and convent, as far as into Linleleghe;[227] and so, ascending westward, along boundary stones placed between <it and> the field of William of Redeschaw and John Bascenthwayt,[228] as far the other side on the northern side of Whynetlelaw; and from there along boundary stones placed between <it and> the field of the said William and John as far as Blakhalcloughe; and then eastward, following that *cloughe*, as far as the boundary on the eastern side of the tenement first mentioned. They also hold 3 acres of land called the Langdale adjoining that tenement; and they lie on the eastern side beside a piece of the free tenement of William of Redeschaw that he holds of the prior, as is said below.[229]

---

[223] See document 20. This entry is translated in *HHN*, IV [part 2, vol. 3], pp. 356-7.
[224] The Lucy family became lords of half of the barony Langley as a result of the marriage of Thomas de Lucy to Isabel, daughter of Adam de Boltby, sometime before 1282: Sanders, p. 127.
[225] This entry is translated in *HHN*, IV [part 2, vol. 3], pp. 384-5.
[226] *Devotland, HHN*.
[227] *Lineloghe, HHN*.
[228] *Bastenthwayt, HHN*.
[229] *superius* (instead of *inferius*).

The Black Book of Hexham

DEMISE: <...>[230]

FREE <LAND> THERE: William of Redeschawe holds by fealty a tenement there called Holdeneslande and pays 2s. 6d. a year. He also holds by fealty another tenement called Milnersland, formerly called Perotisland,[231] and pays 22d. a year.

PASTURE THERE. They also have there <pasture> for themselves and their tenants for eight oxen, and for twenty-four cows, and for a hundred <i.e. 120> ewes, and for five mares, and for five sows, with the one-year-old offspring of all those <animals>.

<21> HAYDEN*[232]

They also hold in the township of Hayden 7½ acres of land; of which, four acres lie round Hayden church; and 2½ acres lie at the eastern end of Haydentoun toward the north by the *lonyng*; and 1 acre lies in Ratonraw* field on the eastern side of the *lonyng* there, and it is called the Crosacre. And Thomas Smyth holds those lands and pays 4s. a year. It used to pay 6s. 8d.

THE TITHE BARN. They also have 1 tithe barn built there standing at the *northest* by the churchyard there; and it is demised.

PASTURE IN HAYDEN. They also have common pasture for thirty working beasts and a hundred <i.e. 120> sheep with their offspring, as is specifically contained in charters.

<22> ALLEWASSHE* MILL[233]

They also hold Allerwasshe mill with the millpond and the *modirdame* of that mill, with suit and multure of every kind of grain growing in Allerwasshe and Allerwasseschelez*, whose tenants will mill their grain at a toll of one thirteenth; and they should

---

[230] The missing text is represented by a dash in the printed edition.
[231] *Scrotisland*, HHN.
[232] This entry is translated in *HHN*, IV [part 2, vol. 3], p. 385.
[233] This entry is transcribed in *SANT* and translated in *HHN*, IV [part 2, vol. 3], p. 399.

make, repair and maintain the millpond as many times as necessary, and should roof the mill, except over the *louthre,* and maintain the walls and other necessities of that mill. And Twedye of Allerwassche holds that mill at lease and pays for it and the lands pertaining to it 10s. a year.

LAND ADJOINING ALLERWASSCHE MILL. They also hold some parcels of land adjoining that mill containing by estimation five roods of land; of which one parcel lies on the western side of the *mylnraw* on either side of the *mylnfleme,* and it is called the *mylndame*; and 1 piece lies by that mill between a burn called the Westburne <missing text> to that mill;[234] and it is demised together with the mill, as above.

<23> OLMERS WITH THE WOOD THERE[235]

They hold a tenement called Olmersse with lands, woods, meadows and pastures in severalty that are contained within these bounds: that is, beginning at the *heuede* of the *heggegarth* on the southern side of Widonlonyng; and westward, along that *heggegarth,* as far as the *croyk*; and from there, along boundary stones placed there, as far as Colpottflatt; and from there due westward as far as the Vepontburn; and southward, following that burn, to an old ditch ascending from the Blakleche; and from there eastward, along that ditch, as far as a ditch on the western side of Redersdyng; <and then> northward as far as the *est ende* of Pesseflattend; and from there, following the enclosure of Olmers, to the door of the hall there; and from there, from the western side of that hall along the *hegegarth,* as far as the *heued* of the *heggegarth* on the southern side of the Wydenlonyng first mentioned.

---

[234] *juxta prædictum molendinum, inter quemdam rivulum vocatum le West-burne dicto molendino.* This reading (except for the spelling *Westburn*) is confirmed by *SANT.* Another possible interpretation is '1 piece lies by that mill between <it and> a burn called the Westburne, <west of> that mill.'

[235] This entry, together with that for *Littil Olmers,* is transcribed in *SANT* and translated in *HHN,* IV [part 2, vol. 3], p. 399. The name common to these two properties survived into the sixteenth century as Owmers: Mawer, p. 154. They were in Warden parish, but are not locatable on modern maps.

<24> LITTIL OLMERS

They also hold there a parcel of arable land and meadow called Litilolmars, as it is enclosed by a ditch; and it lies on the *northest* side of Olmers between the *lonyng* and Allerwesscheles* field. And they are tenanted <for a rent of> 23s.

<25> THE MANOR OF WARDON*[236]

They also hold there the manor of Wardon in which there are various buildings, with lands, woods and pastures, within whose bounds is an enclosed park called Wardonwode, which has the liberties and rights generally pertaining to a park. This manor with all its components is contained within these bounds: that is, beginning at Wardonford; and then westward, ascending along the middle of Tyne water, as far as the Priordyk; and then northward, following the *dyke*, until it reaches the *westrecorner* of Wardonwod; and from there following the enclosure of that *wod* until it reaches the eastern side of Yekesyde; and from there northward, along a *reygne* lying between Wardon field and a parcel of land lying between that *reygne* and Yekesyd, until it reaches the *croftesendes* of Over Wardon;[237] and from there, along boundary stones between those crofts and the manor field, as far as a wooded place called the *hotte*[238] of Ovyrwardon*; and from there along 1 *reygne* until it reaches the road that leads to Walwyk*; and from there northward, following that road, until it reaches the stone bridge that lies at the entrance to Walwykfeld; and from there along a burn running between Walw<yk> field and a parcel of land formerly called Hollemarsse,[239] now called Holmerscrofte, as it falls into the Tyne; and from there following the middle of Northtyne water, until it reaches Wardonford again.

THE CROSFLATT. Outside those bounds they also hold a parcel of land called the Crosflatt in Over Warden field, lying on

---

[236] This entry, is transcribed in *SANT* and translated in *HHN*, IV [part 2, vol. 3], pp. 401-2.
[237] *Wardon Superior.*
[238] An error, perhaps, for *holte.*
[239] *Holk-Marse, SANT*; Holkmarse, *HHN*.

the western side of Walwykwaye, containing by estimation 4 acres of land, and it adjoins the manor.

LANG ACRE. Outside those same bounds, on the northern side, they also hold a parcel of land near Crosflatt, on the road mentioned above;[240] and it contains by estimation 1 acre of land, and it adjoins the manor.

<HARDHALGH>[241] They also hold a parcel of land on the southern side of the South Tyne called Hardhalgh, and it lies between a parcel of Wharnelye* called Eldenhalghe on the western side and Coceleye* *bank* on the southern side, and Tyne water on the northern side. And it contains by estimation 10 acres of land; and it is joined to the cultivated land of the manor.

WARDON TOWNSHIP. There are <...>[242] cottages in the township of Wardon, and each cottage will reap with 1 man for four days each year at harvest time when asked, except that the vicar there performs no service for a parcel of land that he holds from the demesnes there. This land contains 12 acres and 3 roods, and they lie on the southern side of Yekesyde and on the southern side of the *reygne* that separates Over Wardon field from that land.

Father Richard Morlande, the vicar there, holds 12 acres 3 roods of land from the demesnes, as specified above, and they are contained within those bounds; he also holds 1 cottage built in the township there, and 3 acres[243] 1 rood of land, of which 1 acre 1 rood lie on the southern side of those 12 acres 3 roods[244] in the vicar's tenure; and 1 acre lies on the southern side of the park between the park and the water of South Tyne; and 1 acre lies in Hardhalghe, and he pays 4s. a year and labour services and customs.

---

[240] i.e. Walwykwaye.
[241] 'Till some 80 years since, this tract, now called Harhaugh, was an unenclosed common', according to Hodgson, but he places it on the northern side of the South Tyne: *HHN*, IV [part 2, vol. 3], p. 403. The text implies it was on the southern side, like Wharmley and Coastley.
[242] Raine represents the missing figure by a dash. In *SANT* there is a blank.
[243] 3 acres, *SANT*; 4 acres, *HHN*.
[244] 2 roods, *SANT* and *HHN*, but Hodgson reads 12 acres 3 roods in the earlier entry.

(COTTAGES.) Beatrice Wryght holds 1 cottage there and 1 rood of land lying in places corresponding to those in the vicar's holding specified above, [245] and she pays 4s. a year and labour services. Matilda of Paris holds 1 built cottage and 3 acres 1 rood of land lying in various places corresponding to those above, and pays 4s. a year and labour services. John of Schaldfurth holds 1 cottage and 3 acres[246] 1 rood of land in places corresponding to those above, and pays 4s. a year and labour services. John of Ledom holds 1 cottage and 3 acres 1 rood of land, in places as above, and pays 4s. a year and labour services. There is there 1 place called Clerkplace. Gilbert Schephird holds 1 cottage and 3 acres and 1 rood of land adjoining it, as above, and he pays 4s. a year and labour services. There is there 1 cottage with 3 acres 1 rood of land adjoining it, as above.

WARDON BOAT. Alice Coyk <and> Robert Bacward[247] hold Wardon boat for the term of 10 years and pay 20s. a year.

The fruits and revenues of that manor are assigned to the office of the cellarer of the kitchen each year, to be paid at the usual terms, and it pays £6 13s. 4d. a year.

<26> PASTURE IN THE PASTURES OF WALWYK*

They also have common pasture in the pastures of Walwyke for 200 (*i.e. 240*) sheep and sixteen oxen[248] and 10 cows going out from the manor of Wardon*, with free exit and entry to that pasture to common throughout the year, by grant of Richard Comyne, as is specifically contained in charters.

---

[245] *proportionaliter in locis superius in tenura vicarii specificatis*, a reading confirmed by *SANT*. The meaning here and in the following entries is unclear. Perhaps it is a way of repeating 'from the demesnes, as specified above, and they are contained within those bounds'.
[246] 3 acres, *SANT*; 4 acres, *HHN*.
[247] *SANT* represents these two names as connected with a bracket.
[248] *et sexdecim boves*, *PH*; *C sexdecem boves*, *SANT*.

<NORTHUMBERLAND>

<27> SCLAVELEYE*

They also hold various tenements in Sclavelye and half a carucate of land and some other acres, as in the convent's charters, and pastures for some sheep, as is contained in charters.

John Forister of Corbrig* holds freely by fealty 1 messuage with some adjoining acres called Daltonplace (and it lies on the southern side of the township near the eastern end), and he pays 12d. a year. John Dobynson holds 1 built toft there with 1 croft containing in all 3 roods, and various acres of land containing 1 husbandland, of which 1 rood lies on the western side near that croft; and at Wadescroftsendis, ½ acre; and on the Parsonslawe, ½ acre; and on the eastern side by the Foulewell, ½ acre; and on the Thorenknoll, ½ acre, and on the northern side of the Cotegarth, 1 rood; and in Patryding by the Cotegarth, 1 rood; and in Patryding, by the Cotegarth, 5 acres; and on the Chestrez, 1 rood; and at the Hollelech, 1 acre; and at the western end of the Hoghtoncrofte, ½ acre; and <on> the western side of that ½ acre between a parcel of land of Robert of Wollowe, lying on the eastern side, and a parcel of demesne land on the western side, 2 acres; and at the end of Richard Gibbison's croft, 1 acre; and on the Mylnflatte at the southern end of the Hoghtoncrofte, 1 acre; and in the Westcrofte by 6 acres in the tenure of Richard Hunter which he holds of the prior, 2 acres; and on Scheldeschaw* are various waste acres in the tenure of the same tenant. And John holds those tofts and lands for the term of three years, and pays 10s. a year.

PREST PLACE. William Wallar holds 1 toft with 1 adjoining croft called the Prest place containing in all 1½ acres of land for the term of three years, and pays 2s. a year.

LUMBARDS PLACE. Henry Hanson holds a built toft with an adjoining croft containing in all 1 acre called Lumbard Place for the term of three years, and it lies on the western side of the church by the toft already mentioned, and he pays 3s. 4d. a year.

HUSBANDLANDS. Richard Hunter holds 1 waste toft with a croft containing in all 1½ acres, and it lies on the northern side of the township at its western end; and <he holds> various acres constituting 1 husbandland, of which 1 acre is called Matfennesacre lying in the *west syde* of the Northfelde; and in the Westcroftes between a parcel of demesne land on the western side and a parcel of John of Neuton's land on the eastern side, 6 acres; and in the Schelfeld on the eastern side by the Parrok, 1 acre called Prioracre. And the remaining acres pertaining to that husbandland lie waste on Scheldschaw*. And Father Richard[249] holds that toft and lands for the term of three years and he pays 3s. a year.

<PEAT AND TURF.> The prior and convent and their tenants there have <the right> to dig in the peateries and turbaries within the common there, and to take their estovers, and all their necessities, even if the lord of Sclavelye or his tenants do not wish to take <theirs>.

SCLAVELYE SHEEPFOLD. They also have 1 sheepfold on the northern side of the township at its eastern end with 1 adjoining garden containing in all 1 acre of land, and common pasture for commoning there throughout the year; and <the right> to common up to 15 *score <i.e. 300>* of sheep in all sections of Sclavelye at appropriate times. And now they pay nothing because <it is> in the lord's hand for keeping sheep there.

STELE* SHEEPFOLD. They also have 1 sheepfold in the Stele near the western end, with an adjoining garden on its northern side containing in all 1 acre of land, and common pasture for 15 score *<i.e. 300>* of sheep throughout the year, and common in all sections of Stele, as above in Sclavelye. And those sheep, both from Sclavlye and from Stele, will common in either sheepfold, jointly and separately, within the bounds of both Sclavelye and of Stele, as it shall please the prior and convent.

<28> STOKYSFELD*

William Ayrike holds all Stokesfelde by homage and fealty, and pays 13s. 4d.[250] a year; that is, 6s. 8d. at the feast of the Nativity

---

[249] *dominus Ricardus.*
[250] 13s. 8d. in the text.

of St John the Baptist, and 6s. 8d. at the feast of St Cuthbert in September, of which 12d. is for castle guard.

<29> PROUDEHOWE*

They also hold in Proudehowe on the western side of the township, near the northern end, 1 toft and some built acres in the township field with 1 croft, containing in all 1 acre and 1 rood of land; and on the southern side of the Rayhillsyde 1 acre 3 roods called Hexhamland; and on the northern side by the Bradwyner on both sides of the Viner'waye, 2 acres of land; and on the western side of those acres across that road and abutting on the Lytill Viner' at its southern end, 2 acres; and on the Smalrodes abutting on the Bradwellmedoue, 1 rood; and on the Ulyrudes abutting on demesne land there, 1 rood; and on the eastern side by Cokrelliswell, 1 rood; and on the western side near that well, 1 rood; and on the eastern side of the township below Robert Hyne's garden, half a rood. And it pays 8s. a year.

CONCERNING THE FISHERY AT OVYNGEHAM*. <...>[251]

<30> CORBRYG*

They also hold some tenements and rents in Corbryg. The tenants are as follows.

John Meryngton holds 1 free burgage in Sant Maregate* on the western side near the bridge, between John Fayte's burgage on the eastern side and Robert Fayte's burgage on the western side, and pays 3s. a year (to the cellerar).[252] Gilbert Fayte holds 1 burgage in Sydgate on its southern side between Robert Milner's burgage on the western side, and Robert Hudespeth's burgage on the eastern side, and pays 12d. a year. Magot Spryng holds 1 burgage there opposite the *westkyrkstyle* between William of

---

[251] Raine notes that there is a blank space here.
[252] Raine records that the bracketed note is in the margin of the manuscript.

Blenkhowe*'s burgage on the southern side and Thomas Chepman's burgage on the northern side, and pays 12d. a year. William Hogg holds 1 burgage in Fischamblesgat on its northern side, formerly called Mongweskelyplace, between John Fayte's burgage and the burgage of Sir William Heron, knight, on the eastern side, and pays 13s. 4d. a year. John Forestar holds 1 burgage in the same place between John Fayte's burgage on the western side, and William Hunter's burgage on the eastern side, which he holds freely of the almoner, and pays 3s. a year. William Hunter holds freely 1 burgage in the same street between John Forester's burgage and the road which is called Prentstrete, and pays 2s. 6d. a year, and after the term contained in his indentures[253] he will pay 5s. a year. Adam Lauson holds freely 1 burgage in Narowgate on its eastern side, called Adampalmarplace, and pays 3 s. a year. Nichol<as> Walkar holds 1 burgage in Thorneburghgate on its southern side, between the burgage of <...> and he pays 18d. a year; and Robert Walch holds that burgage (to the almoners' office).[254]

They also hold 1 burgage in Colewellchare on its southern side by the vennel that leads to the Tyne, in the lord's hand, and it usually pays 3s.[255] John Forestar of Corbrigg holds 1 burgage formerly in the tenure of Adam of Dyghton, and it usually pays 3s. a year.

<31> BEAUMOND*

They also hold the whole land of Beaumond in the territory of Chollirton*, and it is several throughout the year, and is contained within these bounds; that is, beginning at Eriane bridge*, ascending northward along the Derestrete* as far as Foulebrig; and from there along a siket called Beaumondburne toward the

---

[253] a redundant *and* follows *indentures*.
[254] The relationship between the tenures of Nicholas Walkar and Robert Walch is unclear. Perhaps Walch was a subtenant. Raine records that there is a blank where the adjoining properties should have been noted and that the the bracketed note relating to Walch's rent is in the margin of the manuscript.
[255] *solet reddere*, here and in the next item.

southwest as far as Alexander of Swynburn*'s meadow; and from there toward the *southest* along boundary stones placed between Beaumond and that Alexander's meadow as far as the Sandilandendes;[256] and from there westward, along a small siket between that meadow and a parcel of Beaumond meadow lying between that siket and Eriane water*, as far as the *wythebusk* standing on the eastern side near the Skotisford; and from there following Erian water* as far as Eriane bridge* again. And it is to be noted that that the prior and convent and their tenants dwelling in Beaumond have free egress and entry with all their working beasts to the common pasture of Chollirton* to common on that pasture at all times. And the tenants of the township of Chollirton* hold that <land> with its appurtenances for the term of three years, with the first term of payment at the Feast of St Martin,[257] and they pay 53s. 4d.; they used to pay 5 marks.

<32> CHOLLIRTON*

They also hold various tenements and lands in Chollirton. The tenants are as follows.

Hugh Colstane holds 1 tenement on the southern side of the township next to the churchyard with 1 garden containing by estimation 1 acre and more; the tithe barn stands at the eastern end of this garden. He also holds 27 acres of arable land belonging to that tenement, of which, 2½ acres are on the southern side of Eriane burn* opposite the tithe barn abutting on Cocklaufeld; and on the western side of Kilnflate, ½ acre; and on Horslawspule, ½ acre; <and on> Schothalghbankys and on Nithre<schotlaubankes> ½ acre;[258] and on Overschotlaubankes, ½ acre; and on the eastern side of Blaklaw, ½ acre; and on its western side, 1 acre; and on the eastern side of the Lons<...>ane,[259] 1 rood; and on the eastern side of Bronslauemedoue, 1 rood; and on the western side of Bronslawflate, ½ acre; and on the northern side of Bronslawmedoue, abutting onto it, 3 roods; and on the Canonflatte, on the western side of the

---

[256] *Sandilandes*, SANT.
[257] It is odd not to have a year here; perhaps 1379.
[258] There seems to be errors in the text at this point.
[259] The missing letters are indicated in the printed edition by three dots.

Mosseway that leads to Swynburn*, 1½ acres; and on the *buttes* by the *dyk* at the northern end of the Kilnflatte, ½ acre; and on the *heuedlandes* of Brouneslawflatte abutting on the Canonflatte, 1 rood; and at the head of the Maynflatt on each side of the Messewaye, ½ acre; and on the southern side of the *crosse* on either side of the road there, 1 rood; and on Holmersbank, on the eastern side of that *crosse*, ½ acre; and in Harlawhop abutting on the Messeway, ½ acre; and on the western side by the Harlaw, ½ acre; and on the Mesiway on the same, 1 rood; [260] and on the eastern side of the *lonynghed*, 1 rood; and on the southern side of Aldchestre, 3 roods; and on the western side on the Stobithorn, 1 rood; and on the eastern side of Morelaw, abbutting on the *leche*, ½ acre; and on the northern side of Dueldrigge, ½ acre; and on the eastern side of the Smythehopsyde, ½ acre; and in the middle of Craustrige, ½ acre; and on the eastern side of West<c>raustrige, 1 acre; and on the western side of Est<c>raustrige, 1 rood; and on the eastern side of Fartirmerethorne abutting on Craustermerleche, 1 acre; and on the southern side of that land, 1 rood; and between Faltermere and the *merlpottes*, 1 acre; and on the northern side of the *merlpottes*, 1 rood; and in the middle of Waynrig, 3 roods; and on the eastern side of the Brereryg, 1 rood; and on the eastern side of the Hudesrodes, 1 acre; and between the Kornhilles, 1 rood; and in the middle of the Milnrig, ½ acre; and on Fulrig, 3 roods; and in Swynburnefeld on the northern side of the *crosse*, 1 acre.

He also holds ½ acre of meadow on the southern side of the Eriane burn* by the 2½ acres listed first among his holdings; and 1 acre at the *milndamhede*; and 1 rood on the Prestleche.

He also holds 1 cottage on the northern side of the township at its western end with 1 adjoining croft, containing in all by estimation ½ acre. And there belong to that cottage 3 acres of arable land, of which 3 roods lie at Brouneslaumedoue; and 1 rood lies at the *westsyde* of the Kylnesflate; and on Holmerbankes, ½ acre; and on the northern side of the *crosse* in Swynburnfelde, 1 acre.[261] And

---

[260] *Et super le Mesi-way, super eandem, j roda.*
[261] See the entry for West Swinburn under Colwell, Black Book 40.

the acres specified here are attached to the husbandlands named above.²⁶²

He also holds 1 cottage on the same side of the township <in the>²⁶³ tenure of Alan Hoghyrd with 1 adjoining croft, and it contains in all 1½ roods. And for all the those lands and tenements Hugh pays 28s. a year, of which 25s. for the husbandlands and 3s. for the cottages. He used to pay 4s.²⁶⁴

Alan Hoghird holds 1 built toft with 1 garden and 1 adjoining croft between the cottages already mentioned, and it contains by estimation 1 acre of land; and 28 acres of arable land, of which 1 rood lies on the Kylnflatte; and on Horslawes, 1 acre and 1 rood; and in the *halghe* on the southern side of Ereane burn* by 2½ acres of Hugh of Colstane, 2½ acres; and on Houselauepole, ½ acre; and on Nethrescothalghbank, ½ acre; and on the northern side of the Horslawe abutting on Barensfurthwaye, 3 roods; and on the western side of that road, ½ acre; and on Overschothalghbank, ½ acre; and on the eastern side of the Blaklawe, ½ acre; and on its western side, 1 acre; and on the eastern <side> of Brounslawe-medowe, 1 rood; and on the western side of Bronslauflatte, ½ acre; and on the western side of the Messeway that leads to Swynburn* on the Canonflatte, 1½ acres; and on the *buttes* at the *syk* on the northern side of the Kilnflatte by the Messewaye, ½ acre; and on the *heuedlandes* of Bronslawflatte, 1 rood; and below Schothalghlyn, 1 acre; and at the head of Maynflatte on either side of the Messeway, ½ acre; and on the southern side of the *crosse*, on either side of the road there, 1 rood; and in Harlawhop abutting on the Messewaye, ½ acre; and on the western side by the Harlawe, ½ acre; and near that land on the the Messewaye, 1 rood; and on the eastern side of the *lonyngheuede*, 2 roods; and on the southern side of Agchestre, 3 roods; and on the western side, on the Stobthorne, 1 rood; and on the eastern side, on Morilaw, abbutting on the *leche*, ½ acre; and on the northern <side> of Dueldrige, ½ acre; and on the eastern side of Smethopsyde, ½ acre; and in the middle of

---

²⁶² No husbandlands have been named, and it is not clear how many of them made up Hugh's holding.
²⁶³ Raine represents the missing words by a dash.
²⁶⁴ i.e for the cottages.

Crawstrig, ½ acre; and on the eastern side of Westcrawstrig, 1 acre; and on the western side of Estcrawstrig, 3 roods; and on the eastern side of Fartermerethorne abutting on Crawstrigemereleche, 1 acre; and on the southern side, near that land, 1 rood; and between Fartermerethorne and the *marlpottes*, 1 acre; and in the middle of Waynrige, 3 roods; and on the eastern side of the Breririg, 1 rood; and on the eastern side of Hodesrodes, 1 acre; and between the Cornhilles, 1 acre; and on the southern side of the Cornhilles, 1 acre; and on the Cornhilles, 1 rood; and in the middle of Milnrig, ½ acre; and on Fulrig, 1½ acres.

Alan also holds 1 acre 3 roods of meadow that he shares equally <with Hugh Colstane>, with locations and bounds as specified in the details of Hugh's holdings.

DEMISES. And Alan holds those tofts and lands paying 30s. a year.

And it is to be noted that all the lands listed above in the tenure of Hugh and Alan lie in parcels both together and separately within the locations and bounds specified above.

<33> BAROUSFORD*

They also hold in Barousford 1 built tenement, with 30 acres of arable land and 1 acre of meadow, and this tenement lies on the northern side of the township near the eastern end by the *pole* with 1 adjoining garden containing by estimation 3 roods of land. And of those 30 acres of land, 4 acres lie in the Westegge; and between the *houghes*, 12 acres 3 roods; and in Holfurthhegge, 4 acres; and in Seleegeflatte, 9 acres 1 rood. And those acres of meadow[265] lie in three parts; that is, 1 part in Hardenhole; and the second part in the *karr* which is called Seleeyge; and the third part on the northern side below the garden.

---

[265] There is an obvious but unresolvable discrepancy here between 'those acres of meadow' and the single acre mentioned earlier.

LIBERTIES OF THE TENANTS IN BAROUSFORD. And the prior's tenant of those lands will mill his grain at the lord's mill there without multure, and will be quit of giving pannage.

<TITHE BARN.> They also have there 1 tithe barn on the northern side of the township to the west by the *pottes*, with 1 adjoining garden, and it contains in all ½ acre of land and more; and that barn is in the prior's hands for keeping garb tithes.

<DEMISE.> And the said John of Barassfurd[266] holds those tenements and lands, with the produce of the tithe barn garden, and pays 20s. a year of which 2s. to the bursar's office and 18s. to the abbey's groceries.

<34> GUNWARDTON*

They also hold in Gunwardton 1 built tenement on the southern side of the township and chapel, with 1 garden, on southern side of which stands a tithe barn; and with 1 adjoining croft it contains in all by estimation 4 acres of land; and 2 husbandlands containing as many acres as the other husbandlands there, of which 5 acres called the Priorflatte lie on the southern side by that *croft*; and on the northern side of the road between Barousford* and Chipches*, on the Wyndilandes, 3 acres; and on the Sandilandes on the southern side of Schirrewelstrandes abutting on Tyne water, 5 acres; and on the western side of the *milnsyd*, 2 acres; and on the Scholbrades, 2 acres; and on the eastern side by Fulfurdsyde, 1 acre; and on the Gibbismore, on the eastern side of Michelsbank, abutting on the Sclateford, 8 acres; and on Hardenway, about in the middle, across the road there that leads from Gonwarton to Chipches*, 2 acres; and on the southern side of Mullanwod above the *dyk*, 3 acres.

And at the *heuede* of the Schirrewell, 1 acre of meadow. And in Fulfursyde by the acre of arable land there mentioned above, ½ acre of meadow. And it is tenanted, <and pays> 21s.

---

[266] The tenant's name has not, in fact, been previously mentioned.

<35> BYRTELYE*

They also hold in Byrtelye 1 built tenement on the southern side of the township toward the eastern end, with 1 garden and 1 croft on the southern side of the tenement. And the croft contains 6 acres of arable land that lie between William Lyghtfote's holding on the western side and Adam of Lee's land on the eastern side, and it abuts on Dunley* on the southern side. And the prior's tenants will mill their grain at the lord's mill there without multure, and will be quit of giving pannage. And it is now tenanted, <and pays> 5s.

<36> CHIPCHES*

They also hold in Chipches 1 tithe barn at the eastern end of the township on the northern side of the road that leads to Gonwarton*, and with 1 adjoining garden; and it contains in all less than 1 rood of land; and it is in the lord's hand for putting garb tithes in.

<37> COLDEN*

They also hold all Colden, and it is several throughout the year and contained within these bounds: that is, beginning at the eastern end of the Trowhille; and from there, as the old ditch goes, to the Troweburne; and from there, along Troweburne westward as far as the Leyacredyk; and from there southward, along the *standandstanes* standing between Britle moor and the Newfeld of Colden, as far as the Langesyk; and from there, along the the Langesyk, eastward as far as Coldenburne*; and from there, along an old ditch between Gonwarton* moor and Colden, as far as a small siket on the northern side of a small outcrop of rock; <...>[267] called Coldenkyrk* as far as the Derstrete*; and from there northward along the Derestrete* as far as the Trowhill first mentioned.

---

[267] There appear to be some words missing, and probably at this point since it seems unlikely that as small outcrop of rock (*parva rupis*) would be called Coldenkyrk.

They also have free entry and egress from Colden as far as Gonwarton* moor,[268] for 5 score working beasts, that is oxen and cows, with grazing at this moor for these working beasts at all times. And if these working beasts should enter the Frithe at any prohibited time they should not therefore be impounded for *eschape* but ought to be driven back freely and peacefully without clamour or harm (by an indented charter and concord made between the prior and convent and John son of John of Gonwarton*).[269]

DEMISE. And Colden with all its appurtenances is in the tenure of Alan of the Strothre, and he pays 66s. 8d. a year.

<38> STELDEN[270]

John of Midelton, lord of Swynburn Est*, holds all Steldene by homage and fealty, together with the toft and croft that Samson of Swynburne* once held with all its appurtenances, except the prior and convent's sheepfold in Stelden, and their pasture in Gonwarton* moor with free entry and exit for the prior and convent's sheep accommodated in that sheepfold. And he pays 40s. a year for those lands, of which 33s. 4d. a year to the abbot of

---

[268] *de dicto Colden usque moram de mora de Gonwarton.* The right of common on Gunnerton moor for beasts from Cowden shieling is independently recorded: document 3 (item 18). What is evidently a corrupt text has been amended accordingly. If *de mora* can be allowed to have been wrongly place for some reason the text could be amended to *de mora de dicto Colden usque moram de Gonwarton* ('from Cowden moor to Gunnerton moor').

[269] Raine records that the bracketed note is in the margin of the manuscript. This John son of John of Gunnerton does not figure in the account of Gunnerton in *NCH*, IV, pp. 320-1, 325. Either he was the Sir John recorded in 1279 (on the assumption that the *History* is in error concerning his paternity) or he was Sir John's otherwise unrecorded son and heir. In either case he was dead by 1293: *The Northumberland Eyre Roll for 1293*, ed. C. M. Fraser, Surtees Society 211 (Woodbridge, 2007), nos. 246, 310, pp. 88-9, 120-1.

[270] Stelden was part of the township of Little (alias East) Swinburn: *NCH*, IV, p. 304. The name is lost from modern maps.

Newmostre[271]; and in default of payment, that abbot re-entered and demised Stelden, as his own right and justice required.

<39> SWYNBURN EST*

They also have a parcel of land there for building a tithe barn, measuring 80 feet in length and 80 feet in breadth, and it is at the western end of the churchyard of All Saints' chapel there toward the north. And Jordan of Barousford* holds this plot and pays 1d. a year.

<40> COLLEWELLE*

They also have in Collewelle pasture for four hundred[272] sheep throughout the common pasture there, and for 30 oxen and 10 cows with 1 bull in this township, with free entry and egress from the township of Byngfeld* to that common in that pasture throughout the year [by Gilbert de Umfravill's charter[273]].

They also have there 1 tithe barn with 1 adjoining garden, and it contains in all less than a rood; it stands on the northern side by Chollirtonwaye at the *southwestend* of the township, and abuts on the *southend* of the *meres*. And William Smert holds <right to take> produce grown in that garden, and pays 1d.

DEMISE. The heir of Roger of Wodryngton[274] holds by homage and fealty 1 messuage in the township of Swynburne

---

[271] The abbot of the Cistercian abbey of Newminster, Northumberland. See *Chartularium Monasterii de Novo Monasterio*, ed. J. T. Fowler, Surtees Society LXVI (1878), pp. 71-3, which locates this lost settlement 'in the territory of Swynburn' (p. 73).

[272] *quadringinta*. Four hundred is more likely than forty given the number of other beasts allowed.

[273] Raine records that the bracketed note is in the margin of the manuscript. Umfraville held Colwell of the Heron family, who held the barony of Hadston: *NCH*, IV, p. 291.

[274] Roger of Widdrington died on 13 April 1372. His heir, John de Widdrington, was only one year old at his father's death, and so became a ward of the Crown: *CIPM*, XIII, no. 215, pp. 198-200.

West*, with some acres of land belonging to it in the field there. This messuage lies at the western end on the southern side of the road, and opposite the *northestcorner* of the wall around the castle there.[275] And it was recently in the tenure of Adam Scibald, and pays 3s. a year to the convent's groceries.

TITHE BARN. They also have in the same township 1 tithe barn, and it lies on the *northest* side of the chapel there, and is waste.

AN ACRE OF LAND IN SWYNBURN WEST*. They also have 1 acre of land in the field of this township, and it lies on the northern side by the *crosse*, and it is attached to Hugh Colstane's holding in Chollirton*, as it is set out there.

<41> KYRKHETON* WITH CALDSTROTHRE[276]

They also hold the whole lordship in Kyrkheton and Caldstrothre, that is, in homages, services, reliefs, wardships, escheats, villeinages, with all liberties pertaining to the township, and with all forinsec services whatsoever.

John of Strevelyne, knight,[277] holds some lands in Kyrkheton for homage and fealty. Thomas of Horsle holds some lands there for homage and fealty. John Kemp holds some lands and tenements there for homage and fealty. John of Marlaye holds some lands and tenements there for homage and fealty. Thomas of Beckeburne holds some lands and tenements in Caldstrothre for homage and fealty, and pays 1d each year at Christmas. John of Dalton holds some lands and tenements for homage and fealty. Thomas of Hildreton*, knight, holds some lands and tenements there by homage and fealty. And all those owe suit at the prior's court there.

---

[275] Roger of Widdrington received a licence to crenellate his dwelling at Great Swinburn in May 1346: *CPR 1345-8*, p. 88.

[276] *Caldstrothre* does not appear on modern maps, and its location seems not to be known.

[277] For this man, see D. Cornell, 'Sir John Stirling: Edward III's Scottish Captain', *Northern History*, XLV, no. 1 (2008), pp. 111-24. He died in August 1378.

HUSBANDLANDS. And there are 33 husbandlands in that township,[278] and each land contains 34 acres of arable land and meadow, except for the land in the tenure of Richard Atkynson, for that land contains 7 acres formerly adjoining a cottage, and 18 acres of *forland*, and they are now combined together as a husbandland. The tenants are as follows.

John Hastynsone holds 3 husbandlands, and pays 30s. a year. Richard Atkynsone holds 1 land, which is attached to a husbandland <*or* the husbandlands>, and pays 8s. a year. John of Acome* and Christine Scot hold 1 land, and pay 9s. a year. Roger Johnson holds 2 lands, and pays 20s. a year. John of Esschelez* holds 1 land, and pays 10s. a year. William of Babynton* holds 1 land, and pays 10s. a year. William Gilessone holds 3 lands, and pays 10s. a year. Henry of Schaftow* holds 1 land, and pays 10s. a year. John Wilkynson, a neif of the lord, holds 3 lands, and pays 20s. Robert Seemane holds 1 land, and pays 10s. a year. William Jonson, a neif of the lord, holds 2 lands, and pays 20s.

There are 8 cottages there and 2 crofts. The tenants are as follows.

John Hastynson holds a built cottage with 4½ acres of land, and pays 2s <a year>; he also holds a waste cottage and 5 acres of land, and pays 2s. a year. John Wylkynson, a neif of the lord, holds 1 waste cottage and 3 acres, <and pays> 18d. John of Babynton* holds a cottage and 13 acres of wasteland, and pays 3s. a year. John Morell holds 1 built cottage and 3½ acres of land, and pays 3s. a year. William Dudden holds 1 built cottage and 7 acres, and pays 6s. a year. Christine Scott holds 1 waste cottage and 3½ acres of land, and pays 12d. a year. William Beene holds 1 built cottage and 7 acres of land, and pays 5s. a year. Robert Atkinson holds 1 croft called the Cotgarth and pays 8d. a year; he also holds 1 croft called Natrescrofte and pays 12d. a year.

DEMESNE MEADOW. All the tenants of the township jointly hold 7½ acres of meadow from the demesnes, and pay 6s. a year.

---

[278] Only eighteen are listed below.

WASTE MEADOW. They also have a piece of demesne meadow called the Heghsidlech, and it is waste.

LIBERTIES OF KYRKHETON AND CALDSTROTHRE. And it is to be noted that, according to the confirmation of charters made by ancestors of the present lord earl, neither the earl of Riddesdale, nor his heirs, nor their bailiffs, should make any distraint by their own authority in the township of Little Heton and Caldstrothre for any forinsec service owed to the lord king, nor for any common amercement in the court of the lord king's itinerant justices, nor on any other account.

<42> LITTLE BABYNTON*

They also hold in Little Babyngton 2 built tofts at the western end of the township, and on its northern side, containing in total, by estimation, 1 acre of land; and 1 waste toft near the eastern end of the township on the northern side, with 1 adjoining garden; and 9½ acres of arable land, of which 3 acres lie on the Toftes; and on the Honylandes, ½ acre; and by the Harewell, 1 acre; and on the Chestres near Gibbiskilne, 1½ acres; and on Gosecroft, 1 acre and 1 rood; and on Godilawe, 2 acres; and on the Morilandes, 1 rood.

PASTURE. They also have common pasture in that territory for 15 working beasts and 60 sheep and for 2 horses throughout the year.

And William of Schafthow* of Babyngton holds those tenements and lands at the lord's will, and he pays 2s. a year to the almoner's office.

<43> NEUTON* IN COOKDALE* BY HARBOTELL*

They also hold in Neuton in Cookdale* 1 waste toft with 1 adjoining croft called Dianscroft, and they lie at the western end of Suthre Neuton, on the southern side of the *lonyng* there, between John of Berehalgh's toft and croft, as it is bounded by a *balk* on the eastern side, and a siket between <it and> demesne land of the earl

The Black Book of Hexham

of Angose[279] in Hirbotle* on the southern side, and the common moor of Neuton on the western side, and the *lonyng* that leads to that moor on the northern side; and it contains in all by estimation 4 acres.

They also hold 1 carucate of arable land and meadow in the field there, and it lies at the eastern end of Northnewtonfelde between these bounds: that is, beginning at a little siket between Walter Tailboise's field and North Newton field<; and from there> northward, along boundary stones placed between Northnewton field and that carucate of land, as far as the road that leads from Nethreton* to Alwenton* church; and from there eastward, following that road, as far as a little siket descending between that carucate of land and Buroudon* field; and from there southward along that siket as far as a siket called Diansdene; and then westward, following that siket descending between a piece of John of Berehalgh's land and that field of Walter Tailbose, as far as the boundary stones first mentioned. And John of Berehalgh holds that toft and croft with that carucate of land, and pays 13s. 4d. a year.

<44> TEMPLE THORNTON*[280]

They also hold various tofts and lands in Temple Thornton, of which 1 built toft with 1 garden and 1 adjoining croft lies in Westgat, near the northern end on its western side, containing in all by estimation 5 roods; and another built toft lies just on the southern side of that toft with 1 garden and 1 adjoining croft, containing in all by estimation 3 roods; and a third toft lies waste just on the southern side of that toft with a garden and adjoining croft, containing in all 3 roods; and 2 waste tofts with 2 adjoining gardens lie together in the same street, at the southern end of that road on its eastern side, containing in all 1½ acres of land; and 2 acres of land belonging to those 2 waste tofts, in place of crofts, lie together across Wottondeene, abutting on the Westdeene.

---

[279] Gilbert de Umfraville, third earl of Angus, lord of Prudhoe and Redesdale (died 1381), who held the castle at Harbottle: *HHN* (part 2, vol. 1), pp. 34-46; *NCH*, XII, pp. 100-3, 480-2.

[280] There is a note with details of the entry Temple Thornton in *SANT*.

They also hold various arable lands and meadows, of which 1 acre lies on the Ridyng, abutting on the Westdeene; and on Jakisflatt, on the western side of the Crosselande, 5 acres; and on the Wllepottes,[281] on the northern side of the road called the Monkesway, 2½ acres; and Akewelsyd, on its western side, abutting on the Medoubank, 2½ acres; and in the Hyngandsyde, about in the middle, 1 acre and 1 rood; and on the Kyrkway, on its other side, 1½ acres; and on the southern side by the *well*, 2½ acres; and on the Southdeene abutting on the *deen*, 7 acres called the Southcroft and Northcroft; and on the Toftthorne, 2½ acres; and on the Welmyre on its southern side, 2½ acres; and at the *estend* of the Wellmyre, 3 roods; and at its *estsyde*, 3 roods; and on the western side of that *myre*, 5 roods; and on the southern side of that *well*, 2½ acres; and on the Furlanges, 1½ acres; and at Elgeswell, 5 roods; and on the Southdeenbank, abutting on Hartburn, 5 acres; and on the Milnhill, 5 roods; and on Hildeswell at its *northend*, across Morpethway, 1 acre; and at Aldthornlaw, on the western side there, 5 roods; and on the Flores, 5 roods; and on the northern side of the Flores, 2½ acres; and in the Furthalgh, 5 roods; and on the Twistes, abutting on Brerelawmedou, 2 acres 1 rood; and on the Sevenacresse[282] on their southern side, 5 roods; and on Lyntlawes, about in the middle, 3 acres; and on the Holemedoue on its southern side, 2½ acres; and on the western side of that meadow, 1½ acres; and on the southern side of Haltonlawe, 3 acres; and on Hunguge, on the southern side there, 3 roods; and on the Forlanges by the Milnwaye, 5 roods; and on the Furlandes, on the eastern side there, 5 roods; and on the Threpmore, on the western side there, 3 acres; and on the its northern side, 2½ acres; and on the Schellelawe, 2½ acres; and on the Smalhalfacre, about in the middle, on the southern side of the Morpethway, 2½ acres; and on the western side of the Cotwalles,[283] 5 acres; and in Hesewellcroftes, on the southern side there, 2½ acres; and in Sewellsyd, about in the middle, 2½ acres; and at the Propp, on the southern side of Morpethway, 3 roods; and on the southern side of Cloughlech, 2½ acres. \The sum total of acres/[284] 91 acres and 3 roods of land.

---

[281] *Wellepottes, SANT.*
[282] *Seuenacrosse, SANT.*
[283] *Sotwalles*, SANT.
[284] These words are also in the transcript in *SANT.*

MEADOWS. And in Hessewellstrothre, 3 acres of meadow.

<HUSBANDLANDS>[285] And those tofts and lands are divided into 5 husbandlands. The tenants are as follows.

William Smyth holds one built toft, 1 waste toft and <3> lands belonging to them, and he pays 30s a year, of which 10s. for each husbandland.[286]

DEMISE. Thomas of Hertburn* holds 1 built built toft and 1 waste toft and 2 lands belonging to them, and he pays 20s. a year.

<45> WHALTON*

They also hold in Whalton 1 built toft with 1 adjoining croft and garden, and it lies near the western end on the southern side of the township, and on the eastern side of the common road, and contains in all 4 acres. They also hold in the field of that township land of half a carucate, that is 52½ acres of land; of which on Lindeslawe*, on the western side of that township, lie 4 acres; and on the Flores, on the western side near those acres, 9 acres; and in the Westfeld between Walwyk and Leverchild, 13 acres called the Burnflatt<;> on the southern side of the mill there, 13 acres; and on the Farnelaw, on the eastern side of that township, 13 acres.[287]

MEADOWS. And on the northern side of the mill, between Midrige and the *milndame*, lie 1 acre and 3 roods of meadow; and on Ellisdunsyd, 3 roods.

<COMMON PASTURE.> They also have common pasture for 300 <*i.e. 360*> sheep and their lambs throughout the year until

---

[285] In the printed edition the following sentence is included in the paragraph about meadows.
[286] From the rent he paid, and the fact that there were five husbandlands in all, William Smyth had three husbandlands rather than only the two with which the Black Book credits him, the other two being demised to Thomas of Hartburn.
[287] The insertion of a semicolon after Burnflatt resolves an unnecessary difficulty in the printed edition, but half an acre is missing.

the feast of the Nativity of St John the Baptist. And then it <will be>[288] at their discretion whether to retain the lambs in the same pasture, or to remove <them> from the sheep, depending on the number of lambs.

<DEMISE.> And Robert Milner holds those tofts and lands with appurtenances, and pays 10s. a year to the office of the kitchen.

RENT OF 8s. IN THE TOWNSHIP OF WHALTON. They also have there an annual rent of 8s., issuing annually from the manor of that township, paid by Henry Scrope, lord of that township, to the office of the sacrist.

<46> NEWBIGGYNG SUPER MARE*

They also hold in the township of Newbiggyng, near the eastern end of the township on its southern side, 1 burgage, and it lies between Juliana Puddyng's burgage and Marjory Bane's burgage, and it is waste, and contains 5 roods of land according to the borough standard there.[289]

They also hold 1 burgage there in the *southwestend* of that township between two windmills, and it lies between John of Wangesford's burgage and William Serjant's burgage, and contains 3 roods according to the borough standard there. And <they are>[290] demised for 2s., of which they pay for the free farm of those burgages to the lord of the township 16d. a year, that is 2d. a rood, <and the remaining 8d.> to the office of the cellarer.[291]

---

[288] *erat* should presumably be *erit*.

[289] *juxta moram burg. ibidem* (i.e. 'by the borough moor there') . In the next item this expression occurs as *juxta morem burg. ibidem* (i.e. 'by the borough standard there'), which seems on balance a likelier translation since burgage tenements were usually beside each other, not next to moors.

[290] *dimittitur.* But the payment of 16d. (8 acres at 2d. each) must be for both burgages.

[291] The editorial insertion here sems necessary, since the cellarer of the abbey was not the lord of the township.

<47> STANYNGTON*

They also hold in Stanyngton 1 waste toft at the western end of the Catrawe* with 1 adjoining garden on its northern side, and it contains by estimation 1½ roods. They hold 1 husbandland in the field of that township, and it contains as many acres as the other husbandlands of the same township, of which in the Westfeld on the Castellflatt, on the eastern side of the Castellway and abutting on it, lies ½ acre; and at the eastern end of the ½ acre, 1 rood; and on the Dugknoll, on the western side near Maymmedow, 1 *rud*; and on Esshendoneyard, abutting on the Wodway, 1 rood; and on the western side of the Burnway that leads to Belacys*, abutting on that road, 1 rood; and on the western side, near the Foulbrig by Raysland, 1 rood; and on Dunscale, about in the middle, ½ acre; and at the end of Dunscale are 2 butts, of which 1 butt lies by the *balk* of the *milnfleme*, and the other butt lies at the northern end of Dunscale, <and they> contain 1 rood of land; and on the Flores, on the northern side of the Belasysway, abutting on the Wedloch, ½ acre; and on the western side of the Flores, ½ acre; and on the Wyndyhepes, on the northern side there, 1½ acres; and on the southern side by Belysysway, ½ acre; and on the Overflores, about in the middle, abutting on Whytrigway, ½ acre; and on the southern side, near the Elcrosse, ½ rood; and on the northern side, by the Lamepottis, 1 rood; and on the the western side of Killescrok abutting on Blyth,[292] ½ rood; and on the western side by Grenlawdykes, ½ acre; and on the western side by Blaclawmore, 1 rood; and in the Crok, that is, at the eastern end of the township, 1 rood; and on the northern side of Methrelechbrig, 1 rood; and on Nethrepeslandes, 1 rood; and on the Overpessland by that road, ½ acre; and at the southern end by the Hallflatt, 1 rood; and on the northern side of Brademere, abutting on the *medow*, 1½ roods; and on the eastern side of those 1½ roods, across the Fenneswray, 1½ roods; and on the eastern side of Vikerisflatt, abutting onto it, ½ acre; and on the Heretherne, about in the middle, ½ acre; and on the eastern side of Bradmiere, abutting onto it, 1 rood; and on the eastern side, abutting on Whytthornlech, ½ acre; and on the northern side by the Akinschawe, 1 rood; and on the western side by the Ladydene, 1 rood; and on the southern side of the

---

[292] Meaning, perhaps, the River Blyth.

Ladydenmore, 1 rood; and on the eastern side of the Blaklawe, abutting on the Iles, ½ acre.

And it is to be remembered that the rest of that husbandland, not detailed here, lies among the waste of that field. Wherever there any piece of the land of Raysland lies there, immediately to the west lies an equal piece of the prior's land, throughout the field of that township.

They also hold at the western end of Cliftonmedowe, on its southern side, 2 acres of meadow belonging to that land.

DEMISE. And Richard Addi holds those tofts and lands with all their appurtenances, and he pays 6s. a year to the cellarer.

<48> CLIFTON*

Item, they have one yearly rent in Clifton of 18d., issuing annually from the chantry of the Blessed Mary in Stanyngton* church, for some lands and tenements which the chaplain serving that chantry holds in Clifton by grant of Bernard, formerly prior of Hexham*. And that chaplain, whoever he is at the time, should duly pay that yearly rent at the feast of Peter in Chains. And Roger of Both, chaplain, occupies those tenements and lands belonging to the chantry, and <they are>[293] waste.

<49> SETON WODHORN* BY NEWBIGGYNG*

They also have in the township of Seton one yearly rent of 40s. issuing annually from the whole township of Seton by the gift of Bernard de Balliol. The township is now divided between three lords, that is, Helen of Seton, widow of William de Burgoyne, who holds a third part of that township, Adam of Seton, who holds another third of it,[294] and Robert of Ogle*, John of Wodburne*, and the said Helen, who hold the remaining third part divided

---

[293] *est.*
[294] In 1322 William of Burnton of Newcastle upon Tyne was granted lands in Seaton by Robert of Seaton, with an obligation to pay dues to the Hexham Priory: document 50.

between them; so that each of them should pay to the cellarer's office in proportion to their share in the township.

And it is to be noted that the charters of those lords contain a full specification of the payment of that rent in proportion to the share of each tenure.

<50> BRENKLAWE*

They also have by the gift of Henry of Ferlyngton* one yearly rent of 13s. 4d. from Brenklawe mill, <which is>[295] waste.

<51> NORTH MILNBURN*

They also hold the whole grange of Northmilnburne with all its appurtenances, in meadows, grazings, pastures, marl pits, waters, roads <and> lanes, and it is contained within these bounds: that is, beginning on the eastern side of that grange at a place called the Redehogh; and from there eastward, along a ditch between Hegham field and Milneburne*, until it reaches a ditch called the *mayndyk* of Craklawe; and from there northward, following that *mayndyk* between demesne land of Craklawe and Milnburne*, until it reaches the *estemer* of the Mydilmore; and from there <...>ward,[296], following an old ditch between Craklawe field and Newham, until it reaches the Langsyk; and from there westward, following that *syk*, as far as an old ditch lying at the western end of Milnburne* field, between Newham field and Milnburne* field; and from there southward, following that ditch until it reaches the *burne* called Milnburne*; and from there eastward, following that *burne*, until it reaches the Redehogh first mentioned.

They also have common pasture on Craklaw Moor, and the turbary of Mordesfene belonging to that grange.

They also have by charter a licence to site a mill on the Milnburne *burne** within the lordship there, as and where seems best to them.

---

[295] *quia.*
[296] *versus (—).*

And Robert Horsle holds that grange with appurtenances, and pays £5 6s. 8d. He is also accustomed to have[297] 1 sheepfold there for the lord's use.

<52> BYRESFELD OF MILNBURNE*

They also hold by Milnburne, within the bounds already detailed, a field of arable land and meadow called the Byresfeld, and it is part of that grange and belonging to it, lying within these bounds; that is, beginning at the *fote* of Whytyngdonsyk, where it descends into the Milnburne *burne*; and from there, following that Whyttyndon *syk*, descending southward, between the Southmylnburne and the Byresfeld, until it reaches the Ponteland* *kyrkway*; and from there eastward, following that *waye*, until it reaches the Dedmanisdyk; and from there, following that *dik*, lying between Caldcotes* field and the Byresfeld, as far as the road that leads from Dysyngton* to Caldcotes*; and from there, following that road, until it reaches 1 *siket* at the eastern end of Byresfeld, between that *feld* and Caldecotes*; and from there northward, following that siket until it reaches the Milnburne *burne*; and from there westward, following that *burne*, as far as the foot of Whyttidensyk first mentioned.

And Sir Ralph de Euere holds Byresfield, with allowance of 13s. 4d. for some lands there in the prior's hand, and he pays 18s. a year.

<53. DISSINGTON*>[298]

They also have one rent of two corporal cloths annually through the wife of the lord of Dissington, and the wives of his heirs, to be offered at the feast of St Andrew at the high altar in the priory church, for multure of the prior's men living in the township of Echwyk*, with the exception of multure from the prior's demesne there, in whoever's hands it should be. The tenants of the

---

[297] *sol. habere.* This could be *solebat habere*, i.e. 'used to have'.
[298] This section relating to Dissington is included in the printed edition with the preceding section relating to *Byresfeld de Milnburne.*

demesne lands <shall mill their grain> at Dissyngtone mill next after the lord,[299] and without <giving> multure. And similarly, for this concession of multure, the lord of Dissington, whoever he may be at the time, should stand up when the prior of Hexham comes into court, or wherever else he should be, and offer him his seat, unless prevented by the constraint of a superior.

And, if any of those tenants of Echwyk* withdraws his multure from mill of the lord of the lord of Dissington, he should be brought to justice on that account in the prior's court. And if convicted, he should be compelled by the prior's steward to make restitution of that multure to that lord, and he should make amends to the prior for his forfeiture.

<54> ECHWYK*

They also have 1 capital messuage in Echwyk, with 4 gardens and 2 adjoining tofts, and with 2 crofts belonging to the capital messuage, of which 1 croft lies on the northern side of the Hellilawthornes, and contains ½ acre, and the other lies on the northern side, near that messuage, <and> contains 1 rood of meadow. And 1 other croft lies on the western side on the Hoghlawe, and contains ½ acre.

They also have 88 acres of demesne land there, of which 4 acres and 1 rood lie on the Parkflatt; and on the Strothreflatt, 4 acres; and in the Hope, 2 acres; and at Chereyardsyd and at Daltonhogh, 2 acres and 3 roods; and on Swardonsyde, 2 acres; and on Goseacre, 1 acre; and on Medeburnesyde, 5½ acres; and at the Honnletherne, 1 acre; and on the Bromelandes, 4 acres; and on the Schotwell, 1½ acres; and on the Rasyd, 3 roods; and in Calfstrothre, ½ acre; and at the Lonyngtonheued, ½ acre; and the Harelaw, 1 acre; and on Hobbisflatt, toward the eastern side, 4½ acres; and on either side of the Gladincroke, 4½ acres; and at the Outganges, 6 acres; and on either side of the Gladincrok, 4½ acres;[300] and on the Heghlawes, on the southern side there, 1 acre; and on the northern side of the garden of John of Naffirton*, in two places, 3 acres; and

---

[299] i.e. they will be given priority over other tenants.

[300] This seems to repeat an earlier entry.

on the Staneflatt, 3 acres 1½ roods; and on the northern side of the Bradmedowe, 1 acre; and on the Lamerodes, about in the middle, 1 acre; and on the Southkelawes, about in the middle, 4½ acres; and on the southern side on the Heghlawes in the Langlandes, 3 acres; and on the Treuenbrige, ½ acre; and on Ellybalk, 1 acre; and at the western end on the Northhope, 1 acre; and on the western side on the Harelawe, 1½ acres; and at the western end on the Rasyd, 3 roods.

MEADOWS. They also have in Calfstrothre ½ acre of meadow; and in the Lymkylnemedow, 3 roods of meadow.

DEMISES. And it is to be noted that all that capital messuage, with those gardens, crofts, lands and meadows are divided into four husbandlands.

John of Aynwyk* holds 1 built toft, now called a capital messuage, with 1 garden and an adjoining croft containing ½ acre of meadow, [301] and 29½ acres of arable land and meadow, and he pays 16s. a year

John of Brenklaw*, Robert Watson and Roger Smyth hold all of the rest of those lands, that is 57 acres, with 3 waste tofts, gardens and crofts belonging to them, and they pay for all 17s. a year.

DEMESNE MEADOWS. They also have 7 acres of demesne meadow there in the lord's hand, and they are demised to tenents of the township at the lord's will, and pay 9s. a year. They used to pay 10s. a year.

FREE FARM. John of Brenklawe* holds a cottage and 8 acres of free land by fealty, and pays 8d. a year.

FREMAYDENSLAND, OR BELLINGEHAMSLAND. John Annotson holds 1 built toft called Fremaydensland, with 18 acres of land belonging to it, and pays 6s. a year. He used to pay 12s. a year.

---

[301] *cum j gardino et crofto adjacenti crofto uno cont. di. acr. prati.* This should perhaps be *cum j gardino et crofto adjacenti unde croftum cont. di. acr. prati.*

BONDLANDS.[302] They also have 7 bondlands there, each of which contains 24 acres of arable land and meadow; and they should mill their grain at Dissyngton* mill for a toll of one thirteenth, as noted above under Dissyngton*. The tenants are as follows.

John Syre, a neif of the lord, holds 1 waste bondland with a toft, and pays 8s. a year. Robert Watson holds 1 built bondland, with a toft, and pays 9s. 6d. a year; it used to pay 13s., the charge of this tenant.[303] Adam Milner holds 1 built bondland with a toft, and pays 6s. a year. John Brenklaw holds 1 bondland with a waste toft, and pays 6s. a year. William Hogissone holds 1 bondland with a waste toft, and pays 6s. a year. Matthew Waller holds 1 built bondland with a toft, and pays 8s. a year. John Syre, a neif, holds 1 built bondland with a toft, and pays 10s. 6d. a year.

COTTAGES. There are 8 cottages there with some lands belonging to them; and they may mill their corn wherever it best pleases them. The tenants are as follows.

John Annotson holds 1 cottage with a waste toft, and 2 acres of land called the Brewingland, and pays 2s. a year. Amabel of Rosse holds 2 cottages, 1 of which is built, with 6 acres of arable land and meadow, and pays 3s. 6d. a year. John of Brenklaw* holds 1 cottage with a croft, built, and 3 acres of land, and pays 12d.; John also holds 2 cottages with a waste croft and 6 acres of land, and pays 3s. a year. John Syre holds 2 cottages, 1 of which is built, with 6 acres of land, and pays 2s. a year.

[HUSBANDLANDS.] There are 5 husbandlands there which belonged to John of Faudon*, now granted in mortmain by charter of King Edward III after the Conquest,[304] and each land contains 34 acres of land and meadow. The tenants are as follows.

---

[302] In the printed edition BONDLANDS is placed before the list of tenants in the next paragraph.
[303] *Solebat r. xiijs. oneris isti(us) tenentis.* The translation reads *oneris* as *onus*, but the expression is more than odd, and there must be some more complex corruption of the text.
[304] Cf. document 52.

William Hogisson holds 1 land with a built croft, and pays 5s. a year; William holds 1 land, and pays 5s. a year; John Syre holds 1 land, and pays 6s. a year; John also holds 1 land, and pays 6s. a year. William of Rosse holds 1 built land, and pays 6s. a year.

COTTAGES. There are 2 cottages there belonging to those 5 lands. The tenants are as follows.

William Hogisson holds 1 cottage with an adjoining croft, and pays 3d. a year. Robert Watsone holds 1 cottage and 1 acre of land, and pays 6d. a year.

BREWING. John of Brenklaw* holds the brewing of that township, and pays 12d. a year.

COMMON PASTURE IN WHITCHESTRE*. The prior and convent and their tenants in Echwyk also have common pasture on the common moor lying between Echwyk and Whytchestre to common with their beasts and working beasts there throughout the year.

TURBARY. The prior and convent will take heath and turfs from that moor for all their needs. However, the tenants of Echwyk will not take heath or turfs from that moor except when the tenants of the lord of Whytchestre* may take <heath or turfs> there.

It is to be remembered that John of Faudon*, lord there, granted to one William of Hoghton and the legitimate heirs of his body all his lands and tenements in Whytchestre* and Hirlaw* in exchange for an annual rent of 26s. 8d. payable to John, his heirs and assigns. And if it should happen that William should die without legitimate heirs of his body, the said lands and tenements were to revert entirely to John and his right heirs. And afterwards that John of Faudon* granted the rent of 26s. 8d. to the prior and convent, and also granted the reversion of those tenements and lands, should this become available, to Father Gilbert of Minstreacres*, chaplain, and Thomas of Raneton, their heirs and assigns.[305] Gilbert and Thomas conceded and granted the reversion

---

[305] These two grantees were trustees to hold the land pending a charter to allowing the priory to acquire them in mortmain.

of those tenements and lands to the prior and convent, together with the services of all the free tenents there. And because William of Hoghton died without any children born of his body, the reversion of those tenements and lands should rest with the prior and convent. But they have not yet obtained possession of those lands and tenements for want of licence to enter from the Earl of Angos, the immediate lord, which has not yet been sought. And those tenements and lands were alienated in mortmain to the abbey of Hexham* by the lord king's charter, as may be seen in the royal charter drawn up concerning the alienation in mortmain of lands in Echewyk.[306] And it is to be noted that all those former tenements and lands of John of Faudon*, granted to the prior and convent, lie dispersed throughout the field there, being always nearer the sun in each location.

<55> DALTON*

They also have the whole manor of Dalton, in which there is 1 capital messuage, and various buildings with various adjoining gardens, and 140 acres of demesne arable land and meadow, of which 9 acres lies on the Bernflatt; and on Lintlawes, 4 acres; and on Schibeverlawe, 4 acres; and on Kiplawflatte, 16 acres; and on the Milndykes, 10 acres; and on the Toftes, 12 acres; and on Skuttesklene, 6 acres; and on Dedmanslaucrok, 3 acres; and on Northdemanlawe, 4 acres; and on Halfforlang, 2 acres; and on the Crosflatte, 12 acres; and on Coklawe, 3 acres; and on the Cartrige, 2½ acres; and on Sterlingstrothreflatt, 4 acres; and on the Breches, 4½ acres; and on the Crosflatte 30 acres together lie waste.

MEADOWS. And in the Milnmedowe, 3 acres of meadow; and in the Bradmedowe, 3 acres of meadow; and in Horsepolmedowe, 2 acres 3 roods; and in the Floremedowe, 1 rood; and in the Toft *medowe*, 3 acres; and in Sterlingstrothremedowe, 2 acres.

<DEMISE.> And William Scot, John Bigle, Thomas of Heworth and John Elder hold all the above tenements and lands between them, and they pay 50s. a year.

---

[306] document 52.

John of Dalton holds freely 1 messuage there with some acres of land, that is 7 acres 3 roods of land lately in the tenure of Agnes of Johnby, and he pays 5d. a year, and no more because the said Agnes and William Nippet gave to the prior and convent 11 acres 1 rood of land that were once included in that holding, and they then used to pay 10d. a year.

FREE FARM. Robert Ogle holds freely 1 messuage called Johncolynsonland and 8 acres of land belonging to it, and pays 8d. a year. Agnes Baxter holds freely 2 messuages and 18 acres of land, and pays 18d. a year, but this is remitted to her for her life by the lord because those messuages and lands will remain to the prior and convent after Agnes's death. John of Dalton holds freely 3 acres of land, and pays 3d. a year; John also (holds) freely 1 toft and 1 acre of land, in which toft Robert Batirsuys resides, and he pays 1d. a year.

HUSBANDLANDS. There are 19 husbandlands there, of which 11 contain 2<4>[307] acres and 8 contain 16 acres of arable land and meadow each. And they should carry millstones there, and repair the mill walls and roof it at their own expense. <The tenants are as follows.>

Alan of Galloway holds 1 husbandland, containing 16 acres, and pays 6s. 8d. a year; Alan also holds 1 land, and it contains 24 acres, and pays 4s. a year:[308] it used to pay 9s. 3½d. Thomas of Heworth holds 1 land containing 16 acres, and pays 5s. 8d. a year; he also holds 1 land, containing 24[309] acres of land, and pays 4s. a year. John Eldare holds 2 lands, each containing 16 acres, and pays 12s. a year; John also holds 1 land containing 24 acres, and pays 4s. a year. John Bygglye holds 1 land containing 16 acres, and pays 5s. a year; John also holds 2 husbandlands each containing 24 acres, and pays 10s. a year. John Todde holds 1 land containing 16 acres, and pays 5s. a year; he also holds 3 husbandlands, each containing 24 acres, and pays 18s. a year. William Scotte holds 2 husbandlands each containing 16 acres, and pays 13s. 4d. a year; he

---

[307] *xxiij* (instead of *xxiiij*).
[308] See the correction at *PH*, II, p. 203.
[309] See the correction at *PH*, II, p. 203.

also holds 2 husbandlands each land containing 2<4>[310] acres, and pays 10s. 8d. a year. Alan of Gallewaye holds 1 land containing 24 acres, and pays 5s. a year.

[COTTAGES.] There are 7 cottages there, and each of them should perform labour services to repair the mill, like the husbandlands noted above. The tenants are as follows.

Maurice Scotte holds a built cottage and 3 <acres of land>,[311] and pays 21d. a year; Maurice also holds a cottage with a waste toft and 3 acres of land, and pays 2s. 2d. a year. Alan of Gallewaye holds 1 built cottage and 3 acres of land; he also holds 1 cottage with a waste toft and 3 acres of land and pays 3s. 6d. a year. William Scott holds 1 built cottage and 3 acres of land, and pays 2s. 6d. a year. Alan of Gallewaye holds 1 cottage with a garden, and pays 12d. a year.

WATER MILL. Robert Batirsyse holds a water mill there, and pays 56s. 8d. a year.

<56> TOWNSHIP OF HOGHE*

They have a piece of land in the township of Hoghe called Dedisyd containing 30 acres of arable land and meadow and lying between these bounds; that is, between the road that leads from Heddon* to the township of Hoghe on the western side; and Heddirslawmedow* on the northern side; and Dedisydeleche on the eastern side; and the Langstrothre on the southern side. And John Robinson of the Hoghe holds those lands and 1 toft with a croft in the township of Stanfordham*, as will be set out there below,[312] and he pays 4s. a year.

TENANTS IN HOGHE. They also have in that township various tenements lying on the northern side in the township there, that is, between a holding of the clerks of Baliol, Oxford,[313] on the

---

[310] *xxviij* (instead of *xxiiij*).
[311] *et iij terras* (instead of *et iij acras terræ*).
[312] There is no other reference to lands in Stamfordham in the Black Book.
[313] Balliol College, Oxford, whose foundation is traditionally dated to 1263.

western side, and a holding of Thomas of Falofeld* on the eastern side. And also a tenement lying on the southern side of that township, between a holding of John of Dalton* holding on the eastern side and the holding called Thrillwallesland on the western side. And all those tenements are divided into 7 husbandlands and 2 cottages, as is set out below.

They also have 169½ acres of arable and meadow in the field of that township, of which 2 acres lie in two places on the Lintlawes; and in the Midelkenyll in two plots, 2 acres; and on the Northreyardes of the Hoghe, 1 acre; and on the western side, on the Brerysyde, 1 acre; and on the northern side of Daltonmedowe, 1 acre; and on the northern side of those acres, 2 acres; and on the southern side of Dalton*, <1> rood.

And on the eastern side on the Elichestrez by the march of Dalton*, in various places, 2 acres; and on the southern side of those Chestrez, abutting on the bridge, in various places, 6 acres; and on Lustrelawsyde, about in the middle, across the Dalton* road, 1 acre; and on the western side, by that acre, 1 acre; and on the western side of the Lustrelawsyde, in various places, 2 acres; and in the Eastreleche, abutting on Hecleche, 1 acre; and on the eastern side of that leche, 1 acre; and on the northern side of *lonyng* of Standfordham*, 1 acre 3 roods; and on the western side, by the *mayns* of Standfordham*, 1 acre; and on the eastern side, by the *standdandstane*, 1 acre; and on the western side, by the Kyrkwaye near the township, 1 acre; and on the southern side near that acre, across that road, 1 acre; and at the western end of the township, 1 acre; and on the eastern side, by Mabchestrelawe, 1 acre; and on the Thornelawe, 1 acre; and on the eastern side by the Grenwaye, 1 acre; and below the Blafurlang in various places, 3 acres; and at the Bonyleche and on the Monylaus in two places, 2 acres; and on the western side of the Netlylawe, 1 acre; and on the eastern side of that *lawe*, ½ acre; and in the *strothre* of Nettelilawe, 1 acre; and on the Cranelandes in 2 places, 3 acres; and on the Bakstanes in various places, 4 acres; and on the Rilandes across the Stanfordham* road, 1 acre; and below the Hallyardes, abutting on that yard, 1 acre; and on Scherwentdimpyls in various places, 3 acres; and on the southern side, on Scherwentlaw, 1 acre; and on Scherwentlawsyd, 2½ acres; and on Redelandes in 2 places, 2 acres; and on the Halffurlang in various places, 6½ acres; and on the western side of the Hollawe, 1 acre; and on the western side of Elichestres, 2 acres; and on the eastern side of those acres, 2½ acres; and on Elichestrelaw, 1 acre; and on the Stobbe in various places, 8 acres; and on the Knottlawe, 1 acre; and on the western side, on Blalangfurlangdyk, 1 rood; and on the western side by Heddonway in two places, 2 acres; and on Langstrothresyd in various places, 3 acres; and on that *strothre* at the Florewelle, 1 acre; and below John Nippet's garden, abutting upon it, 1 acre; and at the eastern end of Ovyrgripchestres by the moor, 4 acres; and on the western side, on Dedisyde, by Heddonway in various places, 3½ acres; and on the eastern side of Thrilliswallland, abutting on Wrechitmanmedow, 1 acre; and on the southern side, by that *medow*, 1 acre; and on the Crosfurlang in various places, 5 acres; and on the western side of <the> [314]*crosse*, 1 acre; and on the eastern side of that *crosse*, abutting on Heddoneburne, 1 acre; and in Heathreslawchestres and in the Hemptwystes above that *burne*, in various places, 5 acres; and on Hordlawsyde, on the eastern side there, in various places, 3 acres; and on the western side of the Havyrbalk, 1 acre; and on the Farlaws in various places, 5 acres. And on Goneldchestres, between a piece of Geoffrey of Farlawe's land on the eastern side and a piece of the the demesne lands of that township on the western side, there lies a piece of land containing by estimation 16 acres. And on Wythopp, between a moor called Ravenstanmore on the eastern side and a piece of land called Thrillwallland on the western side, lies a piece of land <containing> by estimation 5 acres. And on Ravenstanmore, on the western side by Fourstanes, lies a piece of land containing by estimation 8 acres. And at the eastern end of that moor lies a piece of land containing by estimation 5 acres. And at the eastern end of the Ybrakes lies a piece of land containing by estimation 5 acres.

MEADOWS. They also have there a (piece) of meadow called the Holmedow containing by estimation 3 acres, and it pays 4d. a year.

PASTURES IN SEVERALTY. They also hold a piece of moor in severalty, and it lies on the eastern side of the Northmore by Yngowlech*. No tenant there should dig turfs or take heath in it without licence from the prior or the terrar.

---

[314] *de* (instead of *le*).

< *Raine notes that here there is a blank page. It presumably was intended to contain matter relating to Matfen that was never entered.*>

<57 MATFEN EST*>

STILL CONCERNING MATFEN EST. It is to be noted that if the current lord of Fenwyk* and the lord of Matfen should wish to put the waste in that field back into cultivation, the prior and convent will receive their due proportionate share by of ploughed land by lot as they did originally in other ploughed lands; that is, according to assertion of elderly men, a third part of the whole throughout.

MEADOWS. They also have, at the western end of Knokerhill, 10 acres of meadow; and in the middle of the large meadow there, 7 acres of meadow; and at the Yles, near the eastern end, 6 acres; and at the Roubrig on its eastern side, in a meadow called the Litilmedow, about in the middle, 1 rood.

They also have there 3 tofts with adjoining gardens <*or an adjoining garden*>, which lie together between a holding called Yngowlande* on the eastern side <and> the holding[315] of Thomas Matfen on the western side. Of which 1 toft is designated[316] of old for 1 husbandland and 2 tofts are designated for 2 cottages.

They also have 7 waste cottages on the southern side of the township there, and at its western end, and they lie together between a holding formerly <called> Knokersland on the eastern side and a holding formerly called Yorkesland on the western side, with 7 adjoining gardens, and they contain in all by estimation, 10 acres of land which, whenever they were tenanted, paid the sums set out below as follows:.

William Troute holds 1 built toft designated for 1 husbandland, and 14 acres of arable land and meadow assigned to

---

[315] *in tenura* (for *et tenuram*).
[316] *limitatur.*

that toft from the land specified above, and pays 13s. 4d. a year. He also holds 2 cottages by that toft, and 4½ acres of land assigned to them from the lands as above, and pays 6s. 8d. a year.

And the 7 waste cottages, as noted above, were formerly <tenanted> as follows:[317]

Ralph Shiph<i>rd held 1 cottage and 1 acre 1 rood of the land as above, and paid 2s. a year. John of Galleway held 1 cottage and 1 acre 1 rood of land as above, and paid 2s. John Kitteson held 1 cottage and 1 acre of land as above, and paid 2s. Isabel of Tynmouth held 1 cottage and 1 acre of land as above, and paid 2s. Agnes of Rome held 1 cottage <and> 2 acres of land as above, and paid 3s. William of York held 1 cottage and 2½ acres of land as above, and paid 3s. John Rue held 1 cottage and 1 rood of land as above, and paid 12d.

DEMISE. And John of Fenwyk*, lord of that <township>, holds all those tenements and lands, and pays £4 13s. 4d. a year.

COMMON PASTURE. They also have common pasture there to common with 24 oxen and four mares, and with 1 horse, and 2 cows of the warden of the grange, and with 1 sheepfold, and with a *flok* of pigs throughout the year.

They also have common pasture there to common from the feast of All Saints until the Feast of the Invention of the Holy Cross each year, with 1 herd whether of bullocks, stirks or cows as it shall please the prior; except that if the lord of Fenwyk* should wish to enclose the land of Westirmostwlflatt from the western side of the moor as far as the new stone cross towards the west he may surely do so, on condition that the prior and convent shall have common rights in that pasture until the enclosure is properly made. And if, through defective enclosure, cattle of the prior and convent or of their men should enter that pasture, they may be driven back without dispute or obstruction.

---

[317] Raine prints a dash here that seems to represent a link to the following paragraph rather than an indication that there is missing text.

They also have common of the *petmyre* there for themselves and their men to dig and take peats on the southern part of that *petmyre* for all their needs.

<58> HAUKEWELL*

They also have 1 acre of arable land in Haukwell field, and it lies toward the eastern end of the field there by the road that leads from Haukwell as far as Dalton*, on the southern side of that road, and it abuts on Cherlawleche on the western side of Charlawe.

<59> ULKESTON*

They also have 1 acre of arable land in Ulkeston field, and it lies on Beryngflatte at the eastern end of that field, on the *northest* side near the Deryngthorne, and abuts on the Warynere, about in the middle.

PEATERY THERE. They also have there 4 acres of peatery that lie in the peatery there, and extend westward to the peatery of Matfen* <and> eastward <to> the common pasture of Ulkeston.[318]

<60> CHESEBURGHE*[319]

They also have the manor of Che<s>eburghe[320] with all its appurtenances, in which there are various buildings, with 1 chapel and 1 dovecote, and whatever is containeded within the following bounds, and it is several throughout the year; that is, beginning at the *southest corner* of the manor wall, and from there, following the road that leads from the manor as far as the road that leads to the township of Nesbit* until it reaches a siket that descends to the eastern end of the Stobflatte* between Echwyk* field and the

---

[318] *Et extendunt se versus occid. ad peteriam de Matfen versus or. et commune pasturæ de Ulkeston.* Neither text nor translation (reading *ad* for the second *et*) can be deemed very reliable.

[319] Raine says he has corrected this from *Chereburghe*.

[320] *Chereburghe* (uncorrected).

maynes of the manor; and from there westward, following the road called Corbrigway,³²¹ along the metes and bounds between Nesbitt* field and the manor field, until it reaches a *balk* that lies between Ulkeston* field and the *mayns* of the manor; and from there northward, following that *balk* along the boundary stones and old boundaries until it reaches the northern end of the Wetflatt; and from there eastward, following 1 *balk* between Haukwell* field and the *mayns* of the manor until it reaches a *law* called Schapplaw; and from there, following 1 *balk* until it reaches a spring flowing as far as the eastern end of the Threpheuedland; and from there, following a small burn descending from that spring, and along the boundary stones there, until it reaches a burn called Cherlawlech; and from there, following that *leche* until it leads to a burn called Pont*; and from there eastward, following that burn, until it leads to the foot of a *leche* descending from a spring in that manor into Pont burn*; and from there southward, following that *lech* until it reaches the *est corner* of the manor wall already mentioned: and from there, following that wall, as far as the *southcorner* first mentioned.

LANDS ON THE EASTERN SIDE OF THE GRANGE. They also have other lands that are not several on the eastern side of that manor; that is, at the southern head of the Helawes, 2 acres; and at the western end, on the *brokes* by the moor, 4 acres; and on that same *flatte*, on the eastern side near those acres, 4 acres; and on Niksflatt, 20 acres; and there is there a *strothre* called Whitlawstrothre, and it is the manor's ox pasture; and between the *lech* that descends from the manor and Daltonway* by the Pont burn*, 4 acres; and on the eastern side, on Whitlawflatte, 4 acres; and between Whitlawthornes, 3 acres; and on the northern side of Whitlawthorns, 2 acres; and at the *estheued* of Whitlawflatte on the Lamerodes, 2 acres; and on the western side of Wartheghe on the Knokes, 3 acres; and on Wartheghe, 4 acres; and on the eastern side of Wartheghe, abutting on <the> Pont*, 2 acres; and at the eastern end of those acres on the Homelthierne, 1 acre; and on the eastern side of that acre, by <the> Pont burn*, 5 acres; and on Lyntlawes, 15 acres; and on the western side of Lyntlaws, 2 acres; and on the

---

³²¹ Though this seems obviously to be the road to Corbridge it is not easy to envisage which road is meant.

northern side of Lyntlaws, abutting on <the> Pont*, 2½ acres; and in Lyntlawhope, 4 acres; and below the Todhoghe in the Halfacremedow by <the> Pont*, 1 rood of meadow.

PESLAW FLATT. And in Nesbit* field there is a *flatt* called Peslawflatt, and it contains by estimation 6 acres, and is demised at lease to the tenant of Nesbitt*, as set out below – and in Grimescrok.[322]

PASTURES AND WASTES. And it is to be noted that all of the wastes lying by the Pont burn* called the Hughs, from the eastern side of Lyntlawhopp as far as the manor wall, are appurtenant and appendent to the lands of the manor.

John Rothrefurth, Richard Clark, Thomas Cristall and John Cristall hold between them the whole manor with its appurtenances, and pay £6 a year. Those tenants will mill at Dalton mill the grain they grow on the lands of the manor, for a toll of one twentieth.

<61> NESBITTE*

They also have the whole township of Nesbit with all its appurtenances and the services of free men there, of which:

FREEHOLD.[323] Richard Freman holds freely 1 messuage and 12 acres of land by homage and fealty, and performs suit of court at the three head courts in Aynwyk*, and pays 4d. a year.

HUSBANDLANDS. And there are there 19 husbandlands, each of which contains 25 acres of arable land and meadow. The tenants are as follows:

William Hamlyn holds 2 lands with a built toft, and pays 18s. a year. John Netehird holds 2 lands with a built toft, and pays

---

[322] It is not clear what the reference to *Grimescrok* signifies; the name does not appear elsewhere in the survey. Raine follows it with a *sic*. The dash is as in the printed version.

[323] *Libera firma.*

15s. a year. John of Pikryng holds 2 lands with a built toft, and pays 16s. a year. John Jacson holds 1 land with a built toft, and pays 8s. a year. Richard Freman holds 1 land with a built toft, and pays 9s. a year. John Michelson holds 1 land with a waste toft and pays 6s. a year. William Thomson holds 1 land with a waste toft and pays 6s. a year; William also holds 1 land with a built toft, and pays 9s. a year. Michael of Whitchestre* holds 2 lands with a built toft, and pays 16s. a year. John Michelson holds 1 land with a built toft, and pays 6s. 8d. a year. William Brade holds 1 land with a built toft, and pays 9s. a year. Richard Freman holds 1 land with a built toft, and pays 6s. 8d. a year. John Jacson holds 1 land with a built toft, and pays 13s. 6d. a year. Robert of Redesdale* holds 1 land with a built toft, and pays 9s. a year. Richard Freman and William Hamelyn hold 1 land with a waste toft, and pay 4s. a year. Robert of Redesdale* holds 2½ acres of meadow called Maldesmedow, and pays 2s. a year.

PESLAWFLATT. All the tenants of the township hold between 6 acres of demesne land called Priorspesflatte.

[COTTAGES]. There are there 4[324] cottages and 1 garden. The tenants are as follows:

William Hamelyne holds 1 garden, and pays 2d. a year. John Nouthird holds 1 waste cottage and 3 acres of land, and pays 15d. a year. William Thomson holds 1 waste cottage called Smythscotage and 3 acres of land, <and pays> 18d. Richard Freman holds 1 waste cottage called Carrouscotage and 3 acres of land, and pays 18d. Richard Freman, junior, holds 1 built cottage and 3 acres of land, and pays a 15d. a year. John Jacson holds 1 cottage and 3 acres of land, and pays 15d. a year.

MULTURE. And each tenant of that township will mill grain grown on the lands of the manor at Dalton mill, for a toll of one thirteenth.

---

[324] The following list contains 5 cottages.

<62> STELLYNG*

They also have the whole manor of Stellyng with all its appurtenances, in which there are various buildings, and it is several throughout the year. And it is contained within these bounds; that is, beginning at the eastern end of the manor field, <and from there> to a spring, called Holburnewell; and from there, ascending westward, along 1 small siket and along boundary stones placed between the manor field and a field of Neutonhall* called the Morehousfelde until it reaches a *balk* lying at the eastern end of the Lampotlech; and from there southward, following that *balk* along boundary stones placed between the manor field and Neutonhall* field until it reaches the Whyewell: and from there, following another *balk*, lying on the western side of Notthynglawe, until it reaches the Thornlawflatt; and from there, following another *balk*, lying on the western side of the Farnelawe between that *law* and a *flatt* called Cokishow, until it reaches Akomleche; and from there eastward, following that *leche* as far as the Stokwell; and from there following 1 old ditch as far as the head of the enclosure of the manor field; and from there northward, following 1 old ditch, until it reaches the spring called Holburnwell first mentioned.

PASTURE. They also have common pasture belonging to that manor throughout the barony of Bywell*, to common that pasture throughout the year with their working beasts of all kinds belonging to that manor.

DEMISE. Aymer of Athedell, knight, holds that manor with all its appurtenances, and pays 4 marks a year.[325]

They also used to have a water mill in Nafferton*, to which belonged the multure of both Nafferton* and Whithill, and 1 cottage there called Milnercrofte, and they are waste.

---

[325] Sir Aymer of Athol was elected four times as knight of the shire for Northumberland (between 1365 and 1381) and served as sheriff of the county (1381-2). See C. H. H. Blair, 'Members of Parliament for the Boroughs of Northumberland (1295-1377)', *AA*, 4th series, 13 (1936), pp. 51-2.

<63> THROKELAW*

They also have in the township of Throkelaw 1 toft and croft containing in all 1 acre, and half a toft and croft there.

They also have in the field of that township 51½ acres ½ rood of land and meadow, of which 3¼ roods lie on the western side of <a> *lonyng*, and they extend as far as the wall[326]; and on the eastern side of that *lonyng* lie 5½ acres 1¼ roods, and <they extend>[327] as far as Schukeslade; and between the walls, 1 acre; and on Throkerige, 1 acre; and on Morige, 5 acres; and on the Fletes, 4 acres 1 rood; and in the eastern side of Midelflatt, 5½ acres; and in the eastern side of Deulawrige*, 2 acres 1½ roods that extend as far as the Bradischawe by the meadow there; and 8 acres lie in the township field, and these are the acres that Woldewes once held, which were given as security to the lepers of Newcastle[328] with a toft; and 6 acres lie in Bakstanschaw; and 4 acres lie in Grunisflatt, by the *law* nearest the east; and 4 acres in the middle of Scheleflatt; and 2 acres in the middle of Siggesflatt; and 2 acres in the Langschawe near Newburne* field.

MEADOWS. They also have 1 rood of meadow in Wallynges, and all the meadow lying between the Bradeschawe and the Bradegate, and a meadow lying between the walls there.

<64> NEWBURNE*

They also have in Newburn 2 fisheries called Fuyle and Drypintille, with a piece of meadow there on the northern side of the Tyne for drying fishing nets, and they lie between a piece of meadow called Grunesgrene on the western side and demesne lands of Esthalgh on the northern side, and a piece of meadowland called the Crokytspechynes on the eastern side, and Bladenbankes on the

---

[326] Hadrian's Wall.
[327] *Et se extendit* (for *Et se extendunt*).
[328] The hospital of St. Mary Magdalene: A. Goodman, 'The Church and Religion in Newcastle, 1080-1540', in D. Newton and A. J. Pollard, eds, *Newcastle abd Gateshead before 1700* (Chichester, 2009), p. 101.

southern side. And that piece of meadow contains by estimation ½ acre.

And Father Richard, the vicar there, holds the fisheries with the meadow, and pays 26s. 8d. a year.

<65> BENWELL*

They also have within the territory of Benwell, a plot called Wodhall in which there is a building, and it contains in all, with a wood, four acres and more, and it is not several at any time of the year. And it is contained within these bounds; that is, beginning at the foot of a small burn descending into the Tyne between that plot and the wood of William Delaval, knight, on the western side; and from there northward, following that burn until it reaches an old ditch situated between that plot and a wood called Harpareswode; and from there eastward, following that ditch, lying between that plot and the wood called Harpareswode,[329] until it reaches the *lonyng* called the Merelonyng; and from there southward, following that *lonyng* as far as the Tyne: and from there westward, following the Tyne bank as far as the foot of the burn first mentioned.

And if no waste is made there it pays 5s. a year.

<66> NEWCASTLE

Thomas Wodman holds 1 burgage in Newcastle, on the western side of the Calecrosse between the Cokerawe and the Souterraw; and it lies between the burgage formerly of Hugh of Sadlyngstanes, now Roger of Fulthropp's, on the southern side, and Laurence Akton's burgage on the northern side, and pays 4s. a year to the office of the sacrist; he also holds 2 burgages on the eastern side of Sandhill*, near the *keye*, formerly Henry Wodman's; and they lie between the Robert of Kellessowe's burgage on the southern side and John of Bulkham's burgage on the northern side,

---

[329] *sicut jacet inter dictam placeam; et per dictum boscum vocatum Harpares-wode.* The translation assumes that *per dictum* should be *predictum* and that Raine's semicolon is misleading.

and pay 4s. a year to the sacrist's office. And note that that that annual rent is truly believed to be owed annually, though Thomas asserts that it should issue from other burgages. Robert Fleshewer holds 1 burgage at the prior's will in Fleshewergate at its southern end, between Richard Scott's burgage on the northern side, and a little vennel, lying between Fleschewergate and Skynnargate, which is the way in from those roads to the Beremarkategate, and pays 20s. a year.

John of Howdene holds freely 1 burgage, and pays 12s. a year; he also holds 1 burgage by that burgage on its southern side, and pays 6s. a year. Henry Barbor, alias Wyngatis, holds freely 1 burgage there, formerly in the tenure of Robert of Penreth*, and he pays 3s. 6d. a year.

They used also to have 1 annual rent issuing from a burgage that was formerly John Cornfurth's, but now <receive> nothing because the location of that burgage is not known. It used to pay 4s. a year.

They used also to have an annual rent from the *stanhous* in Westgate*, <but> now <receive> nothing because location is not known.

THE BISHOPRIC OF DURHAM

<67> GREN HELEY* BY MUGILSWORTH*

They also have 1 toft with 1 adjoining croft in Heley. This croft contains by estimation 1 acre of land and lies on the northern side of the township, on the eastern side near a toft called the Durham Almor' Place.[330] And they have 1 acre of woody land in Aldencrok called Devencrofte; and it lies on the western side nearest the Durham Almonersland there.

They also have 20 acres of arable land and meadow with all easements in pastures, waters, woods, and suchlike, of which 12

---

[330] Perhaps for Almoner's Place.

acres 3 roods lie in the Scele by the Seggestrothre abutting on the Yman <to>[331] the *northwest*. And 7 acres 1 rood lie by the pond of the old mill, descending northward on the eastern side of a small siket called Chapellwell.

DEMISE. John of Strevelyn*, knight, and Lady Jacoba, his wife, hold all those tenements and lands for the whole duration of their lives, and of which of them lives longest, and they pay 5s. a year to the sacrist.

<68> FENHALL IN GRENCROFT*

They also have in Grencrofte a messuage called the Fenhall with some meadows and woods, and they are contained within these bounds; that is, beginning at the northern end of Gregoricroft, where the *hegegarth* descends into Smalhopburne*; and from there northward, following Smalhopp *burne** as far as the *fote* of the Stolerydyingleche; and from there eastward, following that *lech*, along boundary stones placed in the that *lech* between Robert of Kellow's field and Fenhall field, until it reaches a field called Dawblerfeld; and from there southward, following an old ditch until it reaches Holdenburne; and from there to the *southwest*, following 1 old ditch between Fenhall field and Maldesclose and the common pasture there and the Langchestre* *lonyng*, until it reaches the *fote* of the *heggegarth* first mentioned. And everything contained within these bounds is severalty of the prior and convent throughout the year, except that Lanchestre* church has ½ acre of arable land belonging to it within those bounds.

DEMISE [AND] THE SERVICE DUE FROM IT. And Nicholas of Moresyd holds all those messuages and lands, and pays yearly 28s. a year, of which 3s. is a free rent. Of this 3s. <is paid> annually from Fenhall for a fee-farm payable to the lord of Grencrofte. And he will provide sufficient lodging there for the prior and terrar, hay for horses, straw for beds, fuel and a white candle, whenever they should happen to visit there.

---

[331] Raine puts a dash here.

<69> MAYDENSTANHALL* IN LANGCHESTRE*

They also have in Langchestre 1 messuage called Maydenstanhall with appurtenant lands, meadows and woods several throughout the year. And they are contained within these bounds; that is, beginning at the Westlydyete of <Maydenstan-hall> field, situated on Smalhopburn*; and from there ascending toward the *northest*, along an old ditch between demesne land belonging to the dean of Lanchestre and Maydenstanhall field as far as the common street that leads from the township of Langchestre toward Durham;[332] and from there southward, following an old ditch between the common pasture of the township of Lanchestre and a *flatt* in Maydenstan field called the Kemsterleyghes and the Rydynges until it reaches a field of John of Lewyne;[333] and from there, following an old ditch between the already mentioned Rydyng *flatt* and the holding of John Lewyne until it reaches a burn called the Broune*; and from there westward, following that stream as it descended of old between Maydenstanhall field, and Hamstell* field, and the Forthefeld until it reaches the place where the Brone burn* descends into Smalhopburne*; and from there northward, following that *burne* as far as the Westledyate first named.

Richard of Aldwod holds that messuage with the lands, meadows and woods belonging to it, and pays 31s. 4d a year, of which 23s. 4d. <goes> annually to the bishop of Durham's exchequer for the free rent;[334] and 8s. annually for the groceries of the convent of Hexham.

---

[332] This is the old road from Lanchester to Durham, running to the north of Manor House (with which *Maydenstanhall* is identified) and then south-eastwards along Langley Lane.

[333] John Lewyn was the leading architect in northern England in the late fourteenth-century. By 1379 he had already built the Prior's Kitchen at Durham Cathedral (1367-74), and was in charge of works at Carlisle and Roxburgh castles for the Crown, as well having been appointed to build Bolton Castle for Richard, Lord Scrope: J. Harvey, 'Lewyn, John (*fl.* 1364–1398)', revised by. C. Wilson, *Oxford Dictionary of National Biography* (Oxford, 2004) [http://www.oxforddnb.com/view/article/37675, accessed 9 June 2011].

[334] *unde scaccario Dunelm. iiijd.* (in marg.). *Unde scaccario Dunelm. Episcopi, pro libera firma annuatim exeunte xxiijs.*

<70> KYMESWORTHE*

They also have in the township of Kymesworthe 1 built toft <formed> out of three buildings[335] with 1 orchard and 1 adjoining croft; this croft contains by estimation 1 acre, and lies at the southern end of Westrawe; and they have there 3 acres of land on the western side of that toft. And all those are contained within these bounds; that is, beginning on the northern side of that toft at an old ditch between that toft and land of Robert Coksyde*; and from there westward, following that ditch as far as the Langfelde of the Erlehouse*; and from there southward, following an old ditch as far as the Deenburne; and from there eastward, following that *burne* as far as a hedged *balk* between that toft and Robert of Coksyde's land; and from there northward, following that *balk,* as far as the way into the township of Kymelesworth.

ARABLE LANDS AND MEADOWS. They also have by estimation 1 acre of arable land and 2 acres of meadow, lying on the eastern side of the *lonyng* that leads from Kymelesworth to the township of Durham, by the common pasture.

They also hold common pasture for 300 <*i.e. 360*> sheep and 8 oxen for the prior's ploughs or those of his tenants, to common throughout the year, wherever the animals of the lord of that township shall happen to graze. And they have estovers for construction and fuel in the woods of that township for themselves and their tenants, by view and allowance of the forester there, wherever the lord of that township shall happen to take his estovers.

DEMISE. And Sir Ralph de Euere[336] and John Lewyne, *mason*,[337] executor of Thomas of Coksyd*, hold those tenures and

---

[335] *j toftum ædificatum ex iij domibus.*

[336] Ralph Eure was one of the richest knights in northern England, holding lands in Northumberland, Durham and Yorkshire, and serving as sheriff and knight of the shire for Northumberland and Yorkshire: J. S. Roskell, L. Clark and C. Rawcliffe, eds., *The House of Commons, 1386-1421,* 3 vols, The History of Parliament (Stroud 1992), III, pp. 38-43.

[337] See the note on John Lewyn under Lanchester under Black Book 69.

lands for the term specified in Thomas' indentures, and pay 10s. a year.

And they shall provide the prior and terrar with suitable lodging in that place, hay for horses, straw, fuel <and> a white candle as often as they shall happen to visit there.

<71> STAYNTON IN STRATA*

They also have there 2 built tofts with 3 buildings,[338] with 1 adjoining garden, and it lies on the Westrawe near the southern end, between 2 plots called Masonplaces on either side. And another toft lies on that *rawe* between William Smyth's toft on the southern side, and the toft of Thomas of Elstobbe* on the northern side.

BOVATE<S> OF LAND. Item, they also have there 4 bovates of land, and each contains 18 acres of land and meadow; of which on Northmancrofte between Aukelandgate* and Grendenmore*, ½ acre; and on the Moracrefore by Aukelandgate*, near that ½ acre, 1½ acres; and in the Crokes by that gate, ½ acre; and on Nethirozrowe on the northern side there, 1 acre; and on the western side of Durhamgate*, abutting on Ozrowe, ½ acre; and on the eastern side of that *gate*, 1 acre 1 rood; and across on Elstobrode*, 1 acre; and on the northern side of the Grendyke, abutting onto it, 4 acres; and on Brakenbery, on the northern side there, 2 acres; and between the Ledyflatt <and> cottage land,[339] abutting on Stillyngtongate*, 2 acres; and on the Wathornflatt, 3 roods; and on Northdenbank, 1 rood; and on the Langflatt and the Claybothum, 1½ acres; and around the church, 1½ acres; and on the Fichebuttes and the Milnway, abutting on those Fichebuttes, 1½ acres; and on the southern side of Auklandgate*, between that *gate* and the Milnway, 1 acre; and on the Lousylawe 2 acres 1 rood; and on the Leybrakes, 3 roods.

And on the northern side of the Lytilmedowe, 3 roods; and on the southern side of that meadow, 3 roods; and on the eastern side there, ½ acre; and in Okirdenbank, on its northern side, 10

---

[338] *ij tofta ædificata in iij domibus.*
[339] *inter le Ledy-flatt, cum terr. cotag.*

acres; and on either side of Okirdenbank, 2 acres; and on the Potsyde, 1 acre; and on the Bradeley, 1 acre; and on Thomashous, 3 roods; and at the eastern end of Thomashous, 1 rood; and at the eastern end of Sandiflatt, ½ acre; and on the Schortalfacre, ½ acre; and at the western end of Sandiflatt, ½ acre; and on the Meadoussyd, 3 acres; and on the Severell, abutting onto it, 2 acres; and on the Dunwell and the Forgar, 1 acre; and on the Croftes, on the western side of those tofts, 2 acres; and on Gilbertesflatt, 6 acres; and in Lousylawcarre, on its southern side, ½ acre; and on Harthstanflatt, 1 acre; and on Owthorne, 1 rood.

And at the eastern end of Grantirsdaneheued and on the Brigflatt in various places, 3 acres; and on the southern side of Derlyngtonway*, on the Mildilfurlange, 1 acre; and on Redknoll, ½ acre; and on the southern side of Smaldenegrave, 1 rood; and on the eastern side of Crokythalfacre, ½ acre; and on the Redknoll, 1 acre; and on the Schortbothum, on the northern side of Manflatt, 1½ acres; and on Haukslawe, abutting onto it, 1 acre; and on the western side of the Hansmedowe, 1 acre; and on the southern side of Waldyway, 1 rood; and on the Langflatt, 1½ acres; and on the western side of Derlyngtonway*, ½ acre.

DEMESNE MEADOWS. And in the Lytilmedow by Bisschopton*, 1 acre; and in the Forgare, ½ acre; and in the Bradmedow, ½ acre; and at the southern end of Grantirsdenheued, ½ acre; and in Ballokkarre, ½ acre.

And it is to be noted that other pieces of meadow belonging to 2 bovates of land, lie among the *husbanddales* in proportion to what other husbandlands there share between them. And it should be noted that the tenants of the prior and convent there shall have 1 horse pasturing in the *oxenpasture*, besides the oxen belonging to the 4 bovates of land there, though the other tenants there shall keep no horse in that pasture.

And Thomas of Legiard holds all those lands and tenements, and pays 40s. a year to the cellarer's office.

<72> HERTYLLPULL*

John of Hesilden* holds 1 tenement in Hertilpole in the Southgate, and it lies between a tenement formerly of Robert of Seton on the western side and Peter Legeate's tenement on the east, and he pays 12s. a year. John Dible holds 1 tenement, and it lies between Peter Legeate's tenement on the western side and William of Heddone's tenement on the eastern side, and he pays 2s. a year to the cellarer.

FREE FARM. They also have 1 yearly rent in that holding of Peter's, now waste, and <it pays> nothing now, but used to pay 5s. a year.

<73> SILKYSWORTH*

They also have within the territory of Silkysworth a grange, called Farendongrange*, lying between the township of Herryngton* and the township of Silkysworth, and that grange with its arable lands are contained within these bounds; that is, beginning at the southern gate of that grange, and from there southward, following an old ditch, on the western side of the Barncrofte, by the site of an old barn, until it reaches an old ditch descending from Halmerstank; and from there eastward, following that ditch lying between Barncrofte and Silkysworthe lands, as far as Rodesmore; and from there, following a baulk between the husbandlands there and Rodlandes and the Grensyd of that township and a *flatt* belonging to that grange called Stephanesflatt, as far as the Kylnsele; and from there, following a baulk between the Redelandes and a *flatt* belonging to that grange called the Wharellflatt, as far as Grendonrode*; and from there, following that *rode* between Wharellflatte and Redrodes as far as the *northende* of the Redlandes; and <from there> following a baulk <...>wards,[340] between Wharellflatte and Silkisworth field, as far as the road called Castelway; and from there northward, following that road, as far as the Ca<...>;[341] and from there, following the edge of that moor, between the moor and the Wharelflatt, as far as an old ditch between the moor and the Parkflatte; and from there northward, following that ditch as far as the Lourybush; and from there

---

[340] Raine represents the missing letters by a dash.
[341] Raine represents the missing letters by a dash.

westward, following an old ditch between Parkflatte and the moor as far as the Pillemoreflatte; and from there, following the edge of Canonmore along Pilmorflatte and the Milnflatte until it reaches a small siket between the Milnflatte and Bassetflatte; and from there westward, following that siket between Bassetflatte and the Milnflatte, as far as a ditch called the Canondyk; and from there southward, following the Canondyk, as far as a moor called Harlawmore; and from there, following 1 ditch between that *more* and Farondongrange* field, until it reaches the southern gate of that grange first mentioned.

They also have a *more* called Canonmore, and it lies on the eastern side of Farondongrange* toward Wermouth*, between the township of Silkisworth and the *ford*. And it is a severalty of the prior and convent throughout the year, except that the lord of Silkisworth, or whoever shall hold the demesne land there, will have 24 plough oxen pasturing in the moor, without any additional animals of other kinds.

SEVERALTY OF MORHOUSPOTT. They also have there a piece of land, called Morhouspote containing by estimation 2½ acres, and it is a severalty of the prior and convent.

DEMISE. William Mortimer and William of the Hall hold between themselves all those holdings and lands with the pasture, and they pay yearly 73s. 4d. a year.

MULTURE. And those tenants will mill at the prior's mill the grain they grow on the lands of the manor, for a toll of one twentieth.

They also have there a windmill and its revenues, and it pays 26s. 8d. a year.

<HUSBANDLANDS.> They also have in the township of Silkysworth 4 husbandlands lying dispersed among cottages there,[342] and also the tofts of those husbandlands, with the cottages

---

[342] It is odd that these husbandlands, containing many acres of arable land, should be described as 'lying dispersed among cottages' (*inter cotagia*). This may be an error for 'lying dispersed amongst the rest' (*inter cetera*),

The Black Book of Hexham

lying together at the northern end of the township; and each land shall clear the land around the *milnpost*, and shall carry the mill's grindstones and its *post*, and all the timber for the working parts of the mill.[343]

And they will grind at that mill the corn they grow on that land, that is the wheat they consume in their homes, for a toll of one thirteenth. Also <grain grown> on the prior's lands <will be ground> for a toll of one sixteenth. And they will give for each quarter of barley sold ½ <a bushel>[344] of barley for multure. The tenants are as follows:

William Wedowson holds 1 built toft and 61 acres of arable land and meadow, and pays 54s. 3d. a year. Robert Wilkynson of Tunstale* and John of Hoghton* hold between them 1 built rood and 20 acres of arable land and meadow, and pay 20s. a year. Richard of Durham holds 2 tofts, 1 of which 1 is built, and 64 (acres) of arable land and meadow, and pays £10 6s. 8d. a year.

<COTTAGES.> They also have in that township 12 cottages, and each cottager will grind his grains at the prior's mill, as above.

Matilda Marmeduk holds 3 built cottages and 8 acres of land and 3 roods, and pays 2s. a year. Robert of Berdene holds 1 built cottage and 2 acres 3½ roods of land, and pays 4s. a year. William Deye holds 1 built cottage and 5½ acres of land, and pays 7s. 6d. a year. William Wedowson holds 2 built cottages and 5½ acres of land, and pays 7s. 6d. a year. John Souter holds 1 built cottage and 4½ acres of land, and pays 5s. a year. William Wedouson holds 1 cottage and 2 acres 1 rood of land, and 3 roods of land lying[345] on the Langdene, and pays 3s. a year. Richard

---

i.e. intermingled with other husbandlands not belonging to the priory estate.

[343] *et omne meremium versatile sive currens pertinens dicto molendino*. The words *versatile* and *currens* seem to relate to the mill's moving parts.

[344] Raine represents the unit by a dash. Half a bushel represents a toll of one-sixteenth.

[345] *jac'*. This could alternatively be 'and 3 roods of land lie on the Langdene'; it is not clear whether these 3 roods are included in the 2 acres 1 rood or additional.

Hunter holds 1 cottage without a garden and 1 rood of land, and pays 14d. a year. Agnes, Richardswyfe, holds built 2 cottages and 4 acres of land, and pays 6s. <a year.>.

There is there also 1 small waste cottage by the common oven; it used to pay 8d.

<COMMON OVEN.> They also have there a common oven for the prior's tenants.

<BREWING.> They also hold the common brewing there for those tenants.

<MEADOWS.> According to <their> charters they also hold 13 acres of meadow in the township of Westheryngton*, dispersed among the meadows of that township around the *karre*, with free entry and exit to mow and make hay on those acres and to carry it away wherever shall seem expedient, wth all other liberties pertaining to that meadow.

DEMISE OF MEADOWS. William Mortimer and William of the Hall hold between them those meadow, and pay 25s. a year.

<COURT.>[346] They also have a court for their tenants in Silkisworth, with the amercements belonging to it, and also <will receive> all the amercements of those tenants if they are amerced in the court of the lord of Silkisworth unless <the fine is for an offence that> touches that lord's own person.

CLEVELAND*, YORKSHIRE

<74>LITTLE BROGHTON*

They also have all the manor of Little Broghton, with the homage and services of Nicholas of Semer and his heirs, <and> of William of Flaxton* and his heirs, with a mill with its millrace; and with all the suit and soke, and all the meadows and pasture within and without that township; and with wardships and reliefs, escheats,

---

[346] This paragraph, without a separate heading, is included in the preceding paragraph in the printed text.

The Black Book of Hexham

forinsec services, suits of courts and of mills, with all liberties and easements in woods, open lands, meadows, roads, paths, pastures, waters, moors, in all places belonging to that manor. In its demesne toft are various buildings, with 1 orchard in which aspens grow in great number, and with 1 dovecote and 1 adjoining garden called the Barlygarth, with 1 croft adjoining that toft containing by estimation 7 acres of arable land. And <they have> also various *flattes* of arable land and meadow with their wastes, which are several throughout the year; that is, on the Cotesflatte, 20 acres of arable land; and on the Langflatte, 30 acres; and on the Threplandflatte, 20 acres; and on the Whetehill and the Brantthorne and the Scholebrade, 30 acres; and on the southern side by the Whetehill, 2 acres of meadow; and at the northern end of the Brantthornflatte, 1 acre of meadow.

There are also various *flattes* that are not several lying between husbandlands, of which on Moubrayflatte by a demesne toft, 6 acres; and on the other Moubrayflatte, 4 acres; and at the western end of the Spanlangcrofte, 1 acre; and on the Dalebank, 3 acres; and on the Westlangcrofte, on the eastern side of Lindbek, 2 acres; and on the Croftsykflatte, 4 acres; and on the Moresyk, 1½ acres; and on Ravensacre, 1½ acres; and on the Langlandheuedland, 1 acre; and on the Langlandes, 2 acres; and at the *milndore*, 1½ acres; and on the Mecoteheuedland, ½ acre; and on the northern side of the *milne*, abutting on the Milnsyk, 3 acres; and on the Milngote, 3 acres; and on Hastynggarthe, 10 acres; and on Whytlawe on the northern side of the Skaldthornemore, 1½ acres; and on Beskarre, 3 acres; and on Whitlaw, 8 acres; and on Whitlawsyke, 3 acres; and on the the Moresyk, 2 acres; and on the Peslandes, 3 acres; and on Hercotte, 4 acres; and on Cokthorne, 2 acres; and on Bentescrofte and Bentesflatte, 6 acres; and on Halleburnegavell, 3 acres; and on Feldyngwath abutting on Ellerbek, 1½ acres.

CASSEHOLME. And there is there a place called Casseholme, and it contains 2½ acres. It used to pay 10d. a year.

MEADOWS. And in the Trenches and the Dammes <are> 5 acres of meadow; and in Alanesacreyng, 1½ acres; and on Whathill, 2 acres; and on Bentesyng, 1½ acres. And those acres of meadow are quit of payment of tithe, for which a piece of meadow is assigned to the parish church there.

DEMISE. Thomas Hunter holds that demesne toft with those lands, and pays 73s. 4d. a year.

SERVICES OF THE MANOR. And he will also find suitable lodging for the lord prior and the terrar at that manor, and hay for his <or their> horses, and straw, fuel and a white candle when and as often as he happens to visit there.[347]

FREE FARM WITH SUIT OF COURT. Thomas Hunter holds 1 toft <and ...>[348] bovates of free land, formerly Henry Foxdon's, by homage and fealty, and pays 1d. a year. He also holds 1 tenement and 6 bovates of free land, formerly Nicholas Semer's, by homage and fealty, and pays 3s. 8d. a year.

<HUSBAND MESSUAGES AND BOVATES.> And there are also 9 *husband* messuages there and 26 bovates of land, of which each of 24 bovates contains 8 acres of arable land and meadow, and the 2 remaining each contain 9 acres. And each bovate shall share in carrying carry millstones <to the mill>, and will repair its walls, and will roof the said mill except on the *louthre*, at <its tenant's> own cost and expense as often and whenever it shall be necessary, and shall clean the mill pond, and will grind grains for a toll of one thirteenth. The tenants are as follows.

John Whyte holds 1 messuage and 2 bovates of land, formerly in the tenure of Robert Whytheued, and pays 8s. a year. Adam Maner holds 1 built messuage and 5 bovates of land, and pays 18s. a year. John <...>[349] holds 1 built toft and 4 bovates of land, formerly in the tenure of Nicholas Snawball, <and pays> 17s. <a year>; he also holds 1 *flatte* called Moubrayeflatte, and pays 17s. a year; he also holds 2 bovates of land containing 18 acres, and pays 17s. a year; he also holds 1 messuage formerly John

---

[347] The verb is in the singular, perhaps implying that the prior and terrar were not expected to visit at the same time.
[348] Raine represents the missing figure by a dash.
[349] Raine notes the omission of the surname by adding *sic*.

Snowball's and 4 bovates of land, and pays 14s. <a year>; he also holds 1 messuage and 1 bovate of land formerly Thomas of Colte's, and pays 5s. a year. Roger of Berwyk holds 1 built messuage and 1 bovate of land, and pays 5s. a year. John Whyte holds 1 tenement and 2 bovates of land called Carltonplace, and pays 9s. a year. Thomas Gollane holds 1 built messuage and 3 bovates of land, and pays 12s. a year. John Whyte holds 1 messuage and 2 bovates of land that Peter Mody formerly held, and pays 6s. a year.

LABOUR SERVICES. There are also 11 cottages there, and each cottage will grind its corn at the mill there, and will perform labour services and customs at that mill just like the tenants of the bovates specified above, and they will perform services as set out below. The tenants are as follows.

John Whyte holds 1 cottage, formerly John Mek's, and 5 acres of land, and pays 5s. a year; he also holds 1 cottage called Pondarplace and 2½ acres of land, and pays 3s. a year;[350] he also holds 1 cottage, formerly John Gelle's, and 4 acres of land, <and pays> 3s. <a year>; he also holds 1 cottage, formerly Matilda Parlien's, and 5 acres of land with a croft, and pays 3s. a year; he also holds 1 cottage, formerly Robert Netehyrd's, and 5 acres of land with a croft, and pays 5s. a year, and 4 labour services; he also holds 1 cottage, formerly William Milner's, with 1 croft and 3 acres of land, <and> pays 5s. a year, and 4 labour services; he also holds 1 cottage with 1 croft, formerly Christine Skanser's, and pays 18d. a year; he also holds 1 cottage with a croft and 4 acres of land, formerly John Walker's, and pays 3s. 4d. a year and labour services; he also holds 1 cottage with 1 croft and 8 acres of land, formerly Alicia Abbote's, and pays 5s. a year and labour services; he also holds 1 cottage and 4 acres of land, formerly Thomas of Bekke's, <and> pays 4s. a year; he also holds 1 cottage newly appropriated through Thomas Jonson there, <and> pays <...>.[351]

DEMISE. And the said John Whytte holds all those tenements and lands, with those bovates of land, in accordance with

---

[350] Raine records that at this point the manuscript has a marginal note 'Works at harvest time'. It is unclear just why it is there, but it seems to imply that some of these cottagers owed labour services at harvest time.

[351] *Idem t. j cot. de novo appropriatum per Thomam Jonson ibidem, r--.*

their terms of tenure as specified above,[352] and pays in all for everything 70s. 8d. a year.

<WATER MILL.> And there is also a water mill there belonging to that manor, and 3 acres of land called the Milnholme belonging to the mill, lying westward of the mill, and on the northern side of Ellerbek in the field of Great Broghton*, and it pays 13s. 4d a year.

And it is to be noted that the vicar of Kyrkbe* in Cleveland* has there various tenements and 28 acres of land for which he should have a mass celebrated every Friday in St Margaret's Chapel there; and he will also have the gospel read to the parishioners in that chapel every Sunday, and will have holy water with consecrated bread made and administered to them; and each year he shall provide a chaplain to receive the offerings of candles there at the feast of the Purification of the Blessed Virgin Mary and the offerings of palms on Palm Sunday, and also to hear parishioners' confessions there every year during Lent.

<75> BROGHTON*

They also have in Great Broghton 1 built chief messuage lying on the eastern side of the township and on the southern side near the *owtgang* toward Little Broghton*, with 1 garden and 1 adjoining croft, the croft containing 2 acres of meadow.

They also have 3½ bovates of arable land and meadow belonging to that messuage, of which 2 acres and 1 rood of meadow lie dispersed among the common meadows of the husbands there, and each bovate contains 18 acres of arable land and meadow; of which, on the Lynghill, in two places lie 3 acres; and on the eastern side of the Mykilmere on Whitlawe, 1½ acres; and on Mykillmerhill toward the east, with 1 butt on the Post, 1 acre 1 rood; and on Gudemonondayes, on the eastern side there, 1 acre 1 rood; and on the Crossegarthill, about in the middle, 1 acre; and on the eastern side of Hellkarre by Lytilbroghton* *feld*, 1 acre; and on the Postes, ½ acre; and on the Toft, 1 acre; and on the

---

[352] *prout superius specificatur per tenuras suas.*

Standandstane, about in the middle, 1 acre; and on Schoffurdale and the Daleacre, 1 acre; and on Braubiforris, 3 roods; and on Mikilrigge, about in the middle, 2 acres in various places; and on the western side by Transsyke, 1 acre; and at Jacgartheud on Malknoll, ½ acre; and on the Flores, ½ acre; and at the Schorthordes,[353] ½ rood; and on Schortmossefen, ½ rood; and on Langmosfenne, 1 rood; and on the Schortrodes, ½ rood; and at the Ovyrwendikes, ½ acre; and on the Wychbusk, in various places, 1 acre; and on the Milnhill, toward the eastern end, 1 acre; and on the Lathebuttes, about in the middle, 1½ acres; and on the Langlandes, 2½ acres; and on the Lenendales, ½ acre; and on Wyndesherse, ½ acre; and on Smythstedes, ½ acre; and on the Milngavell, 1 acre 1 rood; and on the Morebrek, ½ acre; and on the Smythstedes on the southern side there, 3 roods; and by Hillerbekbrigges on the northern side, 1 rood; and on the Schortrodes <in> 2 *buttes*, 1 rood; and on Sandelandes, 1½ acres in various places; and on Rowcarre, ½ rood; and on Alwardacre in 3 butts, 3 roods; and at the Falucrosse, ½ acre; and on the Thornedyk, ½ acre; and on the Langhalfacre, 1 acre 1 rood; and on the Thornbank, 3 roods; and on Kimacre, 3 acres; and on the Biglandes in various places, 1½ acres; and on Langabbow, 1 acre 1 rood; and on Schortabbow, 1 rood; and on the Canonflatte, 4 acres; and on Nauwarelaw, 3 roods; and on Gosmodre, ½ acre; and on the Layrepittes in various places, 1 acre; and on the Langpole, 1 acre; and Nocthorne, 1 rood; and on the Wattirfall, in various places, 1 acre; and on Grenrige, 1½ acres; and on Swynholmes in 2 places, 1 acre 1 rood; and on Lambelez, 1 rood; and on Estwynholme, 1 acre; and on Skalrige, ½ acre; and on the northern side of that ½ acre, 1 acre; and on Litilholdale, 1 acre; and on the western side of the *cotgarth* in front of the gate of the abbot of Ryvaux*'s grange,[354] abutting on the *milndam*, ½ acre; and on the Mirsyk, 1 acre; and in the middle of the demesne lands of that grange, abutting on the *cote* toward the west and[355] on Ellersyk toward the east, 1 acre; and on Hurigleyse in 2 places, 1 acre; and on the western side by the Grangeflatte, ½ acre; and on Whaythill, 1 rood.

---

[353] Perhaps for *Schorthrodes:* cf. *Schortrodes* (two instances below).
[354] Broughton Grange: C. Platt, *The Monastic Grange in Medieval England* (London, 1969), pp. 193-4.
[355] The translation here assumes that Raine's capitalization of 'et' is misleading.

COTTAGES WITH ADJOINING LAND. They also have there 2 cottages in that township, of which 1 lies, built, near the northern end of the township, between a plot of the abbot of Ryvaux*'s the northern side, and a plot of the Templars' on the southern side. And there are <3>[356] acres <1 rood> of arable land belonging to that cottage, of which on the Hertbreks lies 1 acre; and on the Standandstan, ½ acre; and on the eastern side of Miklerige, 1 acre; and on the Schorthordes, abutting on Transyk, ½ acre; and in the Hellkarre, 1 rood.

And the other cottage called Tabardplace, with 1 adjoining croft, lies by the abbot's grange there toward the west, and pays 18d. a year.

And John of Appilton holds all those tenements and lands, and pays in all 24s. a year.

<LANDS HELD BY JOHN WHYT.> They also have in Great Broghton field 14 acres of arable land without a toft which used to be in the lord's hand because they are demesne lands, to demise by lease to whoever he should please; of which, on Godemononday, on the eastern side there, lie 6 acres; and on the western side of the *crosse*, on one side of Kyrkgate road, 1½ acres; and on the southern side of Lowykkarre, abutting onto it, 2 acres; and on the northern side of that *karre*, 1½ acres; and on the Longmosfene abutting on Transyk toward the west, 1½ acres of arable land and meadow; and on Schortmosfene, on the eastern side there, 2 acres of arable land and meadow.

DEMESNE MEADOWS. They also have there 2 acres 3 roods of demesne meadow belonging to those acres of demesne land, of which in the Langstrothre on its southern side lie 1 acre 3 roods; and on the western side of Lynbek abutting on Lynbekwathe, 3 roods; and on the northern side, by those roods, 1 rood.

DEMISE. And John Whyt holds those lands and meadows with the lands specified in his holding at Little Broghton*, and pays for all in all of them together.

---

[356] Raine gives no indication of a missing figure here.

<76> INGLEBY*

They also have in the township of Ingleby 1 built toft lying at the southern end of the township on its western side, with 1 garden and 1 adjoining croft, containing in all by estimation 1½ acres.

They also have in the field there 1 bovate of arable land and meadow, containing 15 acres of land; of which on the western side of Maybek lie 5 acres; and on Litilredehowe, about in the middle, abutting on Redehowsyk, 3 roods; and on the eastern side of Belrige abutting on Mebek, 3 roods; and on the northern side of Redhowegate, 2½ acres; and on the Brygsyk, about in the middle, abutting southward on the Blindkeld, 1 acre; and on the Watelandes abutting on Esbymarche*, 1 acre; and on Haystangarth on the northern side of Inglebyfeld, 1 acre; and on Haystangarthhill, abutting on Esbywaye*, 1 acre; and on Hastyngarth on the southern side of the Thornes, ½ acre; and on Haystyngarth, on the southern side near that ½ acre, abutting on the Roundholme, 1 acre.

COTTAGES. They also have 1 built cottage there lying on the eastern side of the township at its northern end, containing in all by estimation ½ acre.

They also have 2½ acres of land belonging to that cottage, of which on the Lamcotes lie 1 acre 1 rood; and on Gildrecost, 1 acre 1 rood.

DEMISE. And Peter of Bathebon holds those tenements and lands, and pays 8s. a year; of which 5s. is for the bovate of land, and 3s. for the cottage with the land belonging to it.

<77> KIRKBE IN CLEVELAND*

They also have 1 built tenement with 1 garden and an adjoining croft, containing in all by estimation 1 acre, lying on the eastern side of the township, between a plot of the vicar of that township on the southern side and a plot of John Turim on the northern side.

They also hold 1 bovate of arable land there containing 12 acres of land; of which on Fulburne and the Dykes, 1 rood; and on Haybek, ½ acre; and on Dymples, 1 rood; and in the *sclak* of the *gate*, 1 rood; and at the Wyndmylnhill on either side of the road that (leads) to Stokeslaye*, ½ acre; and across that road at Hellerberkheued, 3 roods; and on Hillerbeklandes, 3 roods; and on the western side of Hillerbeklandes, 1 acre 1 rood; and on Helle in 2 places, ½ acre; and on Langspanhow, ½ acre; and on Schortspanhow, 1 rood; and in the Bothomes, 1 rood; and on Magodesleyse abutting on the *dykes*, ½ rood; and on Wyndynges by the Aldbek in various places, 6 acres; and in the Petpottes, ½ acre; and to the south of Petpottes, 1 rood; and on Wesebek *furlang* in various places, ½ acre; and on the southern side of the Acrethorne, ½ rood; and on the Overtoftes, 1 rood; and on Somerellbuttes, 3 roods; and in the Overbrotes, about in the middle, 1 rood; and on the western side of the Bererige, ½ acre; and in the middle of it, ½ acre; and in the Brotes, 1½ roods; and on Schortberige, 1 rood; and on Langlillynges, 1 rood; and on Schortlillinges, ½ rood; and on the eastern side of the *lonynge* of the Engegates, 1 rood; and at the southern end of the township, on the eastern side of the *dykes*, ½ acre.

MEADOWS THERE. They also have 3 roods of meadow, lying dispersed among the husband <lands> there; that is, in the Flodres, 1 rood; and in the Langrodes, 1 rood; and in the Schortrodes, 1 rood.

COTTAGE. They also have 1 cottage there with 1 adjoining croft, and it lies on the western side of the township, toward its southern end, between a plot of John <...> on the northern side and a plot of John <...> on the southern side.[357]

DEMISE. And Robert of Yngrame holds all those tenements and lands, and pays in all for everything, 9s.

<Raine has a footnote that 'after this there is a blank page, and a leaf has been cut out of the MS.' He nevertheless continues the section relating to Kirkby in Cleveland with text that is in fact an

---

[357] Raine represents the missing surnames by dashe.

alternative version - here called version A - of part of the material relating to Salton. The variants between version A and the more complete survey of Salton (version B) are indicated below in the footnotes to the latter. >

<78> THE MANOR OF SALTON* <VERSION B>

They also have a manor in the township of Salton, where there are various buildings, that is one hall with three chambers and a chapel, a kitchen, bakehouse, brewhouse, large stable, an orchard and a garden called the *pengarth*. And, on the northern side of the manor, <is> a hall called the *gesthall* with a chamber at the end, the *gatehous*, a large barn, woodshed, piggery, a newly-built maltkiln, an orchard called the *kylngarth*, and a garden called the *bengarth*.

There are also 16 bovates of demesne arable land there, each of which contains 9 acres of land: of which 8 bovates lie in four *flattes* called the Dikes and the Milncroft. These *flattes*, called Blapule,[358] lie by Crossowbrigge, between tenants' lands, and are several. And the other 8 bovates of land lie dispersed in various parts among tenants' lands there.

There are also 12½ acres of meadow there in the W<...>[359] in addition to two selions put back to meadow, and they are several throughout the year. There are also 8 acres of meadow there in the Southenge, not several, lying in one flat among tenants' meadows.

There is also there a close, called the Milnclos, and it is several throughout the year.

FRENSHOLME. There is also there a wood called Frensholme, containing, by estimation, 2½ acres, and it is several throughout the year.[360]

---

[358] *in quattuor flattes, vocatis lez Dikes et lez Miln-croft. Istæ predictæ flattæ, vocatæ Bla-pule ...*'.
[359] Raine represents the remainder of this placename by a dash.
[360] The account of the demesne above corresponds almost exactly to the description in document 71 (item 2), where it is said to contain 2 carucates (i.e. 16 bovates), 13 acres of meadow and 2½ acres in *Frensholm*.

SHEEPFOLD NEAR EDESTON* FIELD. There is also in the field there 1 plot of land called Cotegarth, where the lord used to have a sheepfold.

DEMISE. William of Daventre* holds the *gesthall* with all other buildings there on the northern side of that manor, with the *kylngarth* and the *beengarth*, except that the lord will have the southern end of the great barn for bringing in his tithes as often as necessary. And William also holds all those lands and meadows, except that the lord shall have 6 acres of meadow in Westerige for his horses, and except for Frensholme and the plot for a sheepfold by Edeston* field; and he pays 33s. a year at the terms of Martinmas and Pentecost. And he also pays 6 quarters of wheat and maslin, 4 quarters of barley, and 10 quarters of oats yearly, at the Purification of the Blessed Virgin Mary and at Easter by equal shares. And he will mill his grains at the lord's mill for a toll of <...>,[361] and owes suit of court at the court there.

<CUSTOMS.> There are also 73 bovates of land in the township there, of which 54 bovates are bondlands; and 4 bovates by estimation are in the *forlandes* and are held as bondlands; and 15 bovates of land are demesne land.[362] Of these, each bovate in demesne contains 7½ acres of arable land and meadow, and each bovate of the bondlands and the *forelandes* contains 9 acres. And besides these, 2½ bondlands by estimation are divided between the cottages there.

And <the tenant of> each bovate of land, according to the custom of the manor there, shall carry his share of the lord's victuals anywhere within Yorkshire for the lord and his travels on horseback;[363] and will also carry sawn and squared timber for the building of Salton manor and the mill there; and will carry the millstones for the mill, and repair the millpond, and perform all

---

[361] Raine represents the missing figure by a dash.
[362] These seem to be additional to the 16 bovates detailed above, both because of their different number nd because of their different size. But it is impossible to square either the implied size of the demesne or the total number of bovates with document 71 (item 2), which implies only 16 bovates of demesne land and 43 bovates of husbandland.
[363] *pro domino et equitaturis suis.*

customary labour services appertaining to the mill; and will clear the the conduit to that pond on either side; and roof the mill with the lord's roofing material; and will also provide decent beds for the lord's guests whenever he goes there; and will carry stones and stonemasons' lime, and all the timber for constructing and repairing buildings in the manor; and will also elect a suitable servant to be responsible for the manor, and other reeves for collecting money, and *alegraves, wateregraves*, and 4 men sworn <to present> all things to be presented in the court and in the chapter of Salton,[364] and one stockman for keeping the lord's stock. The tenants there should answer for the men so elected. And also no tenant there will carry his grain at harvest before the lord's grain has been carried unless he has sought and obtained the lord's permission. Furthermore, each bovate will share in cleaning the ditch around Frensholme, and will mill his grains at the lord's mill for a toll of one-thirteenth.

BONDLANDS. John of Cravin holds 1 messuage and 2½ bovates of bondland, and pays 10s. a year; John also holds 2 acres of *forland* and pays 9d. a year; John also (holds) 1½ roods of meadow, and pays 2s. a year; John also holds 1 cottage with *foreland*, and pays 2s. 6½d. a year. Roger Bell holds 1 messuage and 3 bovates of bondland, and pays 12s. a year; Roger also holds 1 bovate of demesne land, and pays 6s. a year; Roger also holds 1 grass plot with a messuage and 2 bovates of bondland, and pays 1d. a year.[365] John Elynson holds 1 messuage and 2 bovates of bondland, and pays 8s. a year; he also holds 1 bovate of demesne land with 1 grass plot, and pays 5s. ½d. a year; he also holds at the lord's pleasure 1 plot of land called Hawykescrofte to enlarge his holding because it is of poor quality, and <pays> nothing, but it used to pay 2s. 4d. Robert Watson's widow holds 1 messuage and 4 bovates of bondland with a grass plot and *forland* and pays 16s. 1½d. a year. John son of Robert Watsun holds 1 messuage, <and pays> 12s. 1d. <a year>; John also holds 1 bovate of demesne land, and pays 6s. 1d. a year. Robert of Malteby* holds 1 messuage and 2 bovates of bondland, and pays 8s. a year; Robert also holds 1 bovate of demesne land, and pays 6s. a year; Robert also holds one

---

[364] *et iiij juratos, omnia præsentatilia (sic) in curia et in capitulo de Salton.* The translation is a guess.
[365] Such an improbable rent implies an error in the text.

cheregarth, half a *wodlibusk* and 1 *wildirland*, and pays 14d. John Smyth holds 1 messuage and 3 bovates of bondland with 1 grass plot and pays 11s. 0½d. a year. Alice of Ottrington* holds 1 messuage and 2 bovates of bondland, and pays 8s. a year; Alice also holds 3 bovates of demesne land, with the *forland*, as <recorded> in the court rolls, and pays 17s. 0¼d. <a year>. William of Thirneham holds 1 messuage with 1 enclosed *girsgarth* and 3 bovates of bondland, <and> pays 13s. <a year>. William also holds 1 parcel of *forland* called the Bradetofte,[366] and pays 18d. a year; he also holds 2 acres of demesne land, and pays 2s. a year. Thomas Enysun holds 1 bovate of demesne land, and performs two labour services at harvest time, and pays 5s. <a year>. John of <the> *stable* holds 1 messuage <and> 2 bovates of bondland, and pays 8s. a year; John also holds 1 bovate of demesne land, and pays 6s. a year. William Talyor holds 1 bovate[367] and 2 bovates of bondland and pays 8s. a year. Walter Cattesun holds 1 messuage and 2 bovates of demesne land, and ½ a bovate of bondland, <and pays> 11s. <a year>. John of Craven holds 1 messuage, 3 bovates of bondland with the *forland* <and> 1 grass plot, <and pays> 10s. 6d. <a year>. Henry Wyotte holds 1 messuage <and> 4 bovates of bondland, and pays 16s. a year. John Ganton holds 1 messuage <and> 3 bovates of bondland, and pays 12s. a year; John also holds 4 acres of demesne land and 1 *bradetofte*, and pays 5s. a year. William Durifen holds 1 messuage <and> 3 bovates of bondland, and pays 12s. a year; William also holds 1 bovate <of>[368] demesne land and 1 acre of *forland*, <and> pays 6s. <a year>; William also holds 1 parcel of meadow by the Westyng called Crok, <and pays> 2s. <a year>. William Riotte holds 1 messuage <and> 2 bovates of bondland, of which 1 bovate was formerly in the tenure of Reginald Lowe, with *forland*, and pays 12s. 8d. a year; William also holds 1 acre of demesne land in the Northfeld, and pays 9d. a year; William also holds 1 acre of land called Stoureland, and pays 10d. a year; William also holds 1 butt of land at the Westcroftyet, and pays 2d. a year. Richard Durifen holds 1 messuage <and> 4 bovates of bondland and pays 16s. a year; Richard also holds Bradetoft <or a

---

[366] *le Brade-tofte*. Later instances suggest this was a type of toft rather than a name.
[367] Perhaps an error for '1 messuage'.
[368] The printed text has *et* instead of *de*.

bradetofte> with a parcel of meadow, 6 butts of land on <the> Doufe*, and 5 butts in the Southfeld, and pays 3s. 4d. a year. Father Peter, the vicar, holds 2 bovates of bondland, and pays 8s. a year. And 2 bovates of bondland are in the lord's hand for want <of tenants>; they used to pay 8s. a year. Also in the lord's hand <is> 1 bovate of demesne land with *forland*; it used to pay 5s. 2d. <a year>.

COTTAGES. And there are in that township 39 cottages, of which 17 are built, and 19 not built <and> demised for herbage; and 3 cottages are completely waste and untenanted. And each cottage owes its share of labour services at the mill and its pond like the bondmen, together with other labour services and customs as set out below.

<LABOUR SERVICES AND CUSTOMS AS BEFORE.>
[369] John Talyor holds 1 cottage,[370] and performs 4 labour services at harvest time, and pays 4 hens[371] at Christmas and 20 eggs at Easter, and also pays 12d. a year, at the customary terms. John Drury holds 1 cottage <and> 3 acres of land and meadow, with 1 grass plot, and pays 4s. 5d.[372] a year and labour services. John Kyell holds 1 cottage, and pays 12d. a year and labour services as above. John Colynson holds a cottage <and> 3½ acres of land, and pays 4s. 6d. a year.[373] John Hare holds 1 cottage <and> 2 acres of land, and pays 2s. 6d. a year, and labour services as above. John Kereby[374] holds 1 cottage <and> 3½ acres of land, and pays 3s. 10d. a year and labour services; he also holds holds osiers by the banks of <the> Doufe*, called the Spechyns, and pays 4s.[375] a year, without labour services. Raynald Robertson holds 1 cottage and 1 acre of land, and pays 3s. a year and labour services. Isabel of Stayngrafn[376] holds 1 cottage, and pays 12d. a year and labour services. Nicholas

---

[369] Version A begins here with this heading (*Opera et consuetudines ut prius*), which is omitted from version B.
[370] '1 messuage' in version A.
[371] '20 eggs at Christmas and at Easter' in version A.
[372] '5d.' (not 4s. 5d.) in version A.
[373] 'and labour services' in version A.
[374] *Kyrkbe* in version A.
[375] '6s.' instead of '4s.' in version A.
[376] *Stanegreve* in version A.

Netehird holds a cottage, and pays 12d. a year and labour services. John Lepar holds a cottage, and pays 2s. a year and labour services; John also holds the herbage of gardens at the end of the township, and he pays only[377] 3s. a year at the feast of St Martin without labour services. William Talyor holds 2 gardens, and pays 2s. a year without labour services. Cel<ia>[378] Ferung holds 1 cottage, and pays 2s. a year without labour services. John Waude[379] holds 1 cottage, 4 acres of land and ½ acre of meadow, <and> pays 4s.[380] a year without labour services. John Moris holds a cottage with various gardens under grass at the end of the township, <and> pays 4s. a year without labour services. William Milner holds 1 cottage, and pays 12d. a year and labour services. John Frere[381] holds a cottage and 1 acre of land, and pays 2s. a year and labour services. The vicar[382] holds the Peelegarth, and pays 4d. a year.[383] William Acastre holds 1 cottage by the churchyard, and pays 2s. a year, without labour services. John of Kirkbe holds a cottage and 1 garden at the southern[384] end of the township, <and> pays 20d. a year.[385] Richard Durefene[386] holds 2 gardens at the western end of the township, <and> pays 18d. a year without [labour services]. William Durefa[387] holds Ketilgarth at the lord's pleasure,[388] <and> pays 13d. a year without labour services.

<FORMER RENTS.>[389] And it is to be noted that that each of those cottages standing apart without adjoining land used of old to be demised at farm for 12d. a year and labour services, as is it set

---

[377] *tantum*, omitted in version A.
[378] *Cel'* in version A; *Ceel'* in version B.
[379] *Wayde* in version A.
[380] '3s. 6d.' instead of '4s.' in version A.
[381] *Mere* in version A.
[382] *Dominus vicarius*. In version A this is *Dominus Petrus, vicarius*, i.e. 'Father Peter, the vicar'.
[383] 'without labour services' in version A.
[384] 'western' instead of 'southern' in version A.
[385] 'without labour services' in version A.
[386] *Durefu* in version A.
[387] *Durefu* in version A.
[388] 'at the lord's pleasure' is omitted in version A.
[389] This subheading is taken from version A.

out <in an old roll>.[390] And all those gardens used to be demised at a higher farm.

The vicar holds Adescrofte, containing 2½ acres of land, and pays 4s. 4d. a year without (labour services).[391]

COMMON OVEN. John Morise holds the common oven of the township and pays 4s. 4d.[392] a year, without labour services.

BREWING. And each woman who brews on bondlands or <in> cottages shall give two gallons of ale of every brew, according to custom.

WATER MILL. John of the *stable* holds the water mill[393] there with its suit of multure, and pays £4 6s. 8d. a year.

The vicar of Salton holds a fishery there, and pays 2s. a year.

AGISTMENT IN THE EST MORE. And it is to be noted that the Estmore is the lord's severalty from the feast of the Invention of the Holy Cross until the feast of St Peter ad Vincula, except that by custom during this period each tenant holding 1 bovate in Salton will have 2 bulls and cows there for each bovate he holds. And if any tenant there should have more beasts there than his holding allows he shall pay 6d. for each beast, and for each two-year-old *stirk* 3d. And by custom during that time each tenant there will have 1 mare there for 3 days after foaling.

LABOUR SERVICES AND CUSTOMS. And it is to be noted that each two bovates of bondland there will supply 1 cart for carrying squared timber for the lord. And each bovate of bondland will find 1 horse for carrying the lord's victuals. And 4 bovates of land will find 1 wain for carrying on the Burdland, when need be, without <also> having to do those labour services.

---

[390] 'in an old roll', from version A, is omitted in version B.
[391] 'without labour services' in version A, printed thus in brackets in version B.
[392] '3s. 6d.' instead of '4s. 4d.' in version A.
[393] Version A ends here.

COMMON AID. And those tenants, according to the old custom of that prebend, should share in giving the sum of 10 marks of silver toward the purchase of a palfrey for the lord prior when he is newly elected, or else toward any common aid when necessity compels him to ask it from them, each in proportion to his holding.

OSIER BED WITH WASTE. The community of the township holds the osiers on the banks of the water of Doufe*, and herbage of the waste in Salton field, and pays yearly <...>.[394]

<79> BRAWBY*

In the township of Brawby there are also 51 bovates and 3 acres of land, of which eight bovates and 3 acres are demesne lands, and 43 bovates are bondlands; of these, 3 bovates of land by estimation are divided into *forland*, which is demised among the tenants of the township, as below. There is also there an enclosure in the tenure of Robert Acastre, which contains 1 bovate of land. And each of those bovates contains 9 acres of arable land and meadow. There is also there is a moorland enclosure called the Cotgarth where they used to have a built sheepfold. The lord also has there a common bakery, and it pays a yearly rent as included below. And each of the tenants of those bovates of land shall perform his share of all labour services and customs at Salton* mill, just as the tenants of Salton* do for their bondlands there, as specified above. And each tenant in the township of Brawby should mill his grains at Salton* mill, so long as there is no mill at Brawby, on pain of losing all of the grain to the *multirgrafe*, and the sack to the miller, and an amercement to the lord. And when there is a mill at Brawby, then the tenants there should mill their grains and perform labour services and customs at that mill just as the tenants of Salton* do at the lord's mill at Salton*. And when there is a mill at Brawby, the tenants do not owe any labour services, customs, or suit with their grain at Salton mill, as ordained in the lord's court there. And each bovate of land there will share in performing all labour services and customs, both carriage services and others, as the tenants of Salton* do for bovates of land there, as specified above. And they ought to give common aid and <an aid> for

---

[394] The missing sum is represented by a dash in the printed edition.

purchasing the lord prior's palfrey, each in proportion to his holding, like the tenants of Salton*, as noted above.

William Courtman holds 1 messuage, 4 bovates of land, 1 grass plot, and *forland*, and <a> *horsepoile*, <and> pays 17s. 6d. a year. Thomas Talyor holds 1 messuage <and> 2 bovates of land, with *forland* <and> pays 8s. 6½d. a year. John Wath holds 1 messuage <and> 2 bovates of land with the *forland* containing ½ acre, and pays 9s. a year. John Knapton holds 2 messuages <and> 3 bovates of bondland, with the *forland*, and pays 12s. 9½d. a year; John also holds 1 bovate of demesne land, <and> pays 5s. a year. John Water and John Knapton hold 3 bondlands with *forland*, and pay 12s. 11½d. a year. Thomas Brown holds 1 messuage <and> 2 bovates of land with *forland*, <and> pays 9s. 2d. a year. Thomas Ronfere holds 1 messuage <and> 3 bovates of demesne land with *forland*, <and> pays 15s. 1d. a year. Robert Castre holds 1 messuage, 2 bovates of bondland with *forland*, <and> 3 acres of demesne land with 1 croft, <and> pays 14s. 3½d. a year; Robert also holds 2 bovates of demesne land, <and> pays 10s. a year. John Symson holds 1 messuage, 2 bovates of land and *forland*, <and> pays 8s. 7d. a year. Robert Walsch holds 1 messuage <and> 2 bovates of demesne land with *forland*, <and> pays 10s. 1d. a year. John of Halton holds 1 messuage <and> 3 bovates of land with *forland*, <and> pays 13s. 1d. <a year>. John Huge holds 1 messuage <and> 2 bovates of bondland with *forland*, <and pays> 8s. 6¾d. <a year>. John Raynerson holds 1 messuage <and> 2 bovates of bondland with *forland*, <and pays> 8s. 6¾d. <a year>. Thomas Talyor holds 1 messuage <and> 2 bovates of bondland with *forland*, <and> pays 8s. 6¾d. <a year>. William Symson holds 1 messuage <and> 2 bovates of land with *forland*, <and pays> 8s. 10d. <a year>. Robert Loge holds 1 messuage 2 bovates of land with a bakehouse, <and> 3 bovates of land with *forland*, <and pays> 16s. 3d. <a year>. John Water holds 1 messuage <and> 2 bovates of land with *forland*, <and pays> 8s. 6½d. <a year>. Robert Talyor holds 1 messuage <and> 2 bovates of land with *forland*, <and> pays 8s. 6½d. a year. William Symson holds 1 messuage <and> 2 bovates of land with *forland*, <and> pays 8s. 6d. a year.

COTTAGES OF BRAUBY. LABOUR SERVICES AND CUSTOMS. Adam Schephyrd holds 1 cottage <and> 3 acres of land and pays 21d. a year, 1 hen and eggs; he also holds 1 *gyrsgarth* and 1 acres of land, and pays 15d. a year, without labour services; he also holds a cottage <and> 2 acres of land and pays 13d. a year and labour services. Alice Northyrn holds 1 cottage <and> 3 acres of land, <and> pays 2s. 1d. a year and labour services. John Kent holds 1 cottage <and> 6 acres of land with meadow, and pays 6s. 3d. a year and labour services. John Broune holds 1 cottage <and> 6 acres of land, <and> pays 3s. 10d. a year and labour services. Isolda Berear holds 1 cottage, 6 acres of land <and> 1 acre of meadow, <and> pays 6s. 4d. <a year> and labour services. Cecilia Liepare holds 1 cottage <and> 1 butt of land, <and> pays 2s. 3d. a year and labour services. Thomas Broune holds a cottage, <and> pays 6d. a year without labour services; he also holds 3 acres of land, <and> pays 12d. a year without labour services. The community of the township holds osiers by the water and waste there, <and> pays 11s. 10d. <a year>. Thomas Talyor holds the *cotgarth* in the hermitage,[395] and pays 2s. <a year> at the lord's pleasure. John Water holds 1 waste cottage with 1 croft, <and> pays 2s. <a year>. John Knapton holds 1 waste cottage, <and> pays 12d. a year. Robert Talyor holds 1 waste cottage, and pays 9d. a year and labour services. William Courtman holds 1 waste cottage, <and> pays 10d. <a year> and labour services. John Raynerson holds 1 waste cottage, and pays 12d. a year and labour services. There are also 5 acres of land there called Gildland in the lord's hand. They used to pay 3s. 4d. a year.

    BREWING THERE. <...>

    FISHERY THERE. <...>

    MILNCLOSE. <...>[396]

<80> EDESTON*

There are in the township of Edeston 40 bovates of land, of which each bovate contains 9 acres of land and meadow; they perform no labour services nor customs like other bovates

---

[395] *t. le Cot-garth in heremo.*
[396] Raine prints these three headings on a single line, with a dash following the last of the three, but they are probably on three separate lines in the manuscript.

belonging to the manor of Salton*, because they are not part of the prebend.

DEMISE. Henry Gamill holds 1 messuage and 6 bovates of land, <and> pays 27s. <a year>. John, son of Walter holds 4 bovates of land, and pays 20s. a year. John Wilcocsun holds one messuage <and> 4½ bovates of land <and pays> 20s. 6d. <a year>. John Gamill holds 1 messuage <and> 4½ bovates of land, <and> pays 20s. a year. Robert Oven holds 1 messuage <and> 4 bovates of land and pays 20s. a year. William Arnald holds 1 bovate of land, and pays 4s. a year. Robert Michell holds 1 messuage <and> 4 bovates of land, <and> pays 18s. <a year>. Robert of Oven holds 3 bovates of land, and pays 12s. a year. John son of Alice holds 4 bovates of land, <and> pays 16s. a year. There are also 2 bovates of land assigned by the lord's goodwill to the vicar of Salton to supplement his portion.[397]

Susan Wilkynson holds 1 bovate of land, <and> pays 4s. a year. William son of Walter holds 2 bovates of land, and pays 8s. a year. Alicia Dawson holds 1 butt of land, and pays 2d. a year.

<Raine notes that 'after this there is a blank plage'.>

<81 EDSTONE ?>[398]

There are 9 cottages there.

William Arnald holds 1 cottage, and pays 2s. a year. Father William, vicar there, holds 1 cottage, and pays 2s. a year. Euphemia Wilkynson holds 1 cottage, and pays 2s. a year. William Arnald holds 3 waste cottages; he used to pay 6s. a year.

DEMESNE MEADOWS. John Watsun holds 8 acres of demesne meadow called the Savageyng, and pays 24s. a year.

---

[397] *in relevamen portionis suæ.*
[398] The William Arnald in this section may be the same William Arnald who had a bovate in Edstone.

FREE LAND. Father Pier<s>[399] holds 1 parcel of enclosed land in John Holme's manor, and pays 6s. a year.

<82> GREAT BERGH*

BONDLANDS. There are in Great Bergh 24 bovates of land, and each of those bovates performs in every particular the same services, both at the plough and at Salton* mill, as the bovates of Salton* manor noted above. The tenants are as follows.

DEMISE. Walter Colman holds 1 messuage and 2 bovates of land, and pays 6s. 1d. a year. John Smyth holds 3 messuages <and> 6 bovates of land, and pays 18s. 3d. a year. William Nyghtgale holds 1 messuage <and> 4 bovates of land, <and> pays 12s. 2d. Thomas Carre holds 1 messuage <and> 2 bovates of land, <and> pays 6s. 1d. a year. William Wand holds 1 messuage <and> 4 bovates of land, <and> pays 12s. 2d. a year. John Tynk holds 1 messuage <and> 4 bovates of land, and pays 12s. 2d. a year. Adam Hogh holds 1 messuage <and> 2 bovates of land, <and> pays 6s. 1d. a year.

COTTAGE. There is a cottage there that performs the same services and labour services as the cottages of Salton* manor, as specified above.

DEMISE. Adam son of Hugh holds 1 cottage, and pays 3s. a year.

FREE LAND. Walter of Bergh holds 2 tofts on which his own manor <house> is built,[400] <and> pays 2s. a year; Walter also holds 1 plot of land called Schorplace that lies between his garden and a garden that was formerly Adam of Whytton's, <and> pays 3s. a year.

---

[399] *Dominus Peert.*
[400] *super quæ ædificatum est manerium ipsius Walteri.*

<83> LYTILL BERGH*

BONDLANDS. There are in Little Bergh 4 bovates of land, of which 3 bovates are bondlands and perform labour services and services, as set out below. And <there is> one bovate of land that is not a bondland[401] that was formerly in Walter of Bergh's tenure, as is set out below.

There is 1 bovate of land there formerly in Walter of Bergh's tenure, by charter, which used to pay 11s. 8d a year; and because that seemed to him excessive it lay waste paying nothing, but now it is demised by the warden of the manor to John Proude, <and> he pays 4s. 6d. a year for it.

BOND<LAND>. There are 3 bovates of bondland there each of which performs the same labour services and services, both in carting and at Salton* mill, as the bovates of Salton* manor, as specified above.

<84> FLAXTON*

FREE FARM. Richard Plaice holds by charter 1 toft and 1 bovate of land, <and> pays 8s. a year; and whenever the lord visits he will provide for him and members of his household a suitable and decent chamber, straw for the beds, a white candle, <and> hay for the horses.

ARABLE LANDS. There are also 5 bovates of bondland and each bovate contains by estimation 15 acres of land and meadow, of which 4 acres and 3 roods lie on the Langcrofte in the middle; and on the Stobkeldes, 3½ acres; on the Langlandes in the middle, 3 acres; on the Haggebrekes in the middle, 3 acres; on the Thwaytes on the southern side, 1½ acres; on the Rongefordgates in the middle, 3 acres; and on the southern side of Thorntonmore, abutting on Lillingdik, 1 acre; on Grelemarbuttes in the middle, abutting on that *dyk*, 1 acre; on the Angromes, between Thorntonmore and Flaxtonryse, 2 acres 1 rood; also, in the Brodfeld on the Crascildes, 1 acre; on the Diglandes, 3 acres; on the Aykbuskes, 3 acres; on the Brakanhill, 1½ acres; on the southern

---

[401] *extra bond.*

side of Thorntonmore, abutting on Flaxtondyk, 2 acres; on Flaxtonbuttes on the northern side, abutting on Thorntonfeld, 2 acres; on the Ersbrayth, abutting on Thorntonbalkes, 3 roods; on the western side of the Westilcarris, 1 acre; on the eastern side of the same Ylecarres, abutting onto it, 1 acre; on the Northbrek in the middle, 2 acres 1 rood; on the Medeldales, 3 acres; on the Westbrek 1½ acres; on the Wandales, 3 roods; on the Brotes in two places, 6 acres; also, in the Croftfeld in the *croftes*, 6 acres; on the Scholbrades, 1½ acres; on the Henbaynes, ½ acre; on the Coftheuedeland, 1½ acres; on the Graystanes, 1½ acres; on the Funrodes, 1½ acres; on the Wranglandes, 2 acres 1 rood; on either side of the Greenhill, abutting onto it, ½ acre; on Petirflatte by the Coterkeld, 3 acres; on the Kirkhilles, 3 acres; on the Morebuttes, between the Kirkhill and Bartonflatte, ½ acre; on the Swynstybuttes, ½ acre; on the Clibberres, 1½ acres; on Bartonflatte, 3 acres; on the Lygates, 3 acres; on the Wandales, 1½ acres; and furthermore,[402] on the Sindirlibuttes, ½ acre; and on the Sandlandes, 1½ acres.

MEADOWS. A piece of meadowland lies in the Southyng, and another piece in the Scholebradyng, and a third piece of meadow lies in the Northyng, and in the Wandale ½ acre. And those lands and meadows lie dispersed through those fields, between Richard Bernard's land, and lands of the nuns of Burneholme,[403] as mentioned above.

DEMISE. Richard Plaice holds 2 tofts with 2 gardens near the southern end of that township by Richard Bernard's plot on the northern side, together with 2 bovates of land of the 5 bovates noted above, and pays 12s. a year. William Raynersune holds 2 tofts and the remaining 3 bovates of land of those noted above, and pays 18s. a year. And he used to pay <...>.[404]

CUSTOMS AND SERVICES. And those tenants should perform suit at the court of Salton* every three weeks. And also, if any of them should become incriminated in any offence whose correction involves ecclesiastical jurisdiction, he should be cited to

---

[402] *et ultra.*
[403] We have not identified this nunnery.
[404] Raine represents the missing sum is represented by a dash.

the chapter of Salton* and punished there. And they should also give common aid for purchasing a palfrey for the lord prior when he is newly elected, or <when> they are otherwise asked by the lord prior to contribute to any aid.

<85> MIL(L)INGTON*[405]

There are 2 bovates of land there, each of which contains (…),[406] and 1 waste messuage. This messuage, with a croft, lies on the northern side of the churchyard there. And of those bovates, 1½ acres lie in Dunholme; and on the Wranglandes, 1½ acres; and on the Blalandes, 1½ acres; and on Swyngilmore, 1 acre; and on the Langerodes and the Wodheuede, 1 acre; and on the Suggedales in two places, 3½ acres; and on the Knolles in 2 places, 1 acre; and on the northern side of the church, 3 roods; and at the western end of the township, 1 rood; and at Fukelheued, 3 roods; and on the Swynes, 1 rood; and on the Eggis, 3 roods; and on Kilnwillmilnbuttis, 1 rood; and on either side of Fulkelsyk, 1 rood; and on the Peterhill, ½ rood; and Lillyngbrest, ½ acre; and on Skilburnkeldheued, ½ acre; and at Sclathornheued, ½ acre; and on Cliffton in 2 places, 1 acre; and on the Blandcornland, ½ acre; and at Threledaleheuedes, 1 acre; and on the Houlelandes, ½ acre; and on the Fouldayles, 2 acres; and in the Brotes, 1½ acres; and on Haverflekmore, ½ acre; and in the Dales, 1 acre. And it is to be noted that those plots of land and various pieces of waste land on (…).[407]

<86> GEVELDALE IN LE HOLE*

There is 1 toft there, with various buildings, with 1 garden. This toft lies between a plot of the baron of Greystoke on the eastern side and a plot of St Peter on the western side. And there are 4 bovates of land lying in the <township> field, of which each

---

[405] It is unclear why Raine puts alternative spellings here.
[406] Raine represents the missing acreage by a dash.
[407] Raine represents the missing termination of this sentence by a long dash.

bovate contains <...>;[408] of which in Grindelldikes lie <...> acres;[409] and on the Houlandes, 1 acre; and on the Hullandes, 2 acres; and on the Wandels, 1½ acres; and on the Graynes, 1 acre; and on the Forland, on the southern side, 3 roods; and on the Brekes, 1 acre; and on either side of the Hungirhill, 3 acres; and on the Northwlfeacre, 2 acres; and on the Southpeselandes, 1 acre; and on the Crosselandes, 2 acres; and on the southern side of the Grengatlandes, 2 acres; and on Thornhousbuttes, 1 acre; and on the Staanlandes on the southern side of the Staane, 1 acre; and on the southern side of the Greengate, 2 acres; and on the northern side of the Mykillsyk, 1 acre; and on the Gare, abutting on the *milndam*, 2 acres; and on the Lynakes, ½ acre; and between the Brigkeld and the Keldes, ½ acre; and on the Cattetaylelandes, ½ acre; and below the Prestgarth, 1 rood; and on the Clerkmynlandes, 1 acre; and on the Kapekeldhilles, 1 acre; and on the Gyastlandes, 1½ acres; and on the Buldayles, 1 acre; and on the Overbuldayles, 1 acre; and on the Skalberes, 1 acre; and on the Langlandes toward the Swynkeld, 4 acres; and on the Scherebrath and the Standlandbuttes, 1 acre; and on the Northirskaldberes and the Garthheuedland, ½ acre; and in the Clerkmylndame, 1 acre of meadow. And it is to be noted that the rest of the lands belonging to those 4 bovates lie dispersed among the *husband* lands of that place, but it is not known how many acres they contain.

---

[408] Raine represents the missing acreage by a dash.
[409] Raine represents the missing numeral by three dots.

4. CALENDAR OF ADDITIONAL DOCUMENTS

DOCUMENTING THE HEXHAM ESTATE

The following selection of documents, calendared from printed sources, is designed to make it possible to work backwards from the Black Book to the earlier history of the Hexham Priory estate. All the records are accordingly from before 1379, except for document 4, which illustrates features of the estate not apparent from the Black Book. Apart from the first section ('Various Counties') the documents are in the same groupings as the surveys in the Black Book, starting with records relating to Hexhamshire. Most of the records calendared are various sorts of deeds, recording the grant of rights, authorizing such grants, or confirming that they have taken place. Particular importance attaches to the royal *inspeximus* charter of 1298 (document 3) by which Edward I confirmed the priory's title to most of its properties in Northumberland. Other types of record represented here are contemporary historical work (documents 1, 5), memoranda (document 16), surveys or valuations of property (documents 4, 59, 71), ordinances (document 72), petitions (documents 47, 53, 56, 57), royal commissions (document 54), articles of agreement with other estate owners (documents 6, 32, 35, 67), recognitions of the priory's rights (document 33) and feet of fines (documents 36-41, 43-4). Feet of fines record legally binding settlements established in the king's courts between a challenger (demandant, plaintiff) and a defendant (tenant, or impedient) following either a genuine dispute or a collaborative procedure. In either case the resulting settlement (the 'final concord'), a copy of which was retained in the records of the court, gave as strong a title as medieval law was capable of conferring to one party or the other, and so could strengthen the evidence of private charters or sometimes substitute for it.

VARIOUS COUNTIES

1. Three extracts from Prior Richard's *History of the Church of Hexham* [410]

[A]

[Ch. x.] Moreover, Archbishop Thomas gave the canons 4 hamlets and 1 mill on the River Tyne, with all that pertained to them, as he had held them in his demesne; and 1,000 eels a year; and certain other things, as attested by their charters, drawn up by the archbishop and witnessed by the chapter of the church of St Peter of York. He also conceded to them, for their clothing 100 shillings a year. He also gave them books, vestments, and many other things necessary for the adornment of a house of God. And if he might have lived longer he would have given much more.

PRINTED SOURCE: *PH*, I, p. 56.

NOTE. The Archbishop Thomas in question is Thomas II, which dates this grant to 1108-14: *Handbook of British Chronology*, p. 281. The four hamlets were two Anicks, Sandhoe and Yarrridge: document 16 (item 2). The £5 annuity for clothing was paid from the archdeaconry of the West Riding in Yorkshire: documents 1 (item 2), 64.

[B]

[Ch. xi] But though he [Archbishop Thurstan of York] loved all houses of religion, yet he particularly cherished and protected that of Hexham, and so not only confirmed by his authority its possessions, customs and privileges but even generously increased them. For in addition to relics of several saints, books, vestments, and two pairs of candlesticks, one silver and one gilded copper, and

---

[410] Richard, prior of Hexham, died *c*.1167: *Heads of Religious Houses, 940-1216*, p. 166.

besides many other adornments of the holy church and several other gifts, he gave the church and its canons in perpetual alms, with the advice and consent of the chapter of St Peter of York, a prebend in the church of York, and £5 a year for their clothing from the archdeaconry of the West Riding, and in the township of Hexham a piece of land on which their men dwelt, and a field between Acomb and the River Tyne, and another piece of land there to expand their own house, and land where the hospital is built, and the township of Dotland, and both Grottingtons, and free pannage for their pigs and those of their townsmen on St. Andrew's land. He also gave them some tithes.

PRINTED SOURCE: *PH*, I, pp. 57-8.

NOTE. Thurstan was archbishop of York from his election in 1114 to his death in 1140: *Handbook of British Chronology*, p. 281. The payment of £5 a year was given up to the archbishop in exchange for the grant of Edstone church in 1162 x 1174: document 64.

[C]

[Ch. xii.] There are also many charters and other evidences there [*i.e.* in the priory at Hexham] of lands that were given to that church [of Hexham] by the alms-giving of generous men. Among these, David, king of Scots, and Henry his son, gave them a house in Carlisle, and another house in the same town. Robert of Seaton, with his mother Richalda, gave them half of the township called Eachwick. And Waltheof and his son Alan his son [gave] 4 bovates of land and 1 house for a herring-fishery, in *Eltadala*. And Forne and his son Ivo [gave] 2 bovates of land. And Sunnulfus the priest [gave] a house in York. William son of Ulf [gave] 4 bovates of land in Givendale. Ralph de Merlay [gave] 10s. a year, until he should settle lands on them. Again, Richalda, mother of Robert Delaval gave to God and the church of St Andrew at Hexham, and the canons there serving God, the other half of Eachwick, in perpetual alms, free and quit from herself and from all that belonged to her.[411] Stephen, king of England, £2 a year for buying wine.

---

[411] i.e. freed from any residual claim she might possibly have.

PRINTED SOURCE: *PH*, I, pp. 58-60.

NOTE: The grant of David I of Scotland is noted in *Charters of David I*, no. 238, p. 165, and dated to 1136 x 1152. For the gift of Robert of Seaton and Richalda, see also document 3 (item 44). This must date from before 1161, by which time Robert was dead: *NCH*, IX, pp. 137-8. *NCH*'s dating of the grant to *c*.1138 is unexplained: *NCH*, III, p. 141; XIII, p. 85. Eltadala, the location of the gift of Waltheof and his son, is identified by Raine as Allerdale in Cumbria, thought the identification would be more convincing if the reading were *Elredala*: *PH*, I, p. 59; II, p. xv. If he is right, this is perhaps the property recorded in the Black Book at Ellenborough, by Maryport. Though the location of the land donated by Forne and Ivo is not stated, it can be identified with the 2 bovates of land held by the canons in Millington, Yorkshire, recorded in the Black Book. Forne son of Sigulf held lands in Millington, and is not recorded as holding any other lands which can be identified with land subsequently held by the priory. See the note to *EYC*, II, no. 1236, p. 505, which records a gift of land to Forne by Henry II in the period 1114 x 1123. For the gift by William son of Ulf of 4 bovates in Givendale, see document 61. In the earlier thirteenth century Prior Bernard contended that the 2 bovates in Millington, together with the 4 bovates in Givendale, were held in free alms as of the prebend of Salton: *Abstract*, no. 15, pp. 41-2. Ralph de Merlay, who was planning to give land to the priory, was lord of Morpeth, *c*.1130 until after 1137: Sanders, p. 65. He is not known to have fulfilled this commitment, but Roger de Merlay granted land and rent at Stannington later in the twelfth century: document 3 (items 52, 53). The undated grants mentioned in this passage must be placed before Prior Richard's death in 1167 - that is, before the compilation of Prior Richard's *History of the Church of Hexham*.

2. Confirmation by King Henry III of grants made to the priory
Henry III grants to the church and canons of St Andrew of Hexham:

Calendar of Additional Documents

1. The church of Hexham, a mill on the Tyne, with its suit, and Anick, Sandhoe and Yarridge, in accordance with a charter of Thomas II, archbishop of York.[412]

2. By gift of Archbishop Thurstan, some pieces of land in the town of Hexham where their men dwell, and a piece of land to enlarge their mansion, and Dotland, being the land of Robert Calin, and arable land between Eachwick and the Tyne, and pannage for their pigs and those of their men and villeins dwelling in the land of St Andrew, together with a prebend in the church of St Peter, York.[413]

3. By gift of John de Normanville, the advowson of the church of St Wilfrid of Stamfordham; and a toft and 2 carucates of land there.[414]

4. By gift of John de Cauz and Aline, his wife, half the township of Kirkheaton and Coldstrother.[415]

5. By gift of James de Cauz and Alice, his wife, the other half of the township of Kirkheaton and Coldstrother.

6. By gift of Gilbert de Umfraville, all the land of Beaumont, which he had in the territory of Chollerton, by the bounds contained in the charter of gift.[416]

7. By gift of Ivo de Vieuxpont, 2 tofts and all his demesne land in Alston and a toft in Garrigill, pasture for 10 cows and 2 mares, and all the land to the west of the Tyne, by bounds contained in the charter of gift, with rights of common pasture for 40 cows, 10 mares and 100 sheep with their offspring of two years; and all Priorsdale, by the bounds contained in the charter of gift, to dispose of as they will.[417]

8. By gift of the same Ivo, the advowson of Alston church with Garrigill chapel.

---

[412] See documents 1A, 3 (items 1, 2), 5.
[413] This grant has no direct parallel in document 3. Document 1B suggests that 'Eachwick' should be 'Acomb'.
[414] Cf. document 3 (item 58).
[415] For this and the following item, see documents 3 (item 23), 37.
[416] Cf. document 3 (item 15).
[417] Cf. document 3 (items 39, 40).

Granted at Northampton.

PRINTED SOURCE: *CChR 1226-57*, pp. 170-1.

DATE. Dated 21 November 1232

NOTE. The prebend in the church of St Peter, York, referred to in item 2, is the prebend of Salton, in York Minster: document 1B.

3. Inspeximus charter of Edward I

The king at Westminster issued letters patent dated 12 July 1297 setting up an inquest into the rights of the prior and convent of Hexham. He had received plaints from them that they were in danger of losing their rights because all their muniments had been burned in the recent invasion of their priory by the Scots. Wishing to help the prior and convent in this respect, the king ordered Guichard de Charron and Adam of *Crokedayk* to hold sworn inquests in the counties of Northumberland, Cumberland and York, to establish what lands, rents and tenements the prior and convent held at the time of that invasion, for how long they had held them, from whom, and by what services. They should also establish which lands, rents and tenements they held at that time by charters and muniments (and by what charters and by what muniments) and also which lands, rents and tenements they held without charters and muniments. The findings of the inquests were to be sent to the king without delay under the seals of Guichard and Adam. The king ordered the sheriffs of those counties to bring honest and law-worthy men before Guichard and Adam to testify to the truth.

The inquest held in accordance with the above writ before Guichard of Charron and Adam of *Crokedayk* reported from Newcastle upon Tyne on 13 September 1298 on the testimony of the following jurors: William of Halton, Nicholas of Yetholm, William of Sweethope, William of Tynedale, Richard of Buteland, Richard Turpin, Richard son of Alan, William of Eachwick, Thomas of Featherstonehaugh and Thomas his son, Robert

Calendar of Additional Documents

Mangevillein and William Bataill. The jurors said that the prior and convent held the following properties, in free alms except where asterisked:

1. Hexham church and priory with all appurtenances by gift of Thomas II, archbishop of York. They had Thomas' charter, confirmed by the chapter of York, and have held from time out of mind.

2. The manor and township of Anick with the townships of Sandhoe and Yarrridge, and a mill on the Tyne with the suit pertaining to it, and all the tithes arising within the liberty of Hexham from the bishop and from others, by gift of Thomas II, archbishop of York. They had his charter, confirmed by the chapter of York. By gift of Thomas, they also have soc and sac, and other liberties, namely enforcement of the assize of bread and ale, the right for their servants to carry a rod of office for making distraints, summonses and attachments, and jurisdiction in the prior's court over their tenants' trespasses.

3. Lands in the township of Hexham, namely the entire street called Cockshaw, 24 messuages in the street called Priestpopple, 14 messuages in Market Street (*Vicus Fori*), 16 messuages in the street called Hencotes, the township of Dotland with Hazeldean (*Knitelhesell*), both Grottingtons, and all the tithes of animals within the liberty of Hexham, by gift of Thurstan, former archbishop of York. They have held from time out of mind.

4. Half the township of Bingfield with its appurtenances by gift of Germund. They had a charter, and have held from time out of mind.

5. Rent of 6 marks in Bingfield, by gift and feoffment of Robert of Skipton. They had a confirmation charter of the present king, and have held have held for over ten years.

6*. Two water mills with their appurtenances in Hamburn and Newbiggin, and 24 acres of land in those townships, the mills having suit from all new and future assarts, by gift of Walter de Gray, former archbishop of York, for a payment of 12 marks a year. They hold by charter, and have held from the reign of King Henry III.

7*. A rood of land in each of the townships of Acomb, Wall, Hallington, Keepwick, Catton, Ninebanks and Rowley, to hold each for 4d. a year, by gift of Walter de Gray and Walter Giffard, archbishops of York. The rood in Rowley is said to be for a tithe barn. They had charters, and have held from the reign of the King Henry III.[418]

8. The manor and church of Warden, together with its chapels at Stonecroft, Haydon and Langley, by gift of Adam of Tindale. They had a charter, confirmed by the bishop of Durham, and have held from time out of mind.

9. Forty acres of land, 6 acres of meadow, and 2 messuages, in Settlingstones, by gift of Adam of Settlingstones. They had a charter, and have held from time out of mind.

10. Two messuages, 40 acres of land and 10s. of rent in Whinnetley by gift of Adam of Thorngrafton. They had a charter, and have held from time out of mind.

11. The land of the Byers, within determinate bounds, with rights of common pasture beyond those bounds, by gift of Sir Adam of Tindale. They had a charter, and have held from time out of mind.

12. Allerwash Mill by gift of Uchtred of Allerwash. They had a charter, and have held from time out of mind.

13. A carucate of land in Allerwash in a place called Owmers, by gift of Richard, former bailiff of Hexham. They had a charter and have held from time out of mind.

14. Chollerton church with its chapels at Birtley, Chipchase, Gunnerton, East (Little) Swinburn, Kirkheaton and Colwell, 8 bovates of land of the church's endowment in the township of Chollerton, and 5 acres of land, called the *Michelcroft* on the north side of the church, by gift of Odinel de Umfraville. They had a charter and confirmation, and have held from time out of mind.

---

[418] All these plots were for tithe barns: see documents 16 (item 14), 17 (item 7).

15. The hamlet of Beaumont, within determinate bounds, by gift of Gilbert de Umfraville. They had a charter, and they have held from the reign of King Henry III.

16. A toft and 7 acres of land in Birtley, by gift of Richard de Umfraville. They had a charter, and have held from time out of mind.

17. The land and pasture of Cowden, within determinate bounds, by gift of Richard de Umfraville. They had a charter, and have held from time out of mind.

18. Common pasture on Gunnerton moor for 100 working beasts coming from Cowden shieling, both in the closed season and in the open season, by gift of Ralph of Gunnerton. They had a charter, and have held from time out of mind.

19. Two tofts and 30 acres of land in the township of Barrasford, by gift of Margery de Umfraville. They had a charter; and have held from the time of the present king.

20. Two tofts and 2 bovates of land in the township of Chesterhope, by gift of Ralph of Gunnerton. They had a charter, and have held from time out of mind.

21. A carucate of land in Newton in Coquetdale, by gift of Walter de Lisle. They had a charter, and have held from time out of mind.

22. Common pasture for 32 oxen, 10 cows, and 280 sheep in Colwell, by gift of Walter Corbet. They had a charter, and they have held from the reign of King Henry III.

23. The manor of Kirkheaton and Coldstrother, by gift of Aline of Bolam and James de Cauz with his wife Alice. They had a charter, and have held from time out of mind.

24. One toft and 6 acres of land in Little Bavington, by gift of Stephen Bataill, together with 2 tofts and 3½ acres there, with common pasture for 15 working beasts, 60 sheep and 2 horses, by gift of Gilbert of Worcester. They had a charter, and have held from time out of mind.[419]

25. Three tofts, a tithe barn, with 2 bovates and 12 acres of land in the township of Gunnerton, by gift of Ralph of Gunnerton and Thurkill of *Cadeiou*. They had a charter, and have held from time out of mind.

26. Slaley church, 1 carucate of land of the church's endowment, rights of common pasture in the same township for 300 sheep, and common pasture in Steel for 300 sheep, by gift of Gilbert of Slaley. They had a charter, confirmed by the bishop and the chapter of Durham, and have held from the reign of King Henry III.

27. A building and 1 acre of land in the township of Chipchase, by gift of Robert de Lisle. They had a charter, and they have held from the reign of King Henry [III].

28. Rent of £2 3s. 4d. from 8 messuages in the township of Newcastle upon Tyne, by various gifts. They had charters, and have held from time out of mind.

29. Rent of £2 3s. 2d. from 15 messuages in the township of Corbridge, by various gifts. They had charters, and have held from time out of mind.

30. A messuage, 7 acres of land in Haydon and rights of common pasture for 300 sheep, by gift of Adam of Tindale. They had a charter, and have held it from time out of mind.

31. An acre of land in the field of West (Great) Swinburn, by gift of John of Worcester. They had a charter, and have held from the reign of King Henry III.

32. The manor of Milbourne Grange (*Northmilneburne*) with common pasture in *Crekelagh* Moor, by gift of Sir Thomas of Dilston. They had a charter, and the licence of the present king for

---

[419] It is unclear why these two properties are grouped with reference only to a single charter.

Calendar of Additional Documents

alienation in mortmain,[420] and have held from the time of the present king.

33*. The land of Stelden, within determinate bounds, for a rent of £1 3s. per year,[421] by grant of the abbot of Newminster. They had a charter, and have held it from time out of mind.

34. Lordship of the township of Whitfield and rent of 16s. 4d., by gift of William, king of Scots. They had a charter, and have held from time out of mind.[422]

35. A moor called Carraw Side (*Karrauesid*) held in severalty, by gift of William, king of Scots. They had a charter, and have held from time out of mind.

36. A hamlet called Carraw held in severalty, and a carucate of land in *Rischeles*, within determinate bounds, by gift of the Richard Comyn, with common pasture at Henshaw. They had a charter, and have held from time out of mind.

37. A toft and 30 acres of land in Stonecroft, by gift of Richard Comyn. They had a charter, and have held from time out of mind.

38. Six tofts and 1 carucate of land in Thirlwall, and common pasture for 80 working beasts, 80 mares with offspring, 40 pigs and 80 goats, by gift of Brice of Thirlwall and Roger his son. They had charters, and have held from time out of mind.

39. A pasture called Priorsdale held in severalty, within determinate bounds, by gift of Ivo de Vieuxpont. They had a charter, confirmed by King Henry III, and they have held from time out of mind.

40. Eight messuages and 1 carucate of land in Alston, by gift of Ivo de Vieuxpont. They had a charter, and have held from time out of mind.

---

[420] Document 46.

[421] Seemingly an error for £1 13s.4d., as in document 35 and Black Book 38.

[422] Cf. document 23, where the annual payment is stated to b 6 lb. of pepper.

41. Rent of 8s. from Tecket, by gift of Laurence of Tecket. They had a charter, and have held from time out of mind.

42. Rent of 13s. 4d. from Elrington mill, by gift of Ivo de Vieuxpont. They had a charter, and have held from time out of mind.

43. Rent of 8s. from *Aldschel*, by gift of Henry de Graham. They had a charter, and have held from time out of mind.

44. Half the manor of Eachwick, by gift of Robert, son of Hubert Delaval and his mother Richilda. They had a charter, and have held from time out of mind.

45. Ten acres of land in Eachwick, by gift of Thomas of Eachwick, and a further 7 acres of land there by gift of Peter of Fawdon. They had a charter and have held from the reign of Henry III.[423]

46. Rent of 13s. 8d from the township of Stocksfield, by gift of William son of Boso, out of which they pay 7s. per year for castle ward. They had a charter, and have held from time out of mind.

47. Rent of 3s. in the township of Stocksfield, by gift of John son of Elias of Stocksfield. They had a charter, and have held from the reign of King Henry III.

48. Five tofts, 10 bovates of land and 3 acres of meadow in (Temple) Thornton, by gift of William de Lisle. They had a charter, confirmed by Sir Walter de Bolbec, and have held from time out of mind.

49. A manor and 3 acres of land in Benwell, within determinate bounds, by gift of Hugh Delaval. They had a charter, and have held from the reign of King Henry III.

50. Two acres of land and rent of 16s. in the township of Throckley, by gift of Robert of Iveston and Christine of Throckley. They had a charter, and have held from time out of mind.

---

[423] It is unclear why these two properties are grouped with reference only to a single charter.

51. A manor, 6 messuages and 3 carucates of land in East Matfen, by gift of Thomas of Fenwick. They had a charter, confirmed by Robert de Lisle, and have held from the reign of King Henry III.

52. A toft and 2 bovates of land in Stannington, by gift of Roger de Merlay. They had a charter, and have held from time out of mind.

53. Rent of 1s. 6d. from the same township, by gift of Roger de Merlay. They had a charter, and have held from time out of mind.

54. A rent of 1 mark from Brenkley mill, by gift of Henry of Farlington. They had a charter, and have held from the reign of King Henry III.

55. A toft, a croft, and 42½ acres of land in the township of Whalton, with common pasture for 400 (or 480) ewes and their lambs, by gift of Walter son of William and his wife Isabel. They had a charter, and have held from time out of mind.

56. Rent of 8s in the township of Riplington, by gift of the Walter son of William and his wife Isabel. They had a charter, and have held from time out of mind.

57. Two fisheries on the river Tyne,[424] one called *Drippinttell*, the other *Foul*, and a place for drying their nets, by gift of Roger Bertram. They had a charter, and have held from time out of mind.

58. A toft and two carucates of land in the township of Stamfordham, by gift of John de Normanville. They had a charter, and have held from time out of mind.

59. The manor(s) of Cheeseburn and Nesbit, by gift of John de Normanville. They had a charter, confirmed by [John] de Balliol,[425] and have held from time out of mind.

60. The garb tithes of the 5 townships of East Matfen, Nesbit[426], Ouston, Hawkwell and Bitchfield, out of the income of Stamfordham church, by grant and ordination of Nicholas, bishop

---

[424] At Newburn: Black Book, 64.
[425] *habuerunt ... confirmationem domini de Balliolo*: cf. document 42.
[426] See Raine's correction at *PH,* II, p. 203.

of Durham. They had a charter, confirmed by the chapter of Durham, and have held from time out of mind.

61. The manor of Stelling, with 1 toft and 2 acres of land in the township of Newbiggin by the Sea, by gift of Bernard de Balliol. They had a charter, and have held from time out of mind.

62. Rent of £2 in the township of (North) Seaton, by gift of Bernard de Balliol. They had a charter, and have held from time out of mind.

63. A third part of the township of Dalton, by gift of Ralph of Gunnerton, and 4 bovates of land, with a rent of 5s. 6d. from the mill there, by gift of William of Dalton. They had a charter, and have held from time out of mind.[427]

64. A toft and 8 acres of land in Prudhoe, by gift of Richard de Umfraville. They had a charter, and have held from time out of mind.

65. The homage of John of East (Little) Swinburn and his heirs, and an annual rent of 1s. for his capital messuage in East Swinburn, by gift of Hugh de Balliol. They had a charter, and have held from time out of mind.

66. The homage of the heirs of Nicholas of West (Great) Swinburn, and a rent of 3s. a year for the chantry chapel at West Swinburn, by grant of John of Worcester. They had a charter, and have held from the reign of King Henry III.

67. The homage of John of Cambo, for lands and tenements he holds in Kirkheaton and Coldstrother, by gift of Aline of Bolam and James de Caux with his wife Alice. They had charters, and have held from time out of mind.

68. The homage of Richard of Thirlwall, and an annual rent of 3s. for land he holds of them in Thirlwall, by gift of Brice of Thirlwall and Roger his son. They had charters, and have held from time out of mind.

---

[427] It is unclear why these two properties are grouped with reference only to a single charter.

Calendar of Additional Documents 163

69. The homage of Adam of Whitlow, with an annual rent of 4s., by gift of Adam of Tindale. They had a charter, and have held from time out of mind.

70. The homage of Thomas son of Richard son of Brice of Thirlwall, for land he holds of them in Thirlwall, by gift of Adam of Tindale. They had a charter, and have held from time out of mind.

71. The homage of John de Normanville for the land of Stocksfield and Apperley, with an annual rent of 13s. 8d., by gift of William son of Boso. They had a charter, and have held from time out of mind.

72. The homage of Robert of *Ribil*, with an annual rent of 10s. and 3 suits at the prior's court each year, by gift of Theophania Bataill. They had a charter, and have held from time out of mind.

73. The homage of Matthew of Whitfield, for lands and tenements in Whitfield he holds of them. They had a charter of William, king of Scots from time out of mind.

74. The homage of Robert of Throckley, for lands and tenements he holds of them in Throckley, by gift of Robert of Iveston and Christine of Throckley. They had a charter, and have held from time out of mind.

75. A tithe barn with a garden in the township of East (Little) Swinburn, by gift of Hugh de Balliol. They had a charter, and have held from time out of mind.

Following the submission of that report, the king at Newcastle issued a charter of *inspeximus* dated 23 November, 1298, under the great seal. In it he rehearsed the two documents summarized above witnessing and verifying the testimony of the inquest. This charter is witnessed by Walter Langton the bishop of Coventry and Lichfield; Gilbert de Umfraville the earl of Angus, John Tregoz, Walter de Beauchamp the steward of the king's household, William of *Rither*, Walter of Huntercombe, Eustace of *Hache*, Walter of *Teye*, John of *Merk*, and others.

PRINTED SOURCES. *PH*, II, pp. 107-17; *Monasticon*, VI, pp. 181-4; *HHN*, VI [part 3, vol. 2], pp. 156-70; noted in *CChR 1257-1300*, p. 474.

DATE. 23 November, 1298 (rehearsing texts of 12 July 1297 and 13 September 1298).

NOTE. This document is of the greatest importance for evidence not otherwise available from extant charters, though it does not include any reference to properties within the liberty of the bishops of Durham. Moreover, despite the king's letters patent, no inquest appears to have held in either Cumberland or Yorkshire, probably because of the threat of invasion from Scotland that became reality in mid October, following the English defeat at Stirling Bridge. Northumberland and Cumberland were again ravaged and Hexham Priory pillaged: M. C. Prestwich, *Edward I* (London, 1988), pp. 477-8; *PH*, I, Appendix, no. 17, p. xxvi; no. 18, pp. xxvi-xxvii. The destruction of Hexham Abbey by the Scots in 1296 is described in *Chronicon de Lanercost*, pp. 174-5; *PH*, I, Appendix, no. 17, pp. xxiv-xxvi. The evidence collected at Newcastle in September 1298 was presumably compiled from a cartulary, such as the one, now fragmentary, noted in *Abstract*. However, the canons perhaps exaggerated their losses, at least with respect to the charter evidence, since a number of originals seem to have survived: see, for example documents 16, 28, 42, 48. References to charter evidence in the Black Book details concerning Bingfield, Thirlwall, *Langdene*, Haydon, Walwick, Slaley, Cowden, Colwell, Kirkheaton with Colstrother, North Seaton, Milbourne Grange and Silksworth, may conceivably relate to cartulary transcripts but do not seem to do so: Black Book 4, 9, 19, 21, 26, 27, 37, 40, 41, 49, 51, 73. Notes on the donors and dating of individual charters, with cross-references to the Black Book and other documents, are supplied property by property in the section recording Properties of Hexham Priory by 1379 (pp. 239-270).

4A and 4B. Survey of the estates of Hexham Priory made at the Dissolution
[A]

The demesnes of the late monastery of Hexham.

The site of the monastery its buildings; 1 dovecote, 1 barn, 1 orchard, 1 'garthing', containing in all 2 acres. Worth 4s. a year

The hospital of St Giles adjoining the monastery, comprising 1 messuage, 1 close containing 2 acres of pasture; and dispersed in the fields of Hexham 30 acres of arable. Worth 13s. 4d. a year.

The profits of lands belonging to the archbishop of York, lately in the hands of the monastery, comprising various arable lands in Hexham fields, 1 close called *Coufelde*, 1 close called Dotland Park. Rent £23 by year to the archbishop, but with no net income to Hexham Abbey.

Total, 17s. 4d.

Hexham burgages.

The wife of William Herryson: 1 cottage, 1 garth containing 1 rood, with common upon the moors and pastures. Rent, 4s. at Martinmas and Pentecost equally.

Alexander Leisman: 1 cottage, 1 garth, containing 1 rood, with common. Rent 5s.

Thomas Nicholson: 1 tenement, 1 garth, containing 1½ roods, 2 acres in the field, with common and pasture. Rent 10s. 3d.

Thomas Smythe: 1 cottage, 1 garth containing ½ rood, with common. Rent 2s. 8d.

Richard Leisman: 1 tenement with buildings, 1 close containing 1 acre, 3 acres of arable in the fields, with common of pasture. Rent 11s. 5d.

Hugh Iryngton: 1 tenement, 1 garth containing ½ rood. Rent 2s.

John Armestronge: 1 tenement, 1 garth containing 1 rood. Rent 4s.

The wife of John Levenwood: 1 tenement with buildings, 1 garth containing 1 rood, 10 acres in the field,[428] common and pasture, Rent 8s.

The wife of Richard Milner: 1 cottage, 1 little garth. Rent 4s.

Roland Swan: 1 cottage, 1 little garth. Rent 3s.

William Browne: 1 house, 1 little garth. Rent 3s. 4d.

Edmund Gibson: 1 cottage, 1 little garth. Rent 3s. 4d.

Edward Hirste: 1 tenement with buildings, 1 croft containing 1 rood, 2 acres in the fields, common and pasture. Rent 8s.

William Elleson: 1 cottage, 1 little garth. Rent 2s.

Richard Davyson: 1 cottage, 1 little garth. Rent 2s.

John Stevenson: 1 cottage, 1 garth containing 1 rood. Rent 2s. 9d.

John Yarroo: 1 cottage, 1 little garth, and rents by year etc. 1s. 4d.

John Laveroke: 1 shop. Rent 8d.

Thomas Laveroke: 1 cottage, 1 garth containing 1 rood. Rent 2s. 8d.

Robert Stevynson: 1 cottage, 1 garth. Rent 3s.

John Grene: 1 cottage, 1 garth. Rent 3s. 4d.

Robert Wanles: 1 cottage, 1 little garth. Rent 8d.

The wife of Roland Grene: 1 cottage, 1 linen garth containing 1 rood. Rent 3s.

---

[428] The printed edition has *a garth conteining one rode in the feld, and x acre*, misplacing the words *in the feld*, perhaps because they were misleadingly interlined.

Thomas Robson: 1 cottage, 1 little garth containing ½ rood. Rent 1s.

Geoffrey Bell: 1 cottage, 1 little garth. Rent 2s.

Thomas Wallis: 1 cottage, 1 croft containing 1 rood, 2 acres in the fields, with common and pasture. Rent 6s. 8d.

Cooke"s' wife: 1 cottage, 1 croft containing 1 rood. Rent 2s.

Henry Levenwood: 1 cottage, 1 little garth. Rent 3s.

Richard Corbye: 1 cottage, 1 little garth. Rent 1s.

John Whichelles: 1 tenement, 1 little garth. Rent 4s.

Thomas Robson: 1 tenement with buildings, 1 close containing 1 acre, 3 acres of arable, pasture and common. Rent 8s. 8d.

The wife of Roland Crayne: 1 tenement, 1 close containing 2 acres, 4 acres of arable, pasture in the *Westemoore* and common. Rent £1.

John Wilkynson: 1 tenement, 1 close containing ½ acre, 3 acres of arable, with common and pasture in the *Westemoore*. Rent 10s.

Roger Pigges: 1 tenement, 1 close containing 1 acre of meadow, 2 acres of arable, with common and pasture. Rent 8s. 8d.

Thomas Bedell: 1 cottage, 1 linen garth. Rent 12d.

Christopher Leighton: 1 tenement, 1 close containing ½ acre, 2 acres of arable. Rent 6s. 8d.

Edward Litle: 1 tenement, 1 garth containing ½ acre. Rent 4s.

Alexander Armestrong: 1 tenement, 1 close containing ½ acre, 2 acres of arable, with common and pasture in the *Westemore*. Rent 6s. 8d.

William Robynson: 1 tenement, 1 close containing ½ acre, 2 acres of land, with common. Rent 6s.

Robert Lighton: 1 tenement, 1 close containing 3 roods, (*blank*) acres of arable, with common and pasture. Rent 6s. 8d.

John Patenson: 1 tenement, 1 little garth. Rent 1s. 8d.

Thomas Laveroke: 1 tenement, 1 little garth. Rent 1s. 8d.

Robert Johnson: : 1 tenement with buildings, 1 close containing ½ acre, 2 acres of arable, with common and pasture. Rent 8s. 9d.

Alexander Armestronge: 1 cottage, 1 little garth. Rent 2s. 6d.

Edward Ridley: 1 tenement with buildings, 1 little garth containing ½ acre, 2 acres of arable in the fields, with common of pasture. Rent 7s.

Hugh Johnson: 1 tenement, 1 garth containing 1 rood, with common of pasture in the *Westmoore*. Rent 4s.

Edmund Stokeall's wife: 1 cottage, 1 little garth. Rent 4s.

William Ellison: 1 tenement, 1 close containing ½ acre, 2 acres of arable in the fields.[429] Rent 7s.

Nicholas Patenson: 1 tenement with buildings, 1 close containing 1 acre, 2 acres of arable, with common. Rent 6s.

Miles Lesheman: 1 tenement, 1 little linen garth, with common. Rent 3s. 4d.

Anthony Johnson: 1 tenement, 1 little garth. Rent 1s. 6d.

William Johnson: 1 tenement, 1 little garth. Rent 3s. 2d.

Anthony Hudson's wife: 1 cottage, 1 little garth. Rent 2s. 8d.

Robert Hirde: 1 cottage, 1 little garth. Rent 2s.

Robert Pigge: 1 cottage, 1 little garth. Rent 2s. 8d.

John Symond: 1 cottage, 1 little garth containing 1 rood. Rent 2s. 8d.

There are 2 cottages late in the holding of (*blank*). Rent 5s. 9d.

---

[429] The printed edition has w*ᵗ a cloose cont. di. acre in the feldis, ij acrez land arrable*, misplacing *in the feldis*.

Calendar of Additional Documents   169

                Total of the burgages and tenements: £12 13s. 5d.

HEXHAMSHIRE
Sandhoe

John Errington: 1 tenement with buildings, 1 close containing 1 acre in the *Law Inges*, 4 acres of meadow, 24 acres of arable in the town fields, with common. Rent £1 6s. 8d.

Richard Hudchonson: 1 tenement, 1 close containing 1 acre in the *Law Inges*, 4 acres of meadow, 24 acres of arable in the town fields, with common. Rent £1 6s. 8d.

Robert Buteland: 1 tenement, 1 close containing 1 rood in the *Law Inges*, 3 acres of meadow, 18 acres of arable, with common. Rent £1.

Robert Sowreby: 1 tenement, 1 little close, 3 ac. in the *Law Inges*, 18 acres in the town fields, common. Rent £1.

John Stevynson: 1 tenement with *bithe*,[430] 6 acres of arable, 2 acres in the *Law Inges*, with common. Rent 13s. 4d.

                        Total: £5 6s. 8d.

Anick township

Thomas Spayne: 1 tenement with buildings, 2 acres of meadow in *Estmyres*, 14 acres of arable in the fields, with common in *Cotland Moore*. Rent 17s. 10d.

William Huchynson: 1 tenement with buildings, 11 acres of arable, with common of pasture in *Cotland Moore*. Rent 15s. 2d.

John Smythe: 1 tenement with buildings, 14 acres of arable, with common. Rent 16s. 2d.

William Greene: 1 tenement with buildings, 2 acres of meadow, 15 acres of arable, with common. Rent 18s. 3d.

---

[430] Meaning uninterpreted.

Robert Sowerby: 1 tenement with buildings, 2 acres of meadow, 14 acres of arable, with common. Rent 15s. 2d.

John Thomson: 1 tenement, called *Belles Leez* containing 6 acres of arable. Rent 10s.

Roger Robinson: 1 tenement with buildings, 2 acres of meadow, and 18 acres of arable in the fields, with common. Rent £1 7s.

John Sowreby: 1 tenement with buildings, 1 acre of meadow, 15 acres of arable in the 3 fields,[431] with common. Rent 15s. 3d.

John Spayne: 1 tenement with buildings, 2 acres of meadow, and 18 acres of arable, with common. Rent £1 7s.

Thomas Sowerby: 1 tenement, 6 acres of arable, with common of pasture. Rent 11s. 4d.

> Total: £8 13s. 1d.

Yarridge township

Cuthbert Stokehall: 1 tenement, 2 acres of meadow, 5 acres of arable, with common. Rent 10s.

George Tayllor: 1 tenement, 1 acre of meadow, 5 acres of arable, with common of pasture. Rent 10s.

William Wilber: 1 tenement with buildings, 1 acre of meadow, 6 acres of arable, with common. Rent 10s.

George Bell: 1 tenement, 1 acre of meadow, 5 acres of arable, with common of pasture. Rent 10s.

Certain lands held by the tenants. Rent 6s. 8d.

> Total: £2 6s. 8d.

---

[431] *in the iij feldes.*

Calendar of Additional Documents   171

Dotland township

Richard Cokeman: 1 tenement with buildings, 1 acre of meadow in the *Small Inges*, 5 acres of arable, with common in *Depestone More*. Rent 9s. 4d.

Thomas Greene: 1 tenement with buildings, 2 acres of meadow, 7 acres of arable, with common of pasture. Rent 16s. 8d.

George Robson: 1 tenement, 1 acre of meadow, 5 acres of arable, with common. Rent 8s. 4d.

Alexander Rowlle: 1 tenement, 2 acres of meadow, 7 acres of arable, with common of pasture. Rent 16s. 8d.

Alexander Leddell: 1 tenement, 1 acre of meadow, and 5 acres of arable, with common. Rent 8s. 4d.

Hugh Donne: 1 tenement, 1 acre of meadow, and 5 acres of arable. Rent 8s. 4d.

Total: £3 6s. 8d.

Bingfield

Nicholas Herrington: the capital messuage, by indenture, with demesnes containing 90 acres. Rent £2 13s. 4d. Also 4 tenements with 4 *frontes*, 5 acres of meadow, 81 acres of arable, with common of pasture in the fields <and in> *Longemoore* and *Downezmoore*. Rent £4 6s. 8d. In all £7.

Beaufront

Edward Hirste: 1 tenement, 2 acres of meadow, 5 acres of arable, with common of pasture in *Birkeborne Morez*. Rent 10s.

William Leegh: 1 tenement, 2 acres of meadow in the *Myllfall*, 8 acres of arable, with common of pasture. Rent 10s.

Total: £3

Grottington

Thomas Harryngton's wife: 1 tenement, 10 acres of meadow in the *Mooreflate*, 30 acres of arable, with common in *Dounesmoore*. Rent £2.

<NORTHUMBERLAND>
Milbourne Grange

Edmund Horseley: 1 tenement called Milbourne Grange, by indenture under the priory seal, 1 close called *Hyecloose* containing 5 acres in the *Estinges*, 10 acres of meadow, 30 acres of arable in the fields, with common of pasture in the *Longebankes*. Rent £5 6s. 8d.

Kirkheaton township

William Musgrave: 8 tenements, 15 acres of meadow called the *Law Inges*, 45 acres of arable, with common in *Hyndesfell*. Rent £7

Total (of the three): £14 6s. 8d.

Alston Moor

William Lawson: 1 tenement with buildings, 4 acre of meadow in the *Wrange Cloose*, 10 acres in the *Longmedoo*, with common in Alston Moor. Rent £1 3s. 4d.

Henry Teysdalle: 1 tenement with buildings, 1 close containing 5 acres, 15 acres in the *Long Inges*, with common. Rent £1 0s. 8d.

William Walton: 1 tenement, 1 close called *Drye Cloose* containing 5 acres, 12 acres in the *Longe Inges*, with common. Rent £1 4s. 8d.

William Milner: 1 tenement, 1 close called the *Calfecloose*, 15 acres of meadow in the *Longe Inges*, with common. Rent £1 4s. 8d.

Total: £4 13s, 4d.

Calendar of Additional Documents

Dalton township

John Bonnton: 1 tenement with buildings, 3 acres of meadow, 10 acres of arable, with common. Rent £1.

William Wallis: 1 tenement, 2 acres of meadow, 10 acres of arable, with common in *Rowleborne*. Rent 18s.

Robert Atkinson: 1 tenement, 2 acres of meadow and 9 acres of arable, with common. Rent 16s.

John Smyth: 1 tenement, 2 acres of meadow, 10 acres of arable, with common. Rent 18s.

Edward Wayles' wife: 1 tenement, 2 acres of meadow, 9 acres of arable, with common of pasture in *Roulleborne*. Rent 15s.

John Wallis: 1 tenement with buildings, 2 acres of meadow, 12 acres of arable, with common. Rent £1.

Robert Wallis: 1 tenement, 3 acres of meadow, 12 acres of arable, with common of pasture in *Rolleborne*. Rent £1.

The vicar: a water mill for grain. Rent £2. 'over and besides all charges'.

Lands held by those tenants. Rent 6s. 8d.

Total: £8 13s. 4d.

Nesbit

John Akinside: 1 tenement, 4 acres of meadow, 5 acres of arable, with common of pasture in *Matfenmorre*. Rent £1 2s. 1d.

William Butler: 1 tenement, 3 acres of meadow, 12 acres of arable, with common, £1 0s. 1d.

Matthew Richerson: 1 tenement, 3 acres of meadow, 13 acres of arable, with common. £1 1s. 1d.

John Okenwood: 1 tenement, 3 acres of meadow, 13 acres of arable, with common of pasture. Rent £1 2s. 1d.

John Collyngwood, senior: 1 tenement, 3 acres of meadow, 13 acres of arable, with common.   Rent £1 1s.

Total: £5 6s. 8d.

Cheeseburn Grange

Gavin Swyneborne: 1 tenement called Cheeseburn Grange, 5 acres of meadow, 55 acres of arable, with common rights of pasture of *Stonefell* by indenture under the priory seal. Rent £5 6s. 8d. at Martinmas and Pentecost, 'and by the first survey but £4'.

Stelling

Thomas Swyneborne: 1 tenement, 2 closes containing 3 acres of meadow, 10 acres of arable, 18 acres with common of *Wellingmoore*.[432] Rent £1 13s. 4d.

Total (of both): £5 13s. 4d.

Eachwick township

Richard Walters: 1 tenement with buildings, 1 close containing ½ acre of meadow in the *Lawe West Feld*, 5 acres of arable, 12 acres with common rights of pasture in the *Westmore*. Rent 16s. 4d. at Martinmas and Pentecost.

Nicholas Clerke's wife: 1 tenement, 1 close containing 1 rood in the *Westefelde*, 3 acres of meadow, 10 acres of arable, with common of pasture. Rent 13s. 4d.

Robert Bowre's wife: 1 tenement, 1 close containing ½ acre in the fields, 3 acres of meadow, 13 acres of arable, with common. Rent £1 1s. 8d.

Robert Walles: 1 tenement, 1 garth containing 1 rood in the fields, 4 acres of meadow, 10 acres of arable, with common. Rent £1 1s. 6d.

---

[432] *ij cloosis cont. iij acres medoo, x acrez land arr., xviij acres, w^t comon of Welling-moore.*

Thomas Elleson: 1 tenement, 1 croft containing 1 rood in the West Field, 2 acres of meadow, 8 acres of arable, with common in the moor. Rent 12s. 6d.

William Boure: 1 tenement with buildings, 2 acres of meadow in the *Westfelde*, 4 acres of arable, with common. Rent 8s.

Total: £3 6s. 8d.

Ingoe Mill

William Story: the mill. Rent 13s. 4d.

Prudhoe

Edward Bell: 1 tenement, 1 croft containing 1 rood, 2 acres of meadow in the *myllestede*, 7 acres of arable, with common in Prudhoe Moor. Rent 8s.

Whalton

Robert Tolland: 1 tenement with buildings, 1 croft containing ½ acre, 8 acres of arable, 2 acres of meadow, with common in Whalton Moors. Rent 10s.

Total (of the three): £1 11s. 4d.

Newcastle

Thomas Atkinson: 1 tenement with buildings. Rent 12s.

Richard Milner's wife: 1 tenement. Rent 8s.

John Watson: 1 tenement. Rent 7s.

Thomas Benyke: 1 tenement. Rent 4d.

John Almere: 1 cottage. Rent 4d.

Total: £1 7s. 8d.

East Matfen

Gerard Fenwyke: 1 tenement, 1 close containing ½ acre in *Mortonsyde*, 4 acres of meadow in the fields, 15 acres of arable, with common. Rent £1 6s. 8d.

Thomas Rutter: 1 tenement, 2 acres of meadow, 4 acres of arable, with common. Rent 6s. 8d.

Thomas Archer: 1 tenement, 2 acres of meadow, 8 acres of arable, with common. Rent 13s. 4d.

William Rutter's wife: 1 tenement, 1 acre of meadow, 5 acres of arable. Rent 6s. 8d.

Total: £2 13s. 4d.

West Matfen

John Thomson: 1 cottage, 1 little garth. Rent 1s. 4d.

Slaley

George Hirde: 1 tenement, 2 acres of meadow, 5 acres of arable. Rent 5s.

Stocksfield Hall

John Newton: 1 tenement with buildings, 2 acres of meadow, 5 acres of pasture and arable, with common in Slaley Moor. Rent 13s. 4d.

Birtley

Thomas Lee: 1 tenement, 1 acre of meadow, 3 acres of arable, with common of pasture in Birtley Moor. Rent 3s. 4d. and now let to him 5s. 10d.

Newburn

John Dalton: a fishery. Rent 5s. per year 'over all charges'.

Total (of all): £1 8s.

Calendar of Additional Documents 177

Stannington

Thomas Robson: 1 tenement, 2 acres of arable, with common of Stannington Moors. Rent 5s.

Gunnerton

William Cooke: 1 tenement, 1 acre of meadow, 3 acres of arable, with common in the *Westmore*. Rent 6s. 8d.

John Cooke: 1 tenement, 1 acre of meadow, 3 acres of arable, with common. Rent 6s. 8d.

Total: 18s. 4d.

Warden

The vicar of Warden: 1 tenement, 1 close containing 2 acres, 10 acres of arable, with common on the moors. Rent 16s. 8d.

Roland Stokeall: 1 tenement, 1 close containing 1 acre, 10 acres of arable, with common. Rent 16s. 8d.

Thomas Kirsop: 1 tenement, 3 acres of meadow, 11 acres of arable, with common. Rent 19s. 4d.

Robert Kirsop: 1 tenement with buildings, 1 croft, 4 acres of meadow, 10 acres of arable, with common on the moors. Rent 16s. 8d.

Thomas Pickeryng: 1 tenement, 3 acres of meadow, 10 acres of arable, with common. Rent 15s.

John Crake: 1 tenement, 3 acres of meadow, 10 acres of arable, with common. Rent 15s.

Nicholas Ledbitter: 1 tenement, 3 acres of meadow, 10 acres of arable, with common. Rent 15s.

William Ledbitter: 1 tenement, 3 acres of meadow, 10 acres of arable, with common. Rent 15s.

Robert Hesley: 1 tenement, 1 acre of meadow, 2 acres of arable, with common. Rent 4s. 4d.

Total: £6 13s. 8d.

Byers Park

William, Lord Dacre: 1 tenement, meadow and pasture lands. Rent £1 13s. 4d.

Chollerton

The vicar of Chollerton: 1 tenement with appurtenances. Rent £2 5s.

Temple Thornton

Richard Cowper: 1 tenement, 4 acres of meadow, and 8 acres of arable, with common. Rent 13s. 4d.

Robert Helpell: 1 tenement, 4 acres <of meadow?>, 8 acres of arable, with common of pasture. Rent 13s. 4d.

Total: £1 6s. 8d.

Kearsley

William Shaftow: 1 tenement, certain ground and common. Rent 6s. 8d., now let to him for 18s.

Total: £5 6s. 8d.

BISHOPRIC OF DURHAM

Farringdon Grange ('Farnedalle Hall')

William Blakeston: various tenements and lands held by indenture under the priory seal. Rent £5 6s. 8d.

Stainton

John Dubbye: 1 tenement with buildings, certain lands. Rent £1 6s. 8d.

Lanchester

John Smerte: 1 tenement with buildings, certain lands. Rent 13s. 4d.

William Smert: 1 tenement with appurtenances. Rent 13s. 4d.[433]

Thomas Forster: 1 tenement, certain lands called the *Manested Hall*. Rent 8s.

<Total: £1 14s 8d.>

YORKSHIRE

Little Broughton

William Warden: various tenements held by indenture under the priory seal, certain. Rent £12 18s. 3½d.

Ilkley Rectory

Thomas Merring: the parsonage of Ilkley, let by indenture under the priory seal, worth £5 a year 'over all reprises'.

Total: £26 6s. 3½d

<The printed edition notes that at this point a line or two are torn>

†*Corn tithes of Hexhamshire*†

The tithe corns of Anick, £10.

The tithe corns of Sandhoe, 13s. 4d.

---

[433] This is followed by an calculated total of £1 6s. 8d., implying that the rent from Thomas Forster was added later.

The tithe corns in Acomb, £2 13s. 4d.

The tithe corns in the township of Wall, £2 6s. 8d.

The tithe corns in the township of Coastley, 10s.

The tithes of the township of Keepwick, 13s. 4d.

The tithes of Errington, £1

Total: £18 4s 8d.[434]

The tithes and offerings belonging to the chapel of Allendale, let under the priory seal to various persons, £15

Total: £15.

Hexham and Hexhamshire <tithes>

The tithes of lambs from all the parishes in Hexhamshire. Worth £3 6s. 8d.

The tithes of wool of all those parishes. Worth £1 7s. 6d. a year 'over all charges'.

The personal tithes, oblations, Lenten tithes, other profits in those parishes. Worth £9

The tithes and offerings in the chapel of St. John. Worth £2 3s.

<The printed edition notes that at this point a line or two are gone>

The offerings and tithes in the chapel of Our Lady in Bingfield. Worth £3 6s. 8d.

---

[434] 8s. of this sum is unaccounted for in the list above, and implies at least one lost item.

Total: £22 5s. 9d.

Northumberland <tithes>

The parsonage and tithe corns belonging to the church in Alston Moor. Worth £3 6s. 8d.

The tithe corns of Newburgh, lately in the hands of the lord. Worth £1 6s. 8d.

The tithe corns of the town of Allerwash, lately in the hands of priory. Worth £1

The tithe corns of the town of Fourstones, in the hands of the lord. Worth 13s. 4d. 'over all charges'.

The tithes of the town of Slaley with the chapel, let under the priory seal to John Swynborne. Rent £4

The tithe corns of Chollerton, lately in the hands of the lord. Worth £1 6s. 8d.

The tithe corns of Barrasford, lately in the hands of the lord. Worth £1 13s. 4d.

The tithe corns of Chipchase, Cowden (*Stewden*) and Birtley, let under the priory seal to John Heron. Rent £4 6s. 8d.

The tithe corns of Gunnerton. Worth £2.

The tithe corns in the town of Colwell, let without the priory seal to Sir John Widdrington. Worth £2.

The tithe corns of Haydon, various parts of tithe corns in the lordship of Langley, and the parish of Haydon, let by indenture under the priory seal to Sir Reginald Carnaby. Worth £17 13s. d.

Total: £39 6s. 8d.

Cumberland \<tithes\>
The tithe corns of the parish church of Isel in the diocese of Carlisle. Worth £5.

Total £5.

Total of the whole rental of Hexham with appurtenances, £229 14s. 6d.

Payment of rent annual pensions
In annual payment issuing from the lands of Salton to the king for castle ward, 13s. 4d.

An annual pension issuing from the prebendary of Salton to the chapter of York, £2.

An annual pension issuing from the prebendary of Salton to the choristers of York Minster, 4s.

An annual pension issuing from the churches of Warden, Chollerton and Alston to the bishop of Durham, £1 13s. 4d.

An annual pension issuing from the churches of Alston (3s. 4d.) and Ovingham (10s.), to the prior of Durham, 13s. 4d.

An annual pension issuing from the chapel of Slaley to the abbot and convent of Blanchland, £1 3s.

Total: £6 7s.[435]

---

[435] An addition to the record notes that this sum was disallowed at the Court of Augmentations until such time as some warrant could be shown to the chancellor and council there.

Salaries of chaplains

The salary of the curate of the chapel or church of Hexham belonging to the priory, £4.

The salary of a chaplain with cure of souls in the chapel of St John, £4.

The salary of a chaplain with cure of souls in the church of Bingfield, £4.

The salary of a chaplain with cure of souls in the chapel of Slaley, £4.

The salary of a chaplain with cure of souls in the parish church of Allendale, £4.

Total: £20

Total allowances: £20

Net income: £209 14s. 6d.[436]

[B]

<NORTHUMBERLAND>

Ovingham, a cell of Hexham

The site of the manor and the tithe barn, £6 14s. 8d.

Tithes of hay, £10s., of lambs and wool, £2 14s., of calves, 2s., of geese, 6s., of hens, 10s., of salmon, 8s. Small tithes, etc., as in the Easter Book, £2.

Total: £13 4s. 8d.

---

[436] A note by R. Huchonson, the auditor, notes that the sum 'agrees with a rental made at the priory's dissolution'.

Of which in pensions to the bishop of Durham, £1; to the prior of Durham, 10s.; to the archdeacon of Durham for synodal dues and procurations, 12s.

Total: £2 2s.

Net income, £11 2s. 8d.

<YORKSHIRE>

The prebend of Salton

Spiritualities:
Salton Rectory, comprising the grain tithe of Salton, £4 13s. 4d.; of Edstone, £4 13s. 4d; of Brawby, £3. The tithe of lambs and wool at Salton, £1 1s. 4d.
Total value of spiritualities: £13 8s. net.[437]

Temporalities:
The manor of Salton and its lands, now in the tenure of James Ridley. Worth £19 16s. 'over reprises'. Rents from tenants in Edstone and Brawby. Worth £4 4s. 'over reprises'.
Total value of temporalities: £24 net.

Total, sprituralities and temporalities: £37 8s.

PRINTED SOURCE. *PH*, II, pp.157-69.

DATE. 14 July 1536; *PH*, I, p. cxxiii; II, p. 157.

LANGUAGE. English.

NOTE. Raine printed the text of document 4A in English 'from a transcript of the original in the possession of W. B. Beaumont, M.P.', the original being in the records of the Court of Augmentations: *PH*, I, p. clxvii, II, p. 158-69. He prints a short extract from this survey relating to the demesnes of the priory in Hexham 'from the Chapter House papers in the Public Record Office': *Ibid.*, I, pp. clxvii-clxviii (second sequence). He also prints

---

[437] The items add to £12 8s.

in Latin another document from the records of Court of Augmentations comprising summaries of parts of the same survey but with additional material relating to Ovingham and the prebend of Salton: *Ibid.*, II, pp. 157-8. This additional material is calendared above as document 4B. The income due to the priory as recorded in documents 4A and 4B exceeds £200: the rental of 1536 seems to have totalled it at £266 5s. 2d.: *Ibid.*, II, p. 158. However, the priory was dissolved under the Act of Dissolution of March 1536 that related to houses whose income was below that figure on the basis of an earlier valuation, deliberately falsified by Henry VIII's commisioners: Knowles and Hadcock, p. 160.

THE LIBERTY OF HEXHAM

5. Extract from Prior Richard's *History of the Church of Hexham*

[Ch. viii.] For a long time the priest Eilaf the younger held from the canons, in great peace and honour, the cure of souls in the parish [of Hexham] with the greater part of the benefices, and 1 carucate of land with certain houses in the township of Hexham, and 6 bovates of land in Anick, namely the endowment of that church.

PRINTED SOURCE. *PH*, I, p. 54.

NOTE. Eilaf II, vicar of Hexham, in succession to his father, Eilaf I, was a married priest. His position was undermined by ecclesiastical reform, and he retired to Durham in 1138: R. Walterspacher, *The Foundation of Hexham Priory, 1070-1170* (Middlesbrough, 2002), p. 11.

6. An agreement or draft agreement between the archbishop of York and the bishop of Durham relating to Allendale church (extract)

The chapel and cemetery of Allendale are to be in the hand of the prior of Hexham, so that the archbishop shall not compel anyone to be buried there, nor the bishop prohibit it. The church of Hexham is to receive chrism and oil from the church of Durham as accustomed, and the prior is to attend the Durham synod; Hexham clerks and canons are to receive ordination from the bishop of Durham; Hexham parishioners are to visit the church of Durham at Pentecost if they wish, without compulsion from the bishop or his men or prohibition. The prior of Hexham is to hold all ecclesiastical pleas of the parish, without financial penalty, and he is to impose penances. On the departure of Prior Richard, the bishop is to have such authority in the appointment of a successor as Prior Richard, the prior of Guisborough and Peter the brother of the prior of Bridlington shall swear the church of Durham had in the appointment of the same prior Richard.

... ...

The names of those who were present: A[ilred] abbot of Rievaulx, Ralph treasurer of York, John son of Letold archdeacon of the church of York, John archdeacon of Durham, G[erman] prior of Durham, Master Mainard, William the chaplain, Jeremiah canon of York, Master Vaccarius, Robert son of Stephen, Alan the chaplain, Peter de Carcass', Richard steward of the bishop of Durham, and Theobald de Musterville, John de Rana, Hugh de Sarz, Ralph Noble, Simon the chamberlain.

> PRINTED SOURCE. *The Historians of the Church of York and its Archbishops*, ed. James Raine (Rolls series, 3 vols., 1879-94), III, pp. 79-81; calendared, with a note on textual transmission and publication history, in *Episcopal Acta Durham 1153-95*, pp. 140-1.
>
> DATE. 1162 x 1166. This is the date given by Snape in *Episcopal Acta Durham 1153-95*.

NOTE. This extract is part of a record of the settlement reached between Archbishop Roger de Pont l'Évêque of York and Bishop Hugh du Puiset of Durham, concerning various long-disputed jurisdictional issues. These included Durham's claims to control of Hexham, which were now abandoned in return for the concessions set down on this occasion: G. V. Scammell, *Hugh du Puiset, Bishop of Durham* (Cambridge, 1956), pp. 168-71, 181-2.

7. Grant of Eshells to the priory by Thomas of Dilston

Thomas of Dilston grants to the church of St Andrew at Hexham and the canons there the whole of Eshells to hold in free and perpetual alms for the salvation of his own soul and those of his ancestors and heirs, saving the service due to the archbishop of York and his successors. Witnesses: Richard de Umfraville, Hugh de Bolbec, Othver de Lisle, Robert Delaval, Robert his brother [*sic*], David de Graham, Matthew of Whitfield, Peter de St Clair, William of Halton, Ranulph of Dilston, Robert Bertram, Adam Bertram, Elias of Frinton of Catton, and others.

PRINTED SOURCE. *PH*, II, pp. 89-90.

DATE. 1203 x 1211. Thomas of Dilston inherited his father's lands in 1203 and died in 1211 or 1212: *NCH*, X, pp, 236-7; Hedley, pp. 144-5. The witness Robert Bertram is probably Sir Robert Bertram, baron of Bothal, who died in 1211: Hedley, pp. 192-3.

NOTE. Document 8 describes the canons of Hexham as having purchased this land, and also explains why it occurs neither in the *inspeximus* of 1298 (document 3) nor in the Black Book.

8. Exchanges made by the priory with Walter de Gray, archbishop of York

Prior William and the convent of Hexham quitclaim all their right in the township of Eshells, purchased from Thomas of Dilston, to

Walter [de Gray], archbishop of York, and surrender to him the charter relating to their acquisition. In exchange the archbishop gives them 85 acres of land whose bounds are described in the archbishop's charter. They also quitclaim to him all right in annual rents of 1,000 eels and 4s. in Beverley, which they exchange for 30 acres of land by the burn below Yarridge to the north. They also quitclaim to him all right in 3½ acres 16 perches of land by St Andrew's well in exchange for the same area of land in the ploughed land called *Sele*. Witnesses, Robert de Gray, Adam of Tindale, William Marcel, Peter de Vaux and G. of *Stanlak*, canons of York, R. of *Bereford*, A. of Stanley, Adam Bertram, Richard le Fossur.

PRINTED SOURCE. *PH*, II, pp. 90-1.

DATE. 1216 x 1226. Walter de Gray received the temporalities of York on 19 February, 1216: *Handbook, of British Chronology,* p. 282. William was no longer prior of Hexham by 5 October 1226: *Heads of Religious Houses 1216-1377*, p. 390. Adam (II) de Tindale was baron of Langley: see document 31. It is unclear which witnesses were canons of York.

9. Grant of lands and privileges to the priory by Walter de Gray, archbishop of York

Walter de Gray, archbishop of York, grants to the church of St Andrew at Hexham and the canons there 145½ acres of land; of which, 40 acres lie between the township of Anick and the archbishop's hedged enclosure at Oakwood to the north, 90 acres above Dotland to the south, and 15½ acres below Dotland to the north, to hold of the archbishop and his successors freely and in perpetuity, paying 4 marks a year for all services, half at Martinmas and half at Pentecost. The archbishop also grants them a road, measuring 10 perches in width, from the end of their township of Anick through the middle of his hedged enclosure at Oakwood, from their sheepfold due northwards a far as their common pasture beyond Birkey Burn. For this concession, the canons will remit to the archbishop, for themselves, their successors and all their men, all right in the archbishop's hedged enclosure of Oakwood, namely, from the end of the township of Sandhoe along the bounds of [the lands of] Peter de Vaux as far as Birkey Burn, and from Birkey Burn descending as far as Acomb mill. The canons also concede that they will neither make claim to, nor object to, any assart that the archbishop or his successors shall make between Hexham and Dotland. The archbishop further grants the canons a mill he had newly built on the large burn between Dotland and the township of Rowley, with the multure of the archbishop's men in Eshells and of all the men dwelling on his assarts south of the Tyne, both those already made and those which shall be made in the future, except for all Allendale. The canons will hold of the archbishop and his successors at fee-farm paying 10 marks a year. If in time this place should become less suitable for a mill, they shall be allowed to build another mill on the same burn, wherever shall seem most expedient to them, by the counsel of the archbishop and his successors, or his chief steward. Issued at Knaresborough.

PRINTED SOURCE. *PH*, II, pp. 91-2; noted in *Gray's Register*, p. 224.

DATE. Dated 4 August 1226.

NOTE. *PH* has *Kirkeburn* for *Birkeburn*; for confirmation of the correct initial letter, see Black Book 2 and document 16 (item 18). This is Birkey Burn (NY 950661). The new mill was perhaps Whitley Mill on Rowley Burn (NY 925582), which is within two miles of Eshells (NY 897577). The references to land clearance, and to the suit of mill at Whitley owed by the tenants of these assarts, would explain why the Black Book described Whitley Mill as standing in the *Neulandes* and why it ascribes to Whitley Mill (together with Newbiggin Mill) the suit of mill of 'all tenants in (the) *Neulandes*': Black Book 5. The grants in this charter are itemized separately in document 16 (items 7, 18).

10. Grant of the fines and escheats of justices in eyre to the priory by Walter de Gray, archbishop of York

Walter de Gray, archbishop of York, grants to the church of St Andrew at Hexham and the canons there all the fines and escheats which he customarily receives from the canons' men when the archbishop's itinerant justices hear pleas in those parts, that is, whenever the king sends justices in eyre to Northumberland. The pleas that used to be heard before the justices in the canons' own court at the door of the priory church will in future be held before the archbishop's justices in his court, so that there is only one court for all. Penalties will be imposed by the archbishop's justices with the advice of the prior, according to the gravity of each offence, in such a way that the husbandry and property of the canons does not suffer. The canons will receive the sums due to them at the hands of their bailiffs. For this concession, the canons will give to the archbishop and his successors 12 marks whenever the archbishop's itinerant justices hear pleas in those parts. Issued at Knaresborough.

PRINTED SOURCE. *PH*, II, pp. 92-3; noted in *Gray's Register*, p. 224.

DATE. 4 August 1226, the same as document 9.

11. Grant of the land in Dotland to the priory by Walter de Gray, archbishop of York

Walter de Gray, archbishop of York, grants in free and perpetual alms to the church of St Andrew at Hexham and the canons there 64 acres lying between the township of Dotland and their assart of *Tisterl'*, to hold of him and his successors, with all common rights, liberties and easements. Issued at Knaresborough.

PRINTED SOURCE. *PH*, II, pp. 93 noted in *Gray's Register*, p. 224.

DATE. 4 August 1226, the same as document 9.

NOTE. *Tisterl'* recurs as an element in *Thysterleyburne* in document 14. This grant is not listed in document 16.

Calendar of Additional Documents 191

12. Grant of the Hexhamshire tithes to the priory by Walter de Gray, archbishop of York

Walter de Gray, archbishop of York, grants to St. Andrew of Hexham and the prior and canons there all tithes both of corn and legumes in all the assarts which either the archbishop or his men have made, or shall make in future, in Hexhamshire.

PRINTED SOURCE. *PH*, II, pp. 93; noted in *Gray's Register*, p. 224.

DATE. 4 August 1226, the same as document 9.

NOTE. The tithes of Hexhamshire had been granted over a century earlier by Archbishop Thomas: document 16 (item 2). This grant relates to new lands brought into cultivation since that time.

13. Confirmation of documents 9-12 by the prior of Hexham

Prior Bernard and the convent of Hexham confirm the arrangements agreed by charters 21-4 above. Witnesses: Nicholas, formerly bishop of Man and the Isles, Master Richard the chancellor, Godard the penitentiary and Walter de Tany canons of York, William the chaplain and Adam of Staveley canons of Southwell, Peter de Vaux, William of *Widindon*, Peter Harang, Adam Bertram, Roger of Bingfield and Thomas of Whittington, and many others. Issued at Knaresborough.

PRINTED SOURCE: *PH*, II, pp. 93-4.

DATE: 5 August 1226.

14. Grant of lands in Dotland to the priory by Walter de Gray, archbishop of York

Walter de Gray, archbishop of York, grants in free and perpetual alms to the church of St Andrew at Hexham and the canons there 60 acres of land lying between the township of Dotland and their assart of *Torneby*. The 60 acres lie between *Ormeslecche*, *Smaleburne*, *Thysterleyburne* and that assart. This is given to make up the rent[438] they pay him for a mill they hold of him near Dotland. The archbishop also grants in free and perpetual alms the remaining 34 acres lying within those bounds, with all common rights, liberties and easements, for a rent to him and his successors of 11s. 4d. a year, i.e. 4d. an acre. The canons will hold of the archbishop and his successors freely and quit of all services except that rent.

PRINTED SOURCE. *PH*, II, p. 95.

DATE. Dated 31 August 1229.

NOTE. The assart of *Torneby* is perhaps the same as the assart of *Thornleye* in document 16 (item 17). The grants in this charter are itemized separately in document 16 (items 9, 17).

15. Lease by Walter de Gray, archbishop of York, to Hexham to the priory of his demesne lands in Hexham

Walter de Gray, archbishop of York, leases for 15 years to the prior and convent of Hexham all his demesne land of Hexham within the following ploughed lands: in the large ploughed land between the archbishop's demesne manse and the Tyne, 62 acres sown with oats; in the ploughed land by the Tyne between the township and the hospital, 6 acres sown with wheat; in Haining Croft, 15 acres sown with wheat; in the ploughed land of *Widhalc*, 20 acres sown with wheat; in the ploughed land by St. Andrew's Well, on the north side of the way out of the township, 6½ acres sown with rye; on the north side of the Tyne, by the bridge, 4 acres sown with rye; on the western and eastern sides of the bridge above the Tyne, 9 acres sown with oats; in the ploughed land by *Harestane* on the south side of the way out of Priestpopple, 7 acres sown with oats; in a ploughland on the south side of Priestpopple, 50 acres of fallow land; with ploughing and harrowing boons and with reaping and harvest works; with pasture for 16 oxen in Oakwood; and with the estovers (?) from *Westwod* such as can be drawn by of two ox

---

[438] *ad emendacionem firme.*

teams, to be taken under the supervision of the foresters;[439] and with all other easements of the demesne except the demesne meadows between the feast of the Purification of the BVM until the hay is taken off. For this the will render a *tawa* of marketable wheat, winnowed and sieved, for each acre of wheat and rye, and a *tawa* of marketable flour for each acre of oats, to be paid half at the feast of the Annunciation of the BVM, half at the feat of St John the Baptist. At the end of 15 years the land will be restored to the archbishop sowed as when they received it. If the prior and convent lose the advantage of the lease through war or any other way through the archbishop's fault, they will receive due compensation upon consideration by approved and law-worthy men.

PRINTED SOURCE. *PH*, II, pp. 96-7.

DATE. 30 May (Pentecost), 1232.

NOTE. The arable land here totals 179½ acres, apparently in a three-course rotation of winter-sown crops (wheat and rye), spring-sown crops (oats), and fallow. It is not clear why the oats acreage is broken into two sections. Perhaps the second section of land under oats, amounting to 16 acres, represents land outside the normal rotation sequence. In that case the sowing may be analysed as 51½ acres in the wheat and rye course, 62 acres in the oats course, 50 acres in the fallow course and 16 acres of 'outland'. The clause relating to estovers seems to relate to an allowance of wood as fuel for the priory. The *tawa* that the lease uses as a measure is not known to the dictionaries, and remains a puzzle.

16. Memorandum regarding lands granted to the priory by the archbishops of York

The canons hold the following properties by gift of archbishops of York.

---

[439] *cum estoveriis (?) ad tractus boum duarum carucarum in West-wod, per visum forestariorum capiendis.*

1 The church and priory of Hexham by grant of Archbishop Thomas II. They have his charter.

2. The two townships of Anick, with Sandhoe and Yarridge, and all the archbishop's tithes and those of other inhabitants of the liberty of Hexham, also by the gift Archbishop Thomas II. They have his charter and a confirmation by the chapter of York.[440]

3. Soc and sac, and the assize of bread and ale, which they exercized until the time the last war with the Scots, also by gift of Archbishop Thomas II.[441]

4. Lands in the township of Hexham, namely the entire street called Cockshaw, 24 messuages in Priestpopple, 14 messuages in Market Street, 16 messuages in Hencotes, the land there where a pilgrim hospital was built, together with the whole township of Dotland with its appurtenances of Hazeldean, both Grottingtons, a field by the River Tyne, and pannage for all their pigs and those of their villagers 'in the land of St Andrew', by grant of Archbishop Thurstan, held free of secular service.[442]

5. 7½ acres of land in a piece of cultivated land called the *Sele*, free of service, by grant of Archbishop Geoffrey.[443] They have his charter.

6. Half the township of Bingfield in free alms, by gift of a certain Germund.[444] They have his charter, together with a confirmation by Archbishop Thurstan and the chapter of York.

7. 145½ acres of land by grant of Archbishop Walter [de Gray], namely 40 acres between Anick and Oakwood to the north, 90 acres below Dotland to the south, and 15½ acres below Dotland to the north, to hold by fealty and a payment of 4 marks a year for all

---

[440] For the four hamlets, see documents 1A, 2 (item 1), 3 (item 2).
[441] See document 3 (item 2).
[442] See documents 1B, 2 (item 2), 3 (item 3).
[443] 1191-1212: *Handbook of British Chronology*, p. 281.
[444] See document 3 (item 4).

services. From these lands they have had no profits from agriculture for the past 30 years.[445]

8. The mills of Hamburn and Newbiggin, with the suit attached to them, held by fealty and a payment of 10 marks a year for all services. The mills are worth nothing, though they used to be worth 30s.[446]

9. 60 acres of land given in free alms, in compensation for the rent of those mills, for which they have to pay 2 marks a year. They have had no profit for 30 years.[447]

10. 27 acres 1 rood of land enclosed within the priory's park at Dotland, for which they pay 9s. 1d. a year for all services. Stephen del Hill and his sister, and John son of Hawise hold 8 acres of land, which the canons were granted by Archbishop John [le Romeyn],[448] to have enclosed in the park. For these lands, the canons have paid a fine of 4d. an acre until now.[449] They believe that Stephen, with his sister, and John pay rent as they do themselves, so they petition the archbishop that they should not be charged the 2s. 8d. due from these two tenancies.

11. 2 acres of waste land by the common peatery, held for 8d. a year for all services.

12. Various tofts enclosed within the *Sele*, held for 4s. 2½d. a year for all services.

13. A land called *Whetewang*, held for 3s. a year, but from which they have received no profit for 30 years. They return it to the archbishop 'by this document', praying his lordship not to take offence.

---

[445] See document 9.
[446] ..l.ez queux molins ne valent nul, an communement xxxs. See document 3 (item 6).
[447] See document 14. This property disappears from the list of rents to the archbishop in document 17.
[448] 1286-96: *Handbook of British Chronology*, p. 282.
[449] ...tantque en cea.

14. 7 tithe barns in 7 townships, held by fealty and 2s. 4d. a year for all services.[450]

15. The land in Bingfield that was Robert of Skipton's, held for fealty and ½ a mark a year for all services.[451]

16. Some small parcels of land and tofts in Hexham, assigned to officers of the priory. They cannot now know just how much land there is, or how much it owes, because they never involved themselves with these offices,[452] but as soon as[453] they know the truth of the matter they will be happy to recognize their obligations in this as in other respects.[454]

17. 34 acres of land between the township of Dotland and the assart of *Thornleye*, as it then was,[455] held by fealty and for 11s. 4d. a year for all services, by the grant of Archbishop Walter [De Gray].[456] This land has lain waste for 30 years.

18. The archbishop also grants them a road, measuring 10 perches in width, from the end of their township of Anick through the middle of his hedged enclosure at Oakwood, from their sheepfold due northwards a far as their common pasture beyond Birkey Burn.[457] For this concession, the canons will remit to the archbishop, for themselves, their successors and all their men, all right in the archbishop's hedged enclosure of Oakwood, namely, from the end of the township of Sandhoe along the bounds of [the lands of] Peter de Vaux as far as Birkey Burn, and from Birkey Burn descending as far as Acomb mill.[458]

PRINTED SOURCE. *PH*, II, pp. 133-6.

---

[450] See document 3 (item 7).
[451] See document 3 (item 5).
[452] *Car nous n'entremedlasmes unques de cels offices.*
[453] Reading *plustost* for Raine's *plus cost*.
[454] Reading *remenaunt* for Raine's *remeraunt*.
[455] *l'assart que adonque feust de Thornleye; cf.* document 14.
[456] 1216-55: *Handbook of British Chronology*, p. 282.
[457] *Birkeburge.*
[458] See document 9.

DATE. c. 1328. As noted by Raine, the memorandum is recorded in the Register of William Melton, archbishop of York, amongst documents for the year 1328. This date fits well with the references to lands being worthless 'for these 30 years past', referring back to the start of the Scottish wars in 1296, and the devastation of Hexhamshire during William Wallace's invasion of 1297: see the note to document 3.

LANGUAGE. The memorandum is linguistically composite. Items **1-6** are in Latin, and **7-17** are in French, while item **18** repeats the original Latin of a charter.

NOTE. The use of the second person plural indicates that the document was prepared by the canons of the priory. The petition in item **10** and the provisions of item **13**, and the fact that the memorandum was copied into the archbishop's register, suggest that it arose from consultations between the canons and the archbishop. Following the peace treaty sealed at Edinburgh in March 1328, in the aftermath of the major Scottish invasion of 1327, there may have been discussions about the dues owed by the priory, as there was some prospect that the priory might now be able to pay them. If so, this may have been a working document prepared by the canons to record what they held of the archbishop, but also to argue the case for their continuing poverty and inability to pay the accustomed dues. Some of the problems caused by the destruction of the priory's muniments are revealed by section **16**. The total dues recorded as owed to the archbishops amounted to £12 13s. 4d. (including 3s. for land which the canons were offering to return, and 2s. 8d. that they disputed). The list of grants does not include document 11.

17. Acknowledgment by the prior of services owed to the archbishop of York

An acknowledgment by the prior of Hexham of the services owed to the archbishop of York for lands and tenements in the liberty of Hexham.

1. For tofts enclosed within the priory, in a place called the *Sele*, 4s. 2d. a year for all services.[459]

---

[459] Cf. documents 8, 16 (item 5, 12).

2. For 145½ acres, namely, 40 acres of land between the wood of Oakwood and the township of Anick, and 90 acres below Dotland to the south, and 15½ acres below Dotland to the north, £2 14s. 4d. in all.[460]

3 For 27 acres 1 rood of land enclosed within the prior's park at Dotland, 9s. 1d. in all.[461]

4. For 34 acres of land between the township of Dotland and Thornley, 11s. 4d. in all.[462]

5. For 2 acres of waste by the peatery, 8d.[463]

6. For diverting water to Whitley Mill, 12d.[464]

7. For 7 pieces of land for tithe barns in 7 hamlets, 2s. 4d. in all.[465]

8. For the lands and tenements in Bingfield that were Robert of Skipton's, 6s. 8d. a year in all.[466]

9. For the mills of Hamburn and Newbiggin, with the suit belonging to them, 10 marks a year in all.

10. For 3 tofts in the hands of the sacrist and almoner lying in St Giles Street, and a toft in Hencotes with 1 rood of land adjacent, 13¾d. a year.[467]

11. For 2 acres of almoner's land called Haining Croft in the field of Hencotes, 2 acres of land called *Coucroft*, a place called *Dudmansknoll*, and a piece of almoner's land called *Beaumond*, 2s. 2d a year in all.

The prior affirmed that if it should be established that any rent was in arrears owing to the muniments having been burned, or from any

---

[460] Cf. documents 9, 16 (item 7)
[461] Cf. document 16 (item 10).
[462] Cf. documents 14, 16 (item 17).
[463] Cf document 16 (item 11).
[464] Cf. document 9.
[465] Cf. documents 3 (item 7), 16 (item 14).
[466] Cf. documents 3 (item 5), 16 (item 15).
[467] Cf. document 3 (item 6), 16 (item 8).

other cause, he would duly inform the archbishop. Issued at Cawood.

PRINTED SOURCE. *PH*, II, pp. 139-40.

DATE. Dated 28 May 1350.

NOTE. The total dues recorded as owed to the archbishop amount to £11 5s. 2¾d.

18. Licence from John Thoresby, archbishop of York, to enclose a park

John Thoresby, archbishop of York, as lord of the liberty of Hexham, licences the prior and convent of Hexham to enclose their wood called Dotland Park, within the liberty, with a higher wall, than the one already there and to make a park there. They are to hold that enclosed wood and park of himself and his successors in perpetuity without impediment, provided that the wood does not lie within the bounds of any forest. Issued at the archbishop's manor by Westminster.

PRINTED SOURCE. *PH*, II, 140.

DATE. 6 October 1354, as noted by Raine in *PH*.

NOTE. For Dotland Park, recorded in Black Book 5, see documents 16 (item 10), 17 (item 3).

THE LIBERTY OF TYNEDALE WITH PRIORSDALE AND ALSTON MOOR

19. Grant of lands in Stonecroft and Henshaw to the priory by Richard Comyn

Richard Comyn, with the assent and counsel of his wife Hextilda, his friends and his men, grants in perpetual alms to the church of St Andrew at Hexham and the canons there the land in the fields of his township of Stonecroft that lies next to the place called Carraw extending westward to the wall of the Romans, by the bounds shown to them. He also confirms the half carucate of land of his fee in Henshaw which Aguilf, his knight, gave to them in alms. He confers this benefice on them because they have received him, his wife Hextilda, his brother Walter, and his heirs into full fraternity, in life and in death. Witnesses: Hugh de Morville, Gilbert de Umfraville, Odinel de Umfraville, William de Somerville, Walter of Ryedale, William of Lindsey, Walter Comyn, Aguilf and Nicholas his brother, Walter son of Rannulf, and many others.

PRINTED SOURCES. *PH*, II, 84-5; *Monasticon*, VI, p. 184; *HHN*, IV [part 2, vol. 3], p. 396.

DATE. The grant can be dated to after Richard Comyn's marriage to Hextilda in 1139 x 1153 and before his death c.1179: *RRS I*, p. 111; *RRS II*, note to no. 287, p. 311.

NOTE. David I of Scotland and Henry, earl of Northumberland had granted Richard and Hextilda land in Tynedale, at Walwick, Thornton, Stonecroft and Henshaw, that previously belonged to Hextilda's father, Uhtred son of Waltheof: *Charters of David I*, no. 277, p. 168. The 'wall of the Romans' is Hadrian's Wall.

20. Grant to the priory of lands of lands in Whitlow by Adam of Tindale

Adam of Tindale grants to the church of St Andrew at Hexham and the canons there the whole of Whitlow, which he had purchased; and with free rights of common pasture throughout the fee of

Featherstone, with wood for building and burning. Witnesses: William of *Ravenest*, Hugh of Grendon, Adam de Thorngrafton, Ranulph his son, Matthew of Whitfield, Odard of Willimontswick, and others.

PRINTED SOURCE: *PH*, II, 85.

DATE. *c*.1165 x 1188. Adam I of Tindale, lord of Langley, first occurs in 1165 and died in 1188: Sanders, p. 127. See also Hedley, I, pp. 231-2.

NOTE. For the location of Whitlow, see the note to Black Book 13.

21. Grant by Countess Ada of Whitfield to Hexham Priory

Countess Ada, mother of the king of Scots, grants in perpetual fee farm to the church of St Andrew at Hexham and the canons there the township of Whitfield with all its lands and the mill, except for the possessions held from her by Robert son of William and Joel of Corbridge, to hold free of all service by the bounds established when she held it from Earl Henry her husband, afterwards from King William, and by which Robert her chaplain held it, being land from the wastes of Earl Henry's demesne that Ada and Robert the chaplain, on her behalf (*per me*) had cultivated and inhabited. They are to pay <...> lb. of pepper a year at Michaelmas. Witnesses: William de *Bolber*, Henry <...>, Regina de *Reneber*, Robert clerk of Heddon, William Giff' clerk, <...> de Mortimer, Gualram son of Ralph Taurium of *Baior'*, Robert de *Belver*.

PRINTED SOURCE. *HHN*, IV [part 2, vol. 3], p. 17 ('from a copy').

DATE. 1166 x 1178, soon after the accession of William I of Scotland: *RRS,* II, no. 79, p. 178.

NOTE. Barrow identifies the source of this copy and notes its close relationship to document 23: *RRS,* II, p. 178.

22. Grant by Countess Ada of the free tenancy of Whitfield to Robert her chaplain

Countess Ada, mother of the king of Scots, grants to Robert her chaplain and his heirs [the township of Whitfield] except the lands of Joel and Robert of Dilston, to hold freely from [the canons of] Hexham. Witnesses: Alexander of St. Martin, William Giffard, Walter clerk.

> PRINTED SOURCE. *HHN*, IV [part 2, vol. 3], p. 17 ('from a copy').

> DATE. 1166 x 1178: the same period as documents 21 and 23.

23. Grant of William I, king of Scots, to Hexham priory relating to Whitfield

William, king of Scots, grants to the church of St Andrew at Hexham and the canons there the whole of Whitfield, with the mill, and all adjacent to the township, except for those lands which Robert son of William and Joel of Corbridge hold of King William's mother. The land is to be held of the king's mother by fee farm in perpetuity, freely and quit of all service, custom, aids and gelds, by the same bounds by which the king's mother held it of Earl Henry, the king's father, and afterwards of the king himself; and by the bounds by which Robert, her chaplain, held it, being land from the wastes of Earl Henry's demesne that the king's mother, and Robert her chaplain on her behalf (*per eam*), had cultivated and populated. They are to render annually to the king's mother and her heirs 6 lbs of pepper at Michaelmas, as the king's mother's charter witnesses and confirms. Witnesses: David the king's brother, Earl Waltheof, Hugh Ridel, Richard Comyn, Roger of Conyers, Walter of Windsor, Hugh Giffard, Liulf son of Maccus, Gilbert son of Richard, Gilbert de Umfraville, William de la Hay, William de Mortimer. Issued at Donkley Haugh,

> PRINTED SOURCE. *RRS, II*, no. 79, pp. 177-8; *PH,* II, pp 86-7.

> DATE. 1166 x 1178, probably 1166. This is the date given by Barrow in *RRS, II*. The canons had acquired Whitfield by 1171

at the latest, for by that date they had enfeoffed it back to Robert the chaplain: document 24.

NOTE. In document 3 (item 34), the prescribed annual render is a cash payment of 16s. 4d.

24. Grant of William I, king of Scots, to Robert the chaplain relating to Whitfield

William, king of Scots, confirms to Robert, chaplain of the king's mother, Countess Ada, the land of Whitfield, to be held to him and his heirs of the canons of Hexham in fee and heredity, freely, quietly and fully, as attested and confirmed by the canons' charter. Witnessess: Countess Ada, David, the king's brother, Nicholas the chancellor, Hugh Giffard, Alexander de St. Martin. Issued at Haddington.

PRINTED SOURCE. *RRS II*, no. 100, pp. 189-90; *HHN*, IV [part 2, vol. 3], p. 19.

DATE. 1165 x 1171, the date attributed by Barrow in *RRS, II*. It presumably post-dates document 23.

25. Grant by the prior and convent of Whitfield to Matthew, son of Robert the chaplain

John, prior of Hexham, and the convent grant in fee to Matthew son of Robert, chaplain of the Countess Ada, all Whitfield, except the land of Hugh and Robert, as freely as they hold it from the countess, i.e. owing her no service, custom, aids and geld, but paying to the canons of Hexham a mark of silver a year, half at Martinmas and half at Pentecost. They also retain in their own hands a toft, six acres of land, an acre of meadow and pasture for 30 cows, given to them by Robert the chaplain in the presence of the countess. They also stipulate that Matthew's heir should pay a mark of silver as a relief. Witnesses: Abraham the priest, Godfrey of Bingfield and Paganerus, Robert Bertram, Cospatrick Homal and his sons Walter and Gregory, Thurkill son of Archill and his son

Adam, Ernebrand of Anick, Benedict the clerk, Brian, Aschetill, John 'of the Castle', John the prior's household servant (*famulus*), Reynold the steward, Horm of Whitfield, and many others.

PRINTED SOURCE. *PH*, II, pp. 87-8; *HHN*, IV [part 2, vol. 3], p. 18.

DATE. 1175 x 1178, or shortly before, presumably antedating document 27. John was prior from 1174 or earlier and last occurs in 1191 x 1194 : *Heads of Religious Houses 940-1216*, p. 166.

26. Lease for 20 years by the prior and convent of Hexham, to Matthew of Whitfield of half of Whitfield and other properties

Prior J[ohn] and the convent of Hexham grant for 200 years to Matthew Witefelde, son of Robert the chaplain of Countess Ada, half of Whitfield and all *Parmontley, Elmlee, Softlaw, Dew Grean, Towne Greene* and *Ould Towne, Hunter Sheels, Hunter Sheels Park* lying between *Harwoodbor'* and *Kingeswoodbor'*, with the wood, for a rent of a mark of silver a year. Witnesses: T. Abraham priest, Godfrey of Bingfield, and Pain, Robert Bertram, Gospatric Homal and Walter [and] Gregory his sons, Thurkill son of Archeleus and Adam his son, Ernbrand of Anick, Benedict clerk, Brian Aschell, John Castel, John the prior's *famulus*, Raynald the steward, Horn of Whitfield, and others.

PRINTED SOURCE. *HHN*, IV [part 2, vol. 3], p. 18.

DATE. Late twelfth century. For Prior John, see document 25.

NOTE. Hodgson reproduces a Latin text he claims to have taken from the original charter, but the forms of the place-names he cites make this implausible. He describes Town Green and Old Town as 'parts of the antient village of Whitfield', and says that Parmontley 'lies on the south side of the burn which gets its name from it, and is otherwise called Car's burn': *HHN*, IV [part 2, vol. 3], pp. 110-11. Elsewhere he renders *Harwoodbor'* and *Kingeswoodbor'* respectively as *Harwood-burn* and *King's-*

wood-burn: Ibid., pp. 98-9. See also the document he cites on p. 111.

27. Grant of William I, king of Scots, to Hexham priory confirming their demise of land at Whitfield to Matthew son of Robert the chaplain

William, king of Scots, confirms the grant which the prior and convent of Hexham made to Matthew son of the king's chaplain Robert and his heirs of the land of Whitfield, to hold freely as the canon's charter witnesses and confirms. He also concedes that Matthew and his heirs may build on and settle the land as fully and well as it was before the time of war. Witnessess: Countess Ada the king's mother, Robert de Quincy, Alexander de St. Martin, William de Mortimer, Bernard son of Brian. Issued at Crail.

PRINTED SOURCE. *RRS II,* no. 172, pp. 234-5.

DATE. 1175 x 1178, the date given by Barrow in *RRS,* II.

NOTE. The war in question was that of 1173-4, whence this dating. The charter confirms document 25.

28. Grant of lands to the priory in Alston by Ivo de Vieuxpont

Ivo de Vieuxpont, for the good of his own soul, and those of his ancestors and successors, grants to the church of St. Andrew of Hexham and the canons there the whole of his demesne land in the township of Alston by these bounds: southward [along] the Natrass Gill burn as it falls to the Tyne; then descending on the west side as far as the bridge; then from the bridge, rising along an old ditch as far as St John's land on the north side; then straight westward by St John's land as far as the long ditch; and then, following the long ditch, as far as to the Natrass Gill burn first mentioned. He also grants rights of common pasture for 40 cows, 10 mares, and 100 sheep with their offspring of two years. He further grants all his land on the west side of the Tyne, within these bounds: beginning at the western end of the upper bridge at Alston; and then going round and upwards along the road and ditch southward as far as a burn by the wooden cross; and then descending along the burn as far as the water of Tyne; and descending along the Tyne on the east side as far as the bridge first mentioned. The canons are to hold freely from him and his heirs, with all liberties, common rights and easements pertaining to the township of Alston, with free entry, transit and egress through the donor's fee of Alston for their men and animals. The priory's tenants shall mill the corn grown on those lands at Alston mill freely and without multure. The canons and their men dwelling there will have timber from the donor's wood in Alston, under supervision of his servants, for building and for maintaining homes and fences. The donor and his heirs will warrant the grant in perpetuity. Witnesses: W[alter] bishop of Carlisle, B[artholomew] prior of Carlisle, Master G. archdeacon of Carlisle, Walter Comyn, Robert of Castle Carrock, Robert parson of Whitfield, John Prat, Ralph of Halton, Nicholas of Willimontswick, Richard son of Alexander, Adam of Thirlwall, John of Whitfield, Laurence de Vieuxpont, William of Kirkhaugh, Hugh of *Buckecastre*, Alan son of Joel, Adam of Elrington, John of Ridley, Richard son of Thurstan, Robert of Elrington, John of Hayton, Robert Marshal, Ughtred of Cheeseburn, John of Stillington clerk, and others.

PRINTED SOURCE. *PH*, II, pp. 120-1; *CChR III: 1300-26*, p. 89.

DATE. 1223 x 1232. Walter Mauclerc was bishop of Carlisle from 1223 to 1246: *Handbook of British Chronology*, p. 235. Bartholomew, prior of Carlisle, died in 1231 or 1232: *Heads of Religious Houses 1216-1377*, p. 359. The text of the charter derives from a royal inspection and confirmation at Carlisle, 20 March, 1307.

NOTE. The boundaries and other details of this grant are rehearsed in the Black Book entry for Alston: Black Book 15. Members of the Vieuxpont family were lords of the manor of Alston by grant of William I of Scotland: *RRS II*, nos. 84, 468, pp. 181-2, 432. For other gifts of Ivo de Vieuxpont in and around Alston, see document 2 (items 7 and 8), and document 3 (item 40).

29. Grant of lands between Langhope and Elrington to the priory by Walter De Gray, archbishop of York

Walter de Gray, archbishop of York, grants in free and perpetual alms to the church of St. Andrew of Hexham and the canons there 245 acres of land between Langhope and Elrington for an annual rent of 4d. an acre, payable to the archbishop and his successors. He also grants in free and perpetual alms 40 acres of land there for an annual rent of 2d. an acre. He further grants 20 acres there for the tithe of hay from all his demesnes in Hexhamshire. The archbishop and his successors will warrant the land against all men in perpetuity, and they will not grant or lease to anyone any other land between the said land and the township of Catton except with the assent of the canons. Issued at Hexham, written by Master Simon.

PRINTED SOURCE. *PH*, II, p. 95.

DATE. Dated 1 September 1229.

NOTE. This is a substantial grant, but its location is unclear. It does not seem to relate to any property recorded in the Black Book.

BARONY OF LANGLEY

30. Grant of lands in Featherstonehaugh to the priory by Elias of Featherstonehaugh

Elias of Featherstonehaugh grants to the church of St Andrew at Hexham and the brothers there from his fee at Featherstonehaugh, as enclosed within stated bounds. The brothers have received him and his son and heir into the fraternity of the church. Witnesses: Eustace, Papedi, Benedict and William, chaplains, Richard the archdeacon, Robert, Roger and Walter Hamel, Uhtred of Errington, Ranulf of Elrington, Reginald of Warden, William Lovell, and others.

PRINTED SOURCE. *PH*, II, p. 89; *HHN*, IV [part 2, vol. 3], p. 355.

DATE. 1212 x 1217, so dated by Hodgson from the time when Richard Marsh was archdeacon of Northumberland, before his election as bishop of Durham: *HHN*, IV, p. 354.

31. Grant of lands in Featherstonehaugh to the priory by Thomas of Featherstonehaugh

Thomas of Featherstonehaugh grants to the church of St. Andrew in Hexham a parcel of land in the territory of Featherstonehaugh. Witnesses: Sir Nicholas of Boltby, Peter de Lisle, Theobald of Boltby, Robert de Lisle, Richard son of Alexander, Adam of Thirlwall, Randal of Blenkinsop, Hugh of Settlingstones, Randal of Grendon, Hugh of Kelloe, Hugh of *Morriley*, Ralph Solar', Walter of Featherstonehaugh, Richard of *Hunterschelis*, and others.

SOURCE. *HHN*, IV [part 2, vol. 3], p. 355-6.

DATE. *c*.1242-3. The *Liber Feodorum* records a moment in 1242-3 when Randal of Blenkinsop, Thomas of Featherstonehaugh, Richard son of Alexander, Ralph Solaz, Richard of *Hunterschelys* and Randal of Grendon and Hugh of Settlingstones all held land of Nicholas of Boltby as of 'the barony of Boltby': *Liber Feodorum. The Book of Fees Commonly Called Testa de Neville*, ed. H. C. Mazwell-Lyte, 2 parts (London, 1920-3), part 2, pp. 1129-30, cf. *HHN*, V [part 3, vol. 1], pp. 220-1. Nicholas of Boltby died in 1272: *EYC*, IX, p. 164; Sanders, p. 127. See also Hedley, I, p. 232.

NOTE. Nicholas of Boltby held Featherstonehalgh as of the barony of Langley (otherwise known as the barony of Boltby or the barony of Tynedale: *Liber Feodorum*, part 2, p. 1111. He had rights in the barony from 1233 by right of marriage to Philippa, daughter of Adam II of Tindale, who died in that year: Sanders, p. 127.

32. Agreement concerning pasture rights between the priory and the convent of Lambley

Agreement by which the prior and convent of Hexham concede to the prioress and nuns of Lambley common rights of pasture for them and their tenants within the bounds of the nuns' tenement of Byers, set out below: from Maiden Way ascending along Black Burn as far as *Morileyburne*, and then ascending along *Morileyburne* as far as *Morileyburnheued*, and from there southwards, outside the wood, straight across the moor as far as Glendue along the boundary stones placed by Glendue, and then along Glendue descending as far as Maiden Way, and then northwards along Maiden Way as far as Black Burn first mentioned. And neither the nuns nor their servants are to take anything or cause any damage anywhere in the wood belonging to the prior and canons. The prioress and nuns are to hold these rights from the prior and convent at fee-farm for an annual render at Hexham on St Andrew's day of one altar cloth suitable for the prior's chamber. The prioress did fealty to the prior and convent and her successors shall do so similarly. Witnesses: Master A[lan] archdeacon of Northumberland, Henry dean of Newcastle, Hugh vicar of Ovingham, Richard son of Alexander bailiff of Hexham, Adam of Thirlwall, Thomas of Featherstone, Adam of Elrington, Hugh of *Calflawe*, Ranulf of Blenkinsop, John of Ingoe, Richard son of Thurstan, Robert Marshal, Robert of Elrington, and others.

PRINTED SOURCE. *PH*, II, pp. 97-8; *HHN*, IV [part 2, vol. 3], p. 94.

DATE. 11 November 1239.

NOTE. The boundaries here relate closely to those described under the Black Book's account of Byers, and to those of Hexham Priory's land with pasture in Knarsdale. For Maiden Way, see the latter entry, note 65. For Lambley Priory, founded by Adam I of Tindale who was also a benefactor of Hexham, see Knowles and Hadcock, p. 260.

33. Recognition of the priory's pasture rights by Lambley priory

Recognition by the prioress nuns of Lambley that they have enjoyed easements of pasture for their working beasts within the lands of the prior and canons of Hexham only by the grace and favour of the prior and canons. Witnesses as in document 32.

> PRINTED SOURCE. *PH*, II, p. 98; Hodgson, *HHN,* IV [part 2, vol. 3], pp. 93-4.

> DATE. About 11 November 1239.

34. The prioress and convent of Lambley grant Hexham Priory the right to a wall

The prioress and convent of Lambley grant that the prior and convent of Hexham may construct and maintain their wall, for which the canons grant rights to the nuns' beasts by escape across *Morleyburne* to the wall on that same burn. Witnesses: Thomas of Featherstonehaugh, William of Kellaw, Robert of Buteland, Gilbert chaplain, Uhtred then serjeant (*serviens*) of Lambley, Henry del Syde then serjeant (*serviens*) of Byres.

> PRINTED SOURCE. *HHN*, IV [part 2, vol. 3], p. 94.

> DATE. Probably thirteenth-century.

> NOTE. Hodgson's text is corrupt, and seemingly incomplete.

NORTHUMBERLAND

35. Agreement between the priory and Newminster Abbey concerning land in Stelden and pasture in Swinburn and Gunnerton

An agreement between the abbot and convent of Newminster and the prior and convent of Hexham, concerning land called Stelden, in the territory of Swinburn. The abbot of Newminster, with the advice of his chapter, grants this land, as specified in the charters of its donors, to the prior and convent of Hexham in perpetual fee farm. He also grants common pasture in Swinburn and Gunnerton for 4 tamed horses, 10 oxen and 30 cows with their calves until they are separated, and 400 ewes with their lambs until separated. He further grants the right to take fuel from Swinburn peatery, to construct a mill, and to take all other profits they should want within these bounds. The canons will hold in free alms, paying the abbot and convent £1 13s. 4d. a year for all services, half at Pentecost, and half at the feast of St Martin in Winter.

PRINTED SOURCE. *The Newminster Cartulary*, ed. J. T. Fowler, Surtees Society lxvi (1876), p. 73.

DATE. Probably earlier thirteenth-century. The grant of this land to Newminster Abbey by Peter of Gunnerton was probably witnessed, but certainly confirmed at the donor's request, by Hugh de Balliol, probably Hugh I, baron of Bywell, between 1200 and 1228, though perhaps Hugh II between 1268 and 1271: I. J. Sanders, p. 25. Stelden is included as a property of the priory in the royal *inspeximus* of 1298, where it is said to have been held from time out of mind: document 3 (item 33). No mill is recorded in the Black Book record of Stelden: Black Book 38.

36. Final concord concerning land in Slaley

Fine made before the king's justices at Westminster between Patrick son of Ylving, demandant, and Bernard, prior of Hexham, vouched to warranty by William son of Waukelin, in a plea of *mort d'ancestor* concerning a messuage and 13 acres of land in Slaley. The prior's right is recognized, for which he gives Patrick two marks of silver. He grants Patrick the messuage and the northern half the land towards the north to hold for a rent of 18d. a year, 9d. at Whitsuntide and 9d. at Martinmas.

SOURCE. *Feet of Fines, Northumberland and Durham*, no. 84, p. 38.

DATE. 25 October, 1224.

37. Final concord concerning the manor of Kirkheaton and Coldstrother

Fine made before the king's justices in eyre at Carlisle between Bernard, prior of Hexham, plaintiff (represented by brother John of Bywell, his canon), and Aline of Bolam, James de Cauz and Alice wife of James, impedients (represented by Everard of Bradford and James of Bolam), in a plea of warranty of charter concerning the manor of Kirkheaton and Coldstrother. The prior and church of Hexham are to hold the manor in free alms, quit of all secular service. Aline, James and Alice warrant the manor to the prior, and the prior admits them to the benefit of prayers to be said in his church of Hexham.

PRINTED SOURCE. *Feet of Fines, Northumberland and Durham*, no. 126, p. 54.

DATE. 24 April, 1235.

NOTE. The royal *inspeximus* of 1298 records a charter of Aline of Bolam and James de Cauz with his wife Alice granting to the priory of the manor of Kirkheaton and Coldstrother: document 3 (item 23). Aline of Bolam was daughter and co-heiress of Gilbert son of James, baron of Bolam, and widow of John de Cauz. Her sister Alice, had married John's brother James: W. P. Hedley, *Northumberland Families*, 1 (Newcastle upon Tyne, 1968), pp, 23-4. See also document 2 (items 4, 5).

38. Final concord concerning land and iron mining in Kirkheaton and Coldstrother

Final concord before the king's justices at Appleby between Robert of Cambo, plaintiff, and Bernard, prior of Hexham, impedient (represented by brother John of Bywell, his canon), in a plea of warranty of charter concerning 7 carucates and 31½ acres of land in Kirkheaton and Coldstrother. Robert is to have, of the prior's gift and with his warranty, the land and half the mining of iron in the common of that township, to hold as one sixth of a knight's fee, paying a fifth of the forinsec service due from the township. Robert releases all right to the remaining land in Kirkheaton and Coldstrother except for lands and tenements held by William Gabraz, Edulf Dud, Simon son of Roger and Thomas son of Robert of Fenwick. This fine is not to annul a previous concord between the two parties concerning the chantry chapel of (Little) Heaton.

SOURCE: *Feet of Fines, Northumberland and Durham*, no. 128, p. 55.

DATE. Morrow of SS Philip and James ('4 May'), 1235.

NOTE. Robert was a successor of John of Cambo, whose land was subinfeudated to the manor of Kirkheaton and Coldstrother at the time the priory acquired the manor: see document 3 (item 67). Robert secured his right to three separate parcels of land in Coldstrother and Little Heaton, totalling 3 carucates and 8 acres, by fines of 19 April, 22 April and 18 May, 1235: *Feet of Fines, Northumberland and Durham*, nos. 122-3, pp. 52-3.

39. Final concord concerning land in Stelling

Final concord made before the king's justices in eyre at Newcastle between Alan of York, smith, and his wife Alice, demandants, and Bernard, prior of Hexham, tenant; in a plea of *mort d'ancestor* concerning 24 acres in Stelling. The prior and his church of Hexham are to have the land, and also the 12 acres of land in Stelling held by Alan and Alice on the day of the making of this concord. The prior is to give Alan and Alice £2 sterling.

PRINTED SOURCE. *Feet of Fines, Northumberland and Durham*, no. 145, p. 64.

DATE. 6 October 1241.

40. Final concord concerning land in Thornton

Fine made before the king's justices in eyre at Newcastle between Thomas son of Robert of Thornton, plaintiff; and Bernard, prior of Hexham, defendant, in a plea of *mort d'ancestor* concerning 4 bovates of land in Thornton. The prior and his church of Hexham are to have the land. The prior is to give Thomas 1 mark of silver.

PRINTED SOURCE. *Feet of Fines, Northumberland and Durham*, no. 146, p. 64.

DATE. 6 October 1241.

NOTE. The Thornton in question is probably Thornton in Tynedale, whose former existence is now attested by the remains of Thornton Tower (NY 874684). This land seems not to be recorded in the Black Book.

41. Final concord concerning land in Newton in Coquetdale

Fine made before the king's justices at Newcastle upon Tyne between Bernard, prior of Hexham, demandant (represented by brother John of Bywell, his canon), and Diana, daughter of Roger of Alwinton, tenant, [in a plea of warranty of charter] concerning a carucate of land in Newton in Coquetdale. The prior is to have the land, but grants it to Diana and the lawful heirs of her body, with his warranty, for a rent of 18s. a year. 9s. at Martinmans and 9s. at Whirsuntide. In default of such heirs the land shall revert to the prior.

PRINTED SOURCE. *Feet of Fines, Northumberland and Durham*, no. 179, p. 73.

DATE. 15 July, 1246.

42. Confirmation by King Henry III of a grant to the priory of the manor of Nesbit

Henry III confirms to the church of St. Andrew of Hexham and the canons there the right to hold in perpetuity, by grant of John de Normanville and Robert de Lisle, the whole manor of Nesbit with all its appurtenances and liberties, together with all right and claim of Walter son of Walter of Nesbit in that property, as testified by the charters of John, Robert and Walter, and the confirmation of John de Balliol. Witnesses: William de Forz, count of Aumale, Hugh le Bigod, Stephen de Mennyl, John of Lexington, Roger Bertram of Mitford, William de Grey, Fulk son of Warin, Bartholomew le Bigod, William Gernon, and others. Issued at Newcastle upon Tyne.

PRINTED SOURCE. *PH*, II, p. 102; *Monasticon*, VI, p. 181 (without witness list); noted in *CChR 1226-57*, p. 450.

DATE. 25 September 1255.

NOTE. The manor of Nesbit had been divided between three co-heiresses by 1213. John de Normanville, Robert de Lisle and Walter son of Walter of Nesbit together represent the three owners of 'the whole manor', as a result of this division: *NCH*, XII, p. 320. John de Normanville's grant must date between 1221, when he inherited from his father, and his death in 1242-3: *Ibid.*, XII, p. 305.

43. Final concord relating to land in Nesbit

Fine made before the king's justices itinerant at Newcastle between Walter son of Walter of Nesbit, plaintiff, and John, prior of Hexham, impedient, concerning a toft and 13½ acres of land in Nesbit. The prior is to have the toft and land, but grants them to Walter, to hold for a yearly rent of a pound of cumin at Easter. The prior warrants the grant, and Walter releases his claim to all lands and tenements held by the prior in the same township, except for that toft and land.

PRINTED SOURCE. *Feet of Fines, Northumberland and Durham*, no. 204, p. 87; *Three Early Assize Rolls*, p. 401.

DATE. Octaves of Michaelmas ('6 Oct.'), 1255.

44. Final concord relating to land in Nesbit

Fine made before the king's justices itinerant at Newcastle between Thomas son of Adam, plaintiff; and John, prior of Hexham, impedient, concerning 2 tofts and 42 acres of land in Nesbit. The prior is to have the tofts and land. Thomas releases all claim to other lands and tenements held by the prior in the same township. The prior will provide Thomas with a servant's provisions for the rest of his life, namely, each day one loaf of wheat and one of oats, one gallon of ale and one dish from the kitchen, and annually at the feast of St Michael one robe or half a mark. After Thomas' death the prior shall have no further obligation.

PRINTED SOURCE. *Feet of Fines, Northumberland and Durham*, no. 205, p. 87; *Three Early Assize Rolls*, pp. 401-2.

DATE. 6 October, 1255.

NOTE. This settlement seems to represent the priory's elimination of the residual right of a member of the family of Walter son of Walter of Nesbit, for whom see also document 43: *NCH*, XII, p. 321.

45. Grant of lands in Stelden by the prior and convent to John of Swinburn

Prior John and the convent of Hexham grant to John, son of Richard of East (Little) Swinburn, for his homage and service, all their land, with the capital messuage, that Richard the ditcher formerly held of them; and all their land, with the toft and the croft, which Sampson of Swinburn held of them in the same township; and all their land of Stelden, except their sheepfold of Stelden, and their pastures on Gunnerton Moor as testified by a charter of the abbot of Newminster. The canons retain free entry and egress for their sheep in that fold. John and his heirs will hold in perpetuity for an annual rent of £2 1s., payable half at Pentecost and half at the feast of St. Martin in Winter, for all customary services and demands, performing such *forinsec* service as pertains to the lands. Witnesses: Hugh de Bolbec, Robert de Lisle, Thomas of Ogle, Thomas of Fenwick, knights, John of West (Great) Swinburn, Walter of Sweethope, William of Colwell, and others.

PRINTED SOURCE. Northumberland Record Office, ZSW 1/5; *PH*, II, pp. 100-1.

DATE. c.1250 x 1269. John of Lasenby occurs as prior in 1250 x 1255 and was superseded as prior in 1269: *Heads of Religious Houses 1216-1377*, p. 390.

NOTE. Though there is no reference in this grant to the final concords recorded in documents 39 and 40, they may have been preparatory to this grant.

46. Licence from Edward I to grant lands in North Milbourne in mortmain

Edward I grants licence for the alienation in mortmain by Thomas of Dilston to the prior and convent of Hexham of land to the yearly value of £20 in North Milbourne (i.e. Milbourne Grange). Issued at Westminster.

PRINTED SOURCE: *CPR 1281-92*, p. 167.

DATE: Dated 25 May 1285.

NOTE. The original grant, together with this licence, is noted in document 3 (item 32).

47. Petition from Hexham Abbey concerning their rights in Stamfordham church

The prior and convent of Hexham relate that John of Normanville, when seized of the manor of Stamfordham and the advowson of the church there, granted in perpetuity by charter some tenements there, together with the advowson, to Bernard, former prior of Hexham, and his successors. Bernard presented one of his clerks, Hugh of Stanbridge, who was received into the church and instituted by the bishop [of Durham], and the priory continued in possession until the time of Bishop Nicholas. Then, because the prior refused the bishop's request to present one of his clerks to Stamfordham church, Nicholas caused them great hardship until the prior submitted. Bishop Nicholas then ordained the advowson to himself and his successors for ever, but allowed the canons' right to the garb tithes of five hamlets. Prior Bernard and his successors have possessed them from that time till now. Afterwards, in 1300-1, King Edward I brought a writ of *quare impedit* before his justices of the Bench against Antony, bishop of Durham, that he should allow him the presentment of a suitable parson to Stamfordham church at each third vacancy, through the forfeiture of one Richard Lovell, a Norman, and Isabel his wife, third daughter and one of the heirs of John of Normanville. The canons petition the king to allow them the tithes of the five hamlets as they and their predecessors have had them from the time of the ordinance of Bishop Nicholas, so that they should not be prejudiced by the judgement made against the bishop, to which they were not party.

PRINTED SOURCE. *Records of the Parliament Holden at Westminster on the Twenty-Eighth Day of February in the Thirty-Third Year of the Reign of King Edward the First, A.D. 1305 [Memoranda de Parliamento]*, ed. F. W. Maitland, Rolls Series 98 (London, 1893), pp. 7-8.

DATE. 1304. The petition must have been presented by 26 July, when the king sent a copy of it to be examined by his council at York: *Calendar of Chancery Warrants Preserved in the Public Record Office, A.D. 1244-1326* (London, 1927), p. 229.

NOTE. the ordinance of Nicholas of Farnham here cited, dated 15 March 1246, is printed in *Episcopal Acta. Durham, 1241-83*, no. 21, pp. 21-2 and in *HHN*, VI [part 3, vol. 2], pp. 105-7, and see document 3 (item 60). It lists the five hamlets in question (here more vaguely described as *loci*, 'places') as Nesbit, Ouston, Hawkwell, East Matfen, and Bitchfield.

48. Edward I grants the advowson of Stamfordham church to Hexham Priory

Edward I having recently recovered in his court the advowson of the church of Stamfordham against Anthony, bishop of Durham, the prior and convent of Hexham have asserted before him that their predecessors had once been the patrons of that church, but that the advowson was arbitrarily seized by Nicholas, former bishop of Durham. Having examined the charters which the prior brought before his council, and for a fine which the prior made before the treasurer and barons of the exchequer, the king grants the advowson to the prior and convent to hold of him and his successors in perpetuity.

Witnesses: R[obert Winchelsey] archbishop of Canterbury, W[alter Langton] bishop of Coventry and Lichfield, J[ohn of Halton] bishop of Carlisle, Henry de Lacy earl of Lincoln, Humphrey de Bohun earl of Hereford and Essex, Aymer de Valence, John de Brittania junior, Hugh the Despenser, Robert of Clifford, John Botetourt, Robert de la Warde steward of the king's household, and others. Issued at Sheen.

> PRINTED SOURCE. *PH*, II, pp. 118-9; noted in *CChR 1300-26*, p. 59.

> DATE. Dated 7 October 1305.

> NOTE. See also C. Fraser, *A History of Anthony Bek, Bishop of Durham 1283-1311* (Oxford, 1957), pp. 119-20. Bek's licence for the priory to appropriate Stamfordham church, dated 2 October, 1307, is printed in *Records of Anthony Bek, Bishop and Patriarch, 1283-1311*, ed. C. Fraser, Surtees Society 162 (Durham, 1953), no. 122, pp. 125-6.

49. Licence from Edward II to grant lands in Kirkheaton in mortmain

Edward II grants licence for the alienation in mortmain to the prior and convent of Hexham by John of Cambo of half the manor of Kirkheaton for a fine of 20 marks. Issued at Beverley.

PRINTED SOURCE: *CPR 1313-17*, p. 109.

DATE. Dated 29 April 1314.

NOTE: The convent already had substantial property in Kirkheaton, described as 'the manor of Kirkheaton and Coldstrother': documents 3 (item 23), 37. The transaction authorized by this record probably implies the recovery by the convent of the 7 carucates and 31½ acres of land enfeoffed to Robert of Cambo in 1235: document 38.

50. Grant of lands in North Seaton bearing services owed to the priory of Hexham

Robert of Seaton grants to William of Burnton of Newcastle upon Tyne, 1 toft and croft and 38 acres of arable land, with the meadow appertaining to the land in Seaton by Woodhorn which John Palfreyman lately held of Robert. William is to pay Robert a rent of one peppercorn a year at Christmas for the first 21 years, then £2 6s. 8d. per year, as well as paying the accustomed services or dues to the prior and convent of Hexham. Witnesses: Sir John of Fenwick sheriff of Northumberland, John Pudding of Seaton, Robert of Cresswell, John of Horsley, Robert of Coventry, Henry of Ardern, John the clerk of Newbiggin, Thomas of Woodburn, and others. Issued at Seaton.

SOURCE. Nottingham Archives, DD/4P/21/101.

DATE. Dated 2 February 1322.

51. Licence from Edward II to Hexham Priory to acquire lands in mortmain in Kirkheaton, Nesbit, East Matfen, Eachwick and Dalton

Edward II, having licenced the prior and convent of Hexham to acquire in mortmain for their relief £20 per year worth of lands and rent, except for lands and rent held of the king, now authorizes the following acquisitions: from William Hetson, 2 tofts and 9 acres of land in Kirkheaton; from Gilbert of Bavington, 1 toft and 9 acres of land in Kirkheaton; from Robert son of Hugh of Cambo, 2 messuages and 18 acres of land in Kirkheaton; from William of Shaftoe, 2 tofts and 55 acres of land in Nesbit; from Henry Derlyng, 3 acres of meadow in East Matfen; from William of Bellingham, 1 messuage and 18 acres of land in Eachwick; from Robert of Appleton and John Fisher, half the township Dalton by Stamfordham. These lands are not held of the king, and are worth in all £2 2s. 8d. a year, except for the said half township which was worth 100s. in time of peace, but is now worth no more than £1, as has been found by inquisitions held at the king's command. Issued at Pontefract.

PRINTED SOURCE. *PH*, pp. 132-3; calendared in *CPR 1321-4*, p. 241.

DATE. Dated 12 February 1323.

NOTE. Already by 1298 the priory had the manors of Kirkheaton, Nesbit and East Matfen, as well as a substantial share of the manors of Dalton and Eachwick: documents 3 (items 23, 45,51, 63), 42. Some acquisitions authorized by this charter may represent the recovery of land previously enfeoffed: cf. document 38. The reduction of the moiety of Dalton from a peace-time value of £5 to its current value of just £1 reflects the devastation inflicted by recurrent Scottish invasions, the latest of which had been in the autumn of 1322. Robert of Appleton and John Fisher may have been acting as trustees for a third party, possibly one of the Normanville family: *NCH*, XIII, p. 165.

52. Licence from Edward III to Hexham Priory to acquire lands in mortmain in Eachwick, Whitchester, Harlow and Dalton

Whereas King Edward II granted licence by letters patent to the prior and convent of Hexham to acquire in mortmain lands and rents worth £20 a year (except for lands and rent held of the king), King Edward III now licences Gilbert le Milnestonacres, chaplain, to grant them 9 messuages, 161 acres of land, 5 acres of meadow and £2 of rent in Eachwick, Whitchester, Harlow and Dalton, worth £3 6s, 8d. a year, in part satisfaction of the £20 per year worth of lands and rent. The inquest taken by Robert Bertram, escheator in the county of Northumberland, has found that these are not held of the king. They are worth in all 8 marks a year. Issued at Reading.

PRINTED SOURCE. *PH*, II, pp. 141-2; *CPR 1345-8*, p. 331.

DATE. Dated 20 June 1347.

NOTE. Gilbert 'le Milnestonacres' of this record is recorded as Gilbert of Minstreacres in the Black Book entry relating to Eachwick: Black Book 54 (q.v.). Gilbert of Minsteracres is also recorded as the vicar of Bywell St Andrew, *c.*1352: *NCH*, VI, p. 247. The valuations here are stated ambiguously, but if the valuation of £3 6s. 8d. excludes the rents of £2, then a total value of eight marks is correct.

53. Petition from the prior and convent to the chancellor relating to boundaries in Corbridge

The prior and convent of Hexham petition the king's chancellor concerning the boundary of their manor of Anick, which they hold in free alms in the franchise of Hexham. The manor borders on the township of Corbridge, in the county of Northumberland, and the lordship of the lord Percy. Quarrels have arisen between the prior and convent, on the one part, and the men of Corbridge on the other, over a portion of land called *Trepenoke*, which the prior and canons claim as part of the manor of Anick. They request that a commission of perambulation should be directed to Sir William of Aldburgh, Henry of Barton clerk, Roger of Fulthorpe, Ellis of Thoresby, John of Mitford and John of Hallington, or some of them.

PRINTED SOURCE. *Ancient Petitions Relating to Northumberland*, ed. C. M. Fraser, Surtees Society 176 (Durham, 1966), no. 62, pp. 80-1.

DATE. 1373

LANGUAGE. French.

NOTE. Fraser notes that 'Threap Nook' means 'debatable corner'. For the ensuing commission, see document 54.

54. Royal commission to perambulate boundaries in Corbridge

15 May 1373, Westminster:

Commission to William of Aldburgh, Henry of Barton, clerk, Roger of Fulthorpe, Ellis of Thoresby, John of Mitford and John of Hallington, to perambulate between the land of Henry Percy in Corbridge, Northumberland, and the lands of the prior and convent of Hexham in Anick, within the liberty of Hexham, as the king understands that there have often been disagreements over these boundaries.

PRINTED SOURCE. *CPR 1370-4*, p. 313.

DATE. Dated 15 May 1373

NOTE This commission is a response to document 53.

55. Licence from Richard II to grant property in mortmain to Hexham Priory

18 May 1378, Westminster:

Licence, at the supplication of Henry de Percy, earl of Northumberland, for Gilbert de Umfraville, earl of Angus, to enfeoff him of the advowson of the church of Ovingham, Northumberland, held in chief. After Henry has obtained seisin, he is authorized to alienate in mortmain to the prior and convent of Hexham both that advowson and the advowson of the church of Ilkley, Yorkshire, also held in chief. The canons are to find three regular chaplains, the vicars of those churches being excepted, to celebrate divine service daily in the church of Ovingham for the good estate of the king, Gilbert and Henry during their lives, and for their souls after death, as well as for the souls of the late king and his progenitors, and of the ancestors of the said Gilbert and Henry and others, according to Henry's ordinance to that effect. Henry alleges that an earlier licence dated 25 April 1377, granted by the late king for the alienation in mortmain by Henry of the advowson of the parish church of Ilkley a yearly rent of 8 marks to the dean and chapter of Lincoln has not taken effect, and offers to surrender that licence to be cancelled.

PRINTED SOURCE. *CPR 1377-81*, p. 218.

DATE. Dated 18 May 1378.

NOTE. The superseded an earlier grant of 25 April, 1377, whose cancellation is recorded at *CPR 1374-7*, p. 456.

THE BISHOPRIC OF DURHAM

56. Petition from the prior and convent to Edward II for financial relief

The prior and convent of Hexham, who have been dispersed for four years and more because the priory has been burnt and destroyed by the Scots, petition the king to ordain something for their sustenance, to be taken from the issues of Barnard Castle or from any other escheat, until they are able to return to their own house. They also ask permission to appropriate the poor church of Alston, of which they hold the advowson, worth 10 marks in time of peace.

PRINTED SOURCE. *NCH*, III, p. 148n.

DATE. *c.* 1319. Barnard Castle was in the king's hands during the minority of the son and heir of the earl of Warwick, who was only two when his father Aske died in 1315: D. Austin, *Barnard Castle* (London, 1988), p. 8.

NOTE. Hexham Priory suffered renewed assault by the Scots in 1312 and was again occupied in 1314: *Chronicon de Lanercost*, pp. 219, 229; *PH*, I, appendix, pp. lviii-lix. In 1292, Edward I's justices had claimed against the prior of Hexham that the advowson of Alston church should belong to the king, on the grounds that Henry I had held it. The prior claimed that King John had granted the advowson to William de Vieuxpont; that William's son, Ivo had granted it to the priory; and that this grant had been confirmed by Henry III. Nevertheless, the jury found in the king's favour, and the advowson, said to be worth 40 marks, came into the king's hands. In 1306, however, when Edward was lying ill at Lanercost Priory in Cumberland, he restored the advowson to the canons in perpetuity. The canons petitioned Edward II for leave to appropriate the church in *c.*1319 by the above document, and subsequently approached Edward III to the same end in the parliament of 1334 : *Rotuli Parliamentorum; ut et Petitiones, et Placita in Parliamento*, 7 vols., Record Commission (n.p., [1783], 1832), II, p. 77. However, it was only in 1378 that the church was finally appropriated: *HHN*, VI [part 3, vol. 2], p. 82; T. H. B. Graham, 'Alston', *Transactions of the Cumberland and Westmorland Archaeological Society*, 31 (1931), pp. 19-20. The rectory of Alston was valued at £8 in the papal taxation of 1291, while the prior of Hexham held an additional 6s. 8d. of the tithes: *Taxatio*, p. 316. In their petition of 1319, the canons valued it at £6 13s. 4d., in time of peace; and at £13 6s. 8d. in their petition of 1334.

57. Petition from the prior and convent to Edward II for a grant of land in Silksworth

The prior and convent of Hexham, who are ruined by the Scottish war, petition the king to grant them the land in the township of Silksworth which has escheated to him by the death of Thomas of Lancaster, to hold of the king at the assized rent to be paid at the Exchequer, in which township the canons held part of the land of Thomas in alms.

PRINTED SOURCE. *Northern Petitions*, no. 135, p. 182.

DATE. *c* . 1323, for reasons explained by Fraser in *Northern Petitions*.

58. Licence from the bishop of Durham to grant lands in mortmain in Lanchester

Thomas Hatfield, bishop of Durham, licences Adam of Bowes, for a fine paid to the bishop, to grant in mortmain to the prior and convent of Hexham a messuage, 60 acres of land, 4 acres of meadow and 16 acres of wood in Lanchester, to be held in chief of the bishop in free alms.

PRINTED SOURCE. *PH*, II, p. 141.

DATE. Dated 1 May 1347.

NOTE. The property in question was presumably *Maydenstanhall*, for which see Black Book 69, document 59, and Watts, p. 75. The prior and convent needed licence from the bishop of Durham because the land was in the bishop's liberty.

59. The priory's property at Manor House, Lanchester

The prior of Hexham holds 1 messuage, called *Maydenstanhall* and 70 acres of land formerly belonging to Simon Dash by forinsec service, and pays 13s. 4d. a year at four terms.

PRINTED SOURCE. *Bishop Hatfield's Survey*, ed. W. Greenwell, Surtees Society 32 (Durham, 1857), p. 125.

DATE. *c.* 1377-80.

NOTE. This Hatfield Survey includes this entry as an item in the survey of Witton Gilbert, Co. Durham.

YORKSHIRE

60. Grant by the prior and convent of Hexham to William of Stonegrave of land in Stonegrave

Charter from Prior Richard and the chapter of Hexham, granting to William of Stonegrave, in fee, the whole land which they had in Stonegrave 'of the prebend of St Peter and ourselves', estimated as 6 bovates, at the yearly rent of 1 mark. Witnesses: Ernisius prior of of Marton, Walter the canon his nephew, Walter the priest of Whelpington, Richard of *Brontone*, and others.

> PRINTED SOURCE. *Abstract*, no. 16, p. 42.

> DATE. Dated 8 September 1141. However, there is perhaps a clerical error in the surviving copy. Ernisius, prior of Marton, a small house of Augustinian canons in North Yorkshire, occurs in the 1150s and was still in office in 1185 x 1191; Richard of Hexham's predecessor resigned in 1141, and Richard himself was not confirmed in office until 1142: *Heads of Religious Houses I*, pp. 166, 175.

> NOTE. Six bovates of land described as a cultivated land called Scarlet in the township of East Newton in the parish of Stonegrave later belonged to the prebend of Salton: document 71 (item 6); *PH*, II, p. 155.

61. Confirmation of a grant to the priory of land in Givendale by William son of Ulf

Notification of Robert, the dean, and the chapter of St Peters, York, that 10 years before the death of King Henry I, William son of Ulf, gave to the church of Hexham 4 bovates of land in Givendale of his fee. He afterwards confirmed that gift in free alms when he offered those 4 bovates on the altar of St Peter, the mother church, with a knife and a penny in the presence of Prior Richard and Benedict, a canon of Hexham church. Witnesses: Hugh the treasurer, Ralph de Sancta Columba, Gernagotus, Gerard, Paulinus, Simon de Sigillo, Nicholas, Simon nephew of Ansfrid, Serle and Gerard his brother, John son of Letald the canon, Gilbert prior of Holy Trinity and

Warin the monk, Ralph de Vestiario, Robert the red, William of Lincoln, Ralph de Aquila, Robert Trenchebis, Roger priest of Salton, Bernard the doctor, Gamell de Cordis and his brother Serle, and others.

> PRINTED SOURCES. *EYC*, I, no. 450, pp. 349-50; *Abstract*, no. 13, p. 41.

> DATE. *c.*1142 x 1154. This is the date attributed to the charter in *EYC*. The original grant was made *c.* 1125, since Henry I died on 1 December 1135.

NOTE. York minster could be regarded as Hexham's mother church because the archbishops of York had been instrumental in establishing the priory. In the earlier thirteenth century Prior Bernard of Hexham contended that these 4 bovates in Givendale, with the 2 bovates in Millington (document 1C) were held in free alms as of the prebend of Salton: *Abstract*, no. 15, pp. 41-2. This is likely to be a proper interpretation of the offering of the Givendale property on the altar of York Minster, as recorded above. A charter of Henry II to William son of Ulf confirming the gift of these 4 bovates to Hexham Priory is recorded in *Abstract*, no. 12, pp. 40-1. The canons also had a mid-twelfth-century confirmation of the grant by Ralph son of Ralph: *Abstract*, no. 11, p. 40. The 4 bovates are described in the Black Book account of Givendale: Black Book 86. See also *The Victoria History of the Counties of England: Yorkshire North Riding*, ed. W. Page, 3 vols (London, 1914-25), I, p. 552.

62. Charter of William, earl of Aumale relating to Edstone church

Charter of William, count of Aumale, to the church of St Andrew of Hexham and the brothers there confirming the donation made to them by Hugh of *Twithe* of the church of Edstone with 5 bovates of land, and a carucate and toft which belonged to Alan the forester, together with another carucate with the men on it, and an annual rent of 6s. from land held in Holme by Richard de Wyville. Witnesses: Philip, abbot of Meaux, Gerard de Samtour, Warin, monk of Meaux, Isaac the clerk, Norman the butler, Roger the earl's clerk, John de Meaux, Henry Foliot, Robert Constable, Engelbert de Mayners, William Samer, William of Galmpton, John of Newcastle, Richard of Bray, John Blunde.

PRINTED SOURCE. *Abstract*, no. 3, p. 39.

DATE. 1160 x 1179. Philip was abbot of Meaux, between 1160 and 1182: *Heads of Religious Houses, I*, p. 138. William, first count of Aumale, died on 20 August 1179: *ODNB*, under William le Gros, count of Aumale and earl of York.

NOTE. The canons had possession of Edstone church by 1174: document 64. The text of the charter is cited by Madden and Nichols from an exemplification by William Greenfield, archbishop of York, dated 11 July 1309 (not included in his episcopal register). A vicarage was established there in 1311, but before them the prior and convent entrusted the church to curates, perhaps as a chapel dependent on their prebendal church of Salton: *The Register of William Greenfield Lord Archbishop of York, 1306-1315*, ed. W. Brown and A. H. Thompson, 5 parts, Surtees Society 146, 149, 151-3 (Durham 1931-40), part 3, p. xliii and no. 1268, p. 59. The canons of Hexham also had a charter of William of Redbourne concerning seven bovates in Edstone. Its text seems not to survive: *Abstract*, no. 4, p. 39. The priory's title to the land in Holme was tested at York in 1284-5 in a an action between the prior and William de Wyville and others. The rent owed from Holme is there said to be 8s. 6d.: *Abstract*, no. 7, p. 40.

63. Charter of William, count of Aumale relating to a lease for life of land in Edstone and Holme

Charter of William, count of Aumale, covenanting with the canons of Hexham that no claim should be made by his heirs after his death to 3 carucates of land in Edstone and Holme granted to him by the canons for the term of his life.

Witnesses: As above.

PRINTED SOURCE. *Abstract*, no. 2, p. 39.

DATE. 1160 x 1179. As document 62: the witness list is identical.

64. Quitclaim by the priory to the archbishop of York of a rent of £5 in exchange for Edstone church.

Prior John and the convent of the church of St Andrew of Hexham quitclaim to Roger, archbishop of York and his successors a customary payment of 100 shillings due from the archdeaconary of the West Riding to the canons for their vestments, as established by his predecessors, archbishops Thomas II and Thurstan. In exchange the archbishop, at the petition of the prior and convent, has confirmed to them in perpetuity the church of Edstone quit of all services and customs, except for 4s. for synodal dues, and 3s. payable annually to Conrad the archdeacon. The prior and convent will present to the archbishop a chaplain who will answer to him for the cure of souls. Witnesses: Robert the deacon, William the cantor, John the archdeacon, Alan, Mainard, Gerald, Hamo, Nicholas and Stephen, canons of York, David and Richard, canons of Hexham.

PRINTED SOURCE. *EYC*, I, no, 146, pp. 127-8; *PH*, II, p. 86; calendared in *English Episcopal Acta 20: York 1154-81*, ed. M. Lovatt (Oxford, 2000), no. 46, pp. 54-5.

DATE. 1162 x *c*.1174, perhaps 1162 x 1164, as dated by Lovatt..

NOTE. Edstone church was granted to the canons by Hugh of Twithe: document 62. For the £5 annuity, see documents 1A and B.

65. Final concord concerning land in Edstone and rent in Holme

Final concord between William, prior of Hexham, plaintiff, and Ralph de Clera, defendant concerning two carucates of land in

Edstone and a rent of 6s. in Holme. Robert Bertram and Mabel his wife had called Ralph to warrant these properties, and there had been a duel between them in court, whereupon Ralph warranted the properties to them and recognized the right of the prior and convent to hold them in free alms. For this recognition the prior gave Ralph 40 marks of silver.

SOURCE. *Pedes Finium Ebor. Regnante Johanne*, ed. W. Brown, Surtees Society 94 (Durham, 1897), no. 428, p. 156; *Abstract*, no. 6, p. 40.

DATE. Dated 29 May, 1209.

66. Grant by the priory of property in York to William the chaplain

Prior John and the convent of Hexham grant to William, chaplain of G[eoffrey], archbishop of York, and his appointed heirs, a messuage (*mansura terre*) in York in the street called Goodramgate as a hereditary fee, to hold from the prior and convent for a payment of 3s. a year, half at Martinmans and half at Pentecost, free of all other services. His heirs who will perform fealty to the prior and convent. Witnesses: Master Simon of Apulia chancellor of York, William archdeacon of Nottingham, Peter de Ros archdeacon of Carlisle, Master Erard and Master Lisiard canons of York, Master Roger Arundel canon of Southwell, Alan the chaplain and Ralph of *Wigethot* canons of Ripon, Master John son of Otes, Nigel the clerk, Benedict the chaplain, Roger de Bavent the archbishop's steward, Ralph of Welwick, Hugh Gernagot, Richard de Wyville, Richard of Luttrington, Richard of Huddlestone and Henry of Mowat, knights, and many other clerks and laymen.

PRINTED SOURCE. *PH*, II, p. 88.

DATE. 1191 x 1194. The charter is so dated by Raine in *PH*. Geoffrey was elected archbishop of York in 1189 and consecrated in 1191: *Handbook of British Chronology*, p. 281. In 1194 Simon de Apulia was obliged to give up the chancellorship on becoming dean: *PH*, I, pp. clii-cliii and 59, note x.

67. Agreement concerning lands in Broughton demised to the priory by William of Mowbray

Agreement made between the prior and convent of Hexham and William de Mowbray, whereby William demised to the prior and convent 5½ acres of land at *Standensternes* in Broughton and a mill freely and quit of all services, until such time as he or his heirs shall assign them 5½ acres at *Brokas* which he had granted to them in alms once they have been recovered from the monks [of Rievaulx] who hold them in pledge.

PRINTED SOURCE: *EYC*, II, no. 801, p. 147; *Abstract*, no. 24, p. 44.

DATE: Dated 24 June, 1194.

NOTE. Farrer in *EYC* identifies the Broughton in question with the lost village of Little Broughton. But *Standensternes* was seemingly the name of a furlong in the fields of Great Broughton: the Black Book records an acre of demesne land there 'on the *Standandstane*' and another half an acre 'on the *Standandstan*' amongst lands attached to the cottages (Black Book 75). The interest of the monks of Rievaulx in Broughton is evident from their cartulary, though it casts no light on their tenure of *Brokas*, which they perhaps held on a lease for years. The royal *inspeximus* of 1298 (document 3) contains no grant from the Mowbrays.

68. William de Mowbray confirms gifts of his father, William, in Broughton

William de Mowbray confirms the gifts of his father William, that is a toft and croft in Broughton beside *Linebec* and land beside that toft by these bounds: to the south, the end of the road that leads from Broughton to Ingleby; to the north the road beside that township of Broughton; to the east, *Linbec*; to the west, bounds marked by standing stones and land that is subdivided. He also confirms the toft and croft formerly Lambert's, half an acre beside it, the toft that Ralph Parvus held, 100½ acres in the same township, that is 24½ acres of land from the donor's demesne, 6 acres of land beside newly broken land by *Linbeck*, 8 acres of *Langalades* towards Greenhow, 4 acres of *Eilwyne*, 4 acres of *Ernaihogas* except for 1 acre 1 rood, 6 acres of *Witelawa*, 1 acre of *Stanylandes*. He also confirms to them in free alms in the same township of his own gift 11 acres of land, that is 5½ acres in *Brokas* that the monks [of Rievaulx] held, ½ acre of *Witelawa* and 2½ acres of *Bessokez*, 1 acre of *Wossa* and 1 acre of *Mossit*. He also allows them to take from his wood in Easby for their needs whenever necessary.

PRINTED SOURCE. *Abstract*, no. 23, p. 44.

DATE. c. 1200?. After document 67, since the monks evidently no longer held *Brokas*, but maybe not long after, since the monks' surrender of that land was expected in 1194.

NOTE. This charters probably describes lands in both Great and Little Broughton (Black Book 74, 75). *Lindbek* or *Lynbek* occurs as a boundary marker on both properties (cf. *Linbec* above), and both properties had land on Whitlaw (cf. *Witelawa* above) and on the *Langlandes* (cf. *Langalandes* above). In the thirteenth century, as by implication for the compiler of the Black Book (Black Book 76) Ingleby and Greenhow were regarded as separate settlements: Ingleby was described as Ingleby by Greenhow in 1285: Watts, p. 331. The canons also had a charter of William de Mowbray, later produced in a legal dispute, 'granting all his demesne messuage with four bovates, and all his other lands, a mill, &c. in Little Broughton, to the church of Hexham in pure alms, free of all service, &c., also an obligation of the same William, aquitting the Prior, &c. of all demands': *Abstract*, no. 29, p. 43.

69. Grant by the priory of land at Newton in Givendale

Prior John and the convent of Hexham grant a tenement and lands in Newton, in Givendale, to John of Newton for a rent of 50s. a year.

> SOURCE. *Abstract,* no. 17, p. 42.

> DATE. Dated 1251

70. Final concord relating to land in Flaxton

Fine before the king's justices at Westminster between John, prior of Hexham, plaintiff (represented by Robert of Belsay), and Nicholas of Flaxton and his wife Emma, impedients, concerning 1 messuage and 2 bovates of land in Flaxton. The prior and his church of Hexham are to have the land, giving Nicholas and Emma 40s sterling.

> PRINTED SOURCE. *Feet of Fines, Northumberland and Durham,* no. 249, p. 102.

> DATE. Three weeks after Michaelmas ('20 October'), 1266

71. A survey of the lands of prebend of Salton

The prebendary of Salton has the following lands and properties.

1. The church at Salton with all the tithes, both great and small, and with jurisdiction in all spiritual cases.

2. In the township of Salton he has a demesne manor with 2 carucates of cultivated demesne land, 13 acres of meadow, and an enclosure called *Frensholm* containing 2½ acres. He has a mill and warren in all his lands. He also has there 20 husbandmen, each of whom holds 1 toft and 2 bovates of land, and pays 8s. per year; and also another tenant who holds 3 bovates of land and pays 12s. a year. All these tenants will carry the lord's timber for constructing and repairing buildings, wherever it shall be bought; they should carry the lord's food to York, and elsewhere, whenever they are asked; they will also repair the mill pond whenever necessary. He also has there 10 *gresmanni*, each of whom holds a toft and an acre of land, and pays 1s. 4d. a year, performs 4 harvest works, and gives a hen and 20 eggs each year.

3. In Brawby he has 11 tenants each of whom has a toft and 2 bovates of land and pays 8s. per year; another 2 tenants each of whom holds 4 bovates of land and pays 17s. a year; and another 3 tenants, each of whom holds 3 bovates of land, and pays 12s. a year. All these perform the same services as the tenants of Salton. He also has there 8 *gresmenni*, each of whom holds 1 toft and 1½ acres of land and pays 1s. 6d. a year, and performs 2 harvest works, and gives a cock at Christmas and 20 eggs at Easter.

4. In Great Barugh he has 4 tenants, each of whom has 4 bovates of land and pays 12s. a year; and also 3 tenants each of whom holds 2 bovates of land, and pays 6s. a year. All these perform the same services as the tenants of Salton. He also has there a tenant who holds 1 bovate of land and pays 3s. a year.[468]

5. In Little Barugh he has a tenant, who holds 2 bovates of land, pays 8s. a year, and performs the same services as the tenants of Salton. He also has there 2 *gresmanni*, each of whom pays 1s. a year.

6. In the township of [East]Newton William of Newton holds 24 bovates of land, pays £2 10s. a year, and performs suit to the court of Salton. Sir J. of Stonegrave holds there a cultivated land[469] called Scarlet containing 6 bovates[470] and pays 13s. 4d. a year.

7. In the township of Flaxton he has 3 tenants, each of whom holds 2 bovates of land and pays £3 6s. 6d. for all services.

8. In the township of Millington, the heirs of Gilbert of Givendale hold 6 bovates of land and pay 10s. a year for all services, except for suit of the court of Salton.

---

[468] Because of the ordering of the information here it is not certain that this last tenant owed services like the rest of the tenants.
[469] MS *cultura*.
[470] See document 61.

PRINTED SOURCE. *PH*, II, pp. 83-4; calendared in 'Extents of the Prebends of York [*c.* 1295] and Extent of Monk Friston, 1320', ed. T. A. M. Bishop, in *Miscellanea, IV,* Yorkshire Archaeological Society, Record Series 94 (1937), pp. 16-17.

DATE. c. 1294-5. The twelfth-century date suggested by Raine in *PH*, from palaeographical appearance, is unlikely to be correct. The survey is recorded in British Library, Cotton MS. Claudius B.III amongst surveys for most of the prebends of York. Though they are written in a archaic hand which resembles that of the early thirteenth century, two are dated 1295 and another 1294. This, with the evidence of personal names that occur elsewhere, suggests that that they all date to about that time: 'Extents of the Prebends of York', ed. Bishop, p. 1. A later version of this survey is printed in *PH*, II, pp. 154-5.

72. Ordinance of the prior of Hexham, as prebendary of Salton, concerning the vicarage of Salton

R[obert], prior of Hexham, as prebendary of Salton, ordains that John of Thwing, perpetual vicar of Salton, shall have all the alterage of that church, in small tithes, oblations and mortuaries, and the tithe of hay of Salton and Brawby, saving to himself and his successors the tithes of wool and lambs and all garb tithes, all the tithes of demesne produce, and Peter's Pence. He also ordains that the vicar of Salton shall pay an annual pension of 10s. owing to the church of Normanby as well as supplying those adornments of the high altar that the priors of Hexham used to supply, lights in the choir, the stipend of clerks, with wine, hosts, and other things required by divine office. The vicar shall be quit of all other charges, ordinary or extraordinary. Issued at Salton.

SOURCE. *Abstract*, no. 1, p. 39.

DATE. Dated 27 August, 1312.

73. Lease by the prior and convent of a tenement in York

John of Cottingham, rector of the church of North Cave, leases to Ellis of Walkington, warden of the house of vicars choral and all the vicars, for 40 years from Pentecost 1366, a place of land with buildings which he had of the demise of the prior and convent of Hexham, appropriated to the prebend of Salton in the church of York, lying in breadth between the tenement of the prebend of Langtoft and that of the prebend of Husthwaite, and in length 89 feet from the street called Ogleforth [in York]. Witnesses: Roger of Hovingham mayor, Robert Barry, William of Leicester and Roger de Moreton bailiffs, John of Acaster, Robert of Holme, John Capron, John of Beverley, and others. Issued at York.

PRINTED SOURCE. *Charters of the Vicars Choral of York Minster: City of York and its Suburbs to 1546*, ed. N. J. Tringham, York Archaeological Society, Record Series 148 (York, 1993), no. 368, pp. 203-4.

DATE. Dated 23 May 1366.

5. PROPERTIES OF HEXHAM PRIORY ACQUIRED BY 1379

Acomb, liberty of Hexham (par. St John Lee): with Black Book 5. The Black Book records a tithe barn and garden. The canons were given a rood of land for a tithe barn by archbishops Walter de Gray (1216-55) and Walter Giffard (1266-79): document 3 (item 7). The Dissolution survey confirms that the priory owned the garb tithes: document 4A.

Aldescheles, in Simonburn township, liberty of Tynedale with Priorsdale and Alston Moor (par. Simonburn): with Black Book 8. The Black Book records rents of 8s. from the 'land of *Aldescheles* by Tecket', granted by Henry de Graham sometime 'time out of mind' before 1298: document 3 (item 43). There were two successive Henry de Grahams as lords of the manor of Simonburn in the mid to late thirteenth century, the latter of whom granted the manor to his brother-in-law in 1291: *NCH*, XV, p. 194. The Black Book reports that the priory was no longer able to collect these rents even before the Black Death.

Allendale, [Northumberland] (par. Allendale): with Black Book 5. The Black Book records the site of a building with a garden and a croft containing ½ acre as glebe of the church. The priory's possession of the chapel and churchyard was confirmed by agreement with the bishop of Durham in 1162 x 1166: document 6. It is not stated precisely when or how the chapel first came into the possession of the priory, but it may have been included in the grant of Hexham church made by Archbishop Thomas II, 1108 x 1114: *NCH*, III, p. 131. The Dissolution survey records the priory's possession of the tithes and offerings belonging to the chapel: document 4A.

Allerdale, Cumbria, see Ellenborough.

Allerwash, barony of Langley (par. Warden): Black Book 22. The Black Book records the mill and 1¼ acres adjoining it. The mill was granted by Ughtred of Allerwash sometime 'time out of mind' before 1298: document 3 (item 12). The priory owned the garb tithes of the township at the time of the Dissolution: document 4A. See also Owmers.

Alston, liberty of Tyndale with Priorsdale and Alston Moor (par. Alston): Black Book 15. The Black Book records lands of unstated extent with definite bounds, and common rights throughout Alston Moor. Eight messuages and a carucate of land were granted by Ivo de Vieuxpont, as confirmed by Henry III in 1232 and again by Edward I in 1298 and 1307: document 2 (item 7), 3 (item 40), 28. Extensive common pasture on Alston Moor is implied both by the Black Book entry for Alston, and in that for Priorsdale: Black Book 17. Ivo de Vieuxpont granted the priory the advowson of the church with the chapel of Garrigill during the early thirteenth century, but their title to the advowson was successfully challenged by Edward I's justices in 1292 : document 2 (item 8), *PQW*, p. 120.[471] The canons petitioned Edward II for leave to appropriate the church *c.*1319, but were granted it only in 1378: document 56 and note. The Dissolution survey suggests that wool was the predominant source of tithe revenue: document 4A.

Anick, liberty of Hexham (par. St John Lee): Black Book 2. The Black Book records a grange containing a garden and 218½ acres of arable and 50 acres of meadow, with a further 40 acres of demesne and 30 acres of several pasture. The demesne also had a detached 30 acres of land in Corbridge, which the Black Book calls the *Bisschopprek*. At Anick there were also 12 husbandlands, 19 cottages and a mill. The church at Hexham held 6 bovates in Anick as the endowment of the church there from its earliest days: document 5. The manor and township, with appurtenances including a mill, were granted with the townships of Sandhoe and Yarridge, by Archbishop Thomas II of York, 1108 x 1114: documents 1A, 2 (item 1), 3 (item 2), 16 (item 2). Documents 1A and 16 (item 2) imply that in the early twelfth century there were two hamlets of Anick, though only one is mentioned in later records. A road from Anick giving access to the pasture beyond Birkey Burn, mentioned in the Black Book account, was granted by Archbishop Walter de Gray of York in 1226: documents 9, 16 (item

---

[471] We have found no warrant for Hodgson's statement that the grant was confirmed by King John in 1215 *HHN*, IV [part 2, vol . 3], p. 41.

18). The Dissolution survey records the garb tithes of Anick as the most valuable in Hexhamshire: document 4A.

Apperley, [Northumberland] (par. Bywell St Peter): no Black Book reference, see Stocksfield.

Barrasford, Northumberland (par. Chollerton): Black Book 33. The Black Book records a tenement, with 30 acres of arable land and 1 acre of meadow. This corresponds closely to the 2 tofts and 30 acres of land granted by Margery de Umfraville in 1272 x 1291 (between Edward I's accession and Margery's death by 1291): document 3 (item 19); *NCH*, IV, pp. 314. The Black Book records a tithe barn there, and the Dissolution survey confirms that the canons had the garb tithe: document 4A.

Barugh, Great and Little, see Great Barugh and Little Barugh, below.

Bavington, Little, *see* **Little Bavington**, below.

Beaufront in Sandhoe township, liberty of Hexham (par. St John Lee): with Black Book 2. Properties here are poorly defined in the Black Book. Two tenements with 17 acres of land, were recorded here at the Dissolution: document 4A. Their earlier history is apparently unknown, unless they were part of the priory's endowment at Sandhoe (q.v.).

Beaumont in Chollerton township, Northumberland (par. Chollerton): Black Book 31. The Black Book records the 'whole land' of Beaumont as a property of unstated size with defined boundaries, and with pasture rights on Chollerton commons. The priory had tenants there. The 'land' or 'hamlet' of Beaumont, with enclosed bounds, in the territory of Chollerton, was granted by Gilbert de Umfraville, lord of Chollerton as of the barony of Prudhoe, in 1226 x 1232: document 3 (item 15). Gilbert inherited the barony of Prudhoe in the former year: Sanders, p. 73. For the terminal date, see document 2, item 6.

Benwell, Northumberland (par. St. John, Newcastle upon Tyne): Black Book 65. The Black Book records a plot of four acres or more with a wood, having defined boundaries, called *Wodhall*. This was granted by Hugh Delaval, probably shortly before 1272:

Edward I's *inspeximus* records the grant as dating from the reign of Henry III, but Hugh is otherwise recorded as living only between 1277 and 1302: document 3 (item 49); *NCH*, IX, p. 167; XIII, pp. 224-5.

Bingfield, liberty of Hexham (par. St John Lee): Black Book 4. The Black Book records a manor, with 254¾ acres of land and 16 acres of pasture, husbandmen and cottagers. A moiety of the township was granted by Germund, about whom nothing seems to be known, sometime before 1140: documents 3 (item 4), 16 (item 6). Further property, said to have a rentable value of £4 (1298) or 6s. 8d. (*c.* 1328 and 1350), was granted by Robert of Skipton before 1288: documents 3 (item 5), 16 (item 15), 17 (item 8).

Birtley, Northumberland (par. Chollerton): Black Book 35. The Black Book records a tenement with a garden and a croft containing 6 acres. This was the toft with 7 acres land granted by Richard de Umfraville, as lord of Prudhoe, c.1192 x 1226: document 3 (item 16); Sanders, p. 73. Birtley chapel was granted to the priory as a dependency of Chollerton (q.v.) by by Odinel I or Odinel II de Umfraville, barons of Prudhoe, before 1182. The priory's possession of the garb tithes there is confirmed by the Dissolution survey: document 4A.

Bitchfield, [Northumberland] (par. Stamfordham): no Black Book reference. In 1246 the priory was given the garb tithes of the township or hamlet of Bitchfield by Nicholas Farnham, bishop of Durham, in part settlement of a dispute over the church of Stamfordham (q.v.): documents 3 (item 60), 47.

Brawby, Cleveland and Yorkshire (par. Salton): Black Book 78. The Black Book records 51 bovates and 3 acres of land (8 bovates and 3 acres as demesne lands, 43 bovates as bondage land), together with 13 cottages and their smallholdings. These belonged to the prebend of Salton (q.v.), granted by Archbishop Thurstan of York, 1114 x 1140: document 71 (item 3). The priory had the township's tithes of grain, wool and lambs, but offerings, small tithes and tithes of hay were assigned to the vicarage in 1312: documents 4B, 72.

Brenkley, Northumberland (par. Ponteland): Black Book 50. The Black Book records a rent of 13s. 4d. from Brenkley Mill by the gift of Henry of Farlington. This is confirmed by charter evidence from 1216 x 1242 (between Henry III's accession and Henry of Farlington's death by 1242): document 3 (item 54); *NCH*, XII, p. 521.

Broughton, Little, see **Little Broughton**, below.

Byers in Hartleyburn township, barony of Langley (par. Haltwhistle): Black Book 18. The Black Book records a property within defined boundaries, and implies predominantly pastoral use. This was the land within defined bounds, with rights of pasture beyond those bounds, granted by Adam de Tindale I (died 1188) or Adam de Tindale II (died 1233), barons of Langley: document 3 (item 11). By the Dissolution it had become Byers Park: document 4A. In 1239, an agreement was reached by which the prior and convent of Hexham conceded rights of pasture to the nuns of Lambley and their tenants, in token of which, the prioress and convent rendered an altar cloth at Hexham on St Andrews day each year: documents 32, 33, and cf. document 34.

Byresfeld **of Milbourne**, see Milbourne Grange.

Carlisle, Cumbria: Black Book 6. The Black Book records 2 tenements and a croft. These were granted by David, King of Scots, and Henry, his son, 1136 x 1152: documents, 1C.

Carraw, liberty of Tynedale with Priorsdale and Alston Moor (par. Warden): Black Book 8. The Black Book records the township with defined boundaries, the pasture of Carraw as a severalty, 'a parcel of the pasture of Carraw' called *Fethreschaue* that the priory leased out, and rights of common pasture. There is no reference to subordinate hereditary tenants. The hamlet of Carraw was granted by Richard Comyn, 1139 x *c.*1179, together with a ploughland in *Rischeles*, (q.v.) with common pasture at Henshaw (q.v.): document 3 (item 36). For the dating, see the note to document 19. The 'pasture all through the pasture of Syde' referred to in the Black Book is Carraw Side Moor, on the north side of Hadrian's Wall, which was granted by William I, king of Scots in 1165 x 1214 (the regnal limits): documents. 3 (item 35). This grant is noted in *RRS II*, no. 538, p. 474, without more precise dating. Richard Comyn's grant may be associated with his grant of nearby properties in Stonecroft (q.v.), similarly bounded by Hadrian's Wall.

Catton, liberty of Hexham (par. Allendale): with Black Book 5. The Black Book records a tithe barn and garden. The canons were given a rood of land for a tithe barn by archbishops Walter de Gray (1216-55) and Walter Giffard (1266-79): document 3 (item 7).

Cheeseburn, Northumberland (par. Stamfordham): Black Book 60. The Black Book records the manor of Cheeseburn, having a chapel and a core of lands ('the grange') with defined bounds but with a further 85½ acres of arable and a rood of meadow dispersed outside these bounds to the east. In addition there were pastures of unstated dimensions and 6 acres of land 'in Nesbit field'. The manor was granted, with Nesbit, by John of Normanvill, 1221 x 1243, probably 1228 x 1243: documents 3 (item 59), 42.

Chesterhope, [Redesdale] (par. Corsenside): with Black Book17. The Black Book records 2 tofts, 2 crofts and 2 bovates 'called a husbandland'. These were the 2 tofts and 2 bovates of land granted by Ralph of Gunnerton, sometime 'time out of mind' before 1298: Black Book 34; document 3 (item 20). A Ralph of Gunnerton held the township of Chesterhope of Gilbert de Umfraville in 1242, but an earlier Ralph of Gunnerton was living *c*.1174 : *HHN*, II [part 2, vol. 1], p. 165n; *NCH*, XIII, p. 164. Chesterhope's positioning in the Black Book, alongside properties in the liberty of Tynedale with Priorsdale and Alston Moor, is misleading.

Chipchase, Northumberland (par. Chollerton): Black Book 36. The Black Book records a tithe barn with a garden. Chipchase chapel was granted to the priory as a dependency of Chollerton (q.v.) by by Odinel I or Odinel II de Umfraville, barons of Prudhoe, before 1182. This was complemented with a building (*domus*), presumably used for the tithe barn, and 1 acre of land, granted by Robert de Lisle, 1261 x 1272: document 3 (item 27). The charter is said to date from the reign of Henry III, so before 1272, but Robert did not inherit until after 1261: *NCH*, IV, p. 331. The Dissolution survey confirms the priory's possession of the garb tithes: document 4A.

Chollerton, Northumberland (par. Chollerton): Black Book 32. The Black Book records two large tenancies in the hands of Hugh

Colstane and Alan Hoghird. Their lands were similarly dispersed in many parcels, and those of Hugh (probably those of Alan as well) were made up of former husbandlands. Chollerton church, with its dependent chapels of Birtley, Chipchase, Gunnerton, Little Swinburn, Kirkheaton and Colwell, together with 8 bovates, of the church's endowment in the township of Chollerton, and 5 additional acres of land there, were granted by Odinel I (died after c.1145) or Odinel II (died 1182), barons of Prudhoe: document 3 (item 14); Sanders, p. 73. The Dissolution survey confirms the priory's possession of the garb tithes: document 4A.

Clifton, Northumberland (par. Stannington): Black Book 48. The Black Book records a rent of 1s. 6d. there, from lands of the Merlay chantry in Stannington Church, that had been granted by Bernard, prior of Hexham, c.1226 x c.1246: *Heads of Religious Houses 940-1216*, p. 390. Robert de Merlay's foundation charter for the chantry records endowments of 10 acres of land in Clifton and 20 acres in Colwell which he had by grant of the prior and convent of Hexham, as well as a grant in free alms of half a carucate in Colwell that he also had by their grant: *HHN*, VI [part 3, vol. 2], pp. 74-5.

Coastley, in the township of West Quarter, liberty of Hexham (par. Hexham): with Black Book 5. The Black Book records a rent of 4 marks annually from the lord of Coastley for licence to have a mill. The Dissolution survey shows that the priory owned the garb tithes: document 4A.

Coldstrother, in Kirkheaton township, Northumberland (par. Kirkheaton): Black Book 41. The Black Book records Coldstrother as combined with Kirkheaton (q.v.) as a single manor. The Dissolution survey records property in the township of Kirkheaton, but does not mention Coldstrother, suggesting that the township lands recorded in the Black Book were in the former: document 4A.

Colwell, Northumberland (par. Chollerton): Black Book 40. The Black Book records rights of pasture in Colwell for 400 sheep, together with 30 oxen, 10 cows and a bull. This corresponds imperfectly with Walter Corbet's grant of pasture for 32 oxen, 10 cows, and 280 sheep, 1216 x 1272: document 3 (item 22). The Black Book also records a tithe barn with a garden attached. Colwell chapel was granted to the priory as a dependency of

Chollerton (q.v.) by by Odinel I or Odinel II de Umfraville, barons of Prudhoe, before 1182, and the Dissolution survey confirms that the canons had the garb tithes of the township: documents 3 (item 14), 4A.

Corbridge, Northumberland, borough (par. Corbridge): Black Book 30. The Black Book records 10 burgages, Corbridge having been reckoned a borough since at least 1201: *CChR*, p. 87b. Rents from 15 messuages in Corbridge were given by various donors at unknown dates before 1298: document 3 (item 29). The Black Book also records 30 acres of land in the territory of Corbridge called the *Bisschopprek*, which were regarded as appurtenances of Anick; their origin is seemingly unrecorded: Black Book 2.

Cowden in the township of Great Swinburn and Colwell, Northumberland (par. Chollerton): Black Book 37. The Black Book records a property of unspecified size with defined bounds under single management, perhaps predominantly pastoral, with rights of common pasture for 100 working beasts on Gunnerton Moor. Land and pasture were granted by Richard de Umfraville, lord of Prudhoe, c.1192 x 1226: document 3 (item 17); Sanders, p. 73. The rights of common pasture on Gunnerton moor were given by Ralph of Gunnerton sometime 'time out of mind' before 1298: document 3 (item 18).

Dalton, Northumberland (par. Newburn, detached): Black Book 55. The Black Book records the whole manor of Dalton, with demesne lands, free tenants and customary tenants, but the canons did not acquire it as such. From 'time out of mind' by 1298 they held a third part of the township by grant of Ralph of Gunnerton, and 4 bovates of land, and a rent of 5s. 6d. from the mill there by grant of William of Dalton: document 3 (item 63). For Ralph of Gunnerton, see under Chesterhope. The gift from William of Dalton was probably made appreciably later, in the second half of the thirteenth century: *NCH*, XIII, p. 165. Subsequently the priory's acquisition in mortmain of half of the township at the hands of Robert of Appleton and John Fisher was authorized by Edward II in 1323: document 51. They were similarly authorized to acquire an unspecified amount of property in Dalton in 1347: document 52.

Dissington, Northumberland (par. Newburn): Black Book, 53. The priory had no property in Dissington, but their tenants at Eachwick owed suit of mill there. in exchange for which the lord of Dissington owed two corporal cloths annually at the high altar of the priory church, as well as an obligation of respect for the prior.

Dotland, liberty of Hexham (par. Hexham): Black Book 5. The Black Book records a complex lordship comprising a park, woodland, demesne lands and customary tenants. The township of Dotland, described as 'the land of Robert Calin', was granted with dependencies at Grottington (q.v.) and Hazeldean (q.v.) by Archbishop Thurstan of York, 1114 x 1140: documents 2 (item 2), 3 (item 3), 16 (item 4). Other lands there or thereabouts to a total of 209½ acres were granted by Archbishop Walter Gray of York in 1226, and a further 94 acres in 1229: documents 9, 11, 14, 16 (items 7, 9, 17). Much of this later acquisition was perhaps land cleared for cultivation quite recently to judge from its proximity to the archbishop's assarts. The Black Book records that 184 acres of the priory's land in Dotland was 'exchequer land'. The small park of 27¼ acres mentioned in the Black Book was in existence by 1296, also by grant of the archbishops of York: document 16, item 10. The canons were authorized to enclose the park with a higher wall in 1354: document, 18.

Eachwick, Northumberland (par. Heddon on the Wall): Black Book 54. The Black Book records a manor with capital messuage, demesne lands, customary tenants and a couple of dependent freeholders. Half the manor was granted by Robert Delaval (of Seaton Delaval), and Richilda, his mother, before 1161: documents 1C, 3 (item 44). In addition the canons also had charters from the reign of Henry III relating to 10 acres of land in Eachwick acquired from Thomas of Eachwick, and a further 7 acres of land from Peter of Fawdon: document 3 (item 45). In 1323 they were licensed to acquire in mortmain a messuage and 18 acres in Eachwick from William of Bellingham, and in 1347 they were similarly licenced to acquire 5 husbandlands that had previously belonged to John of Fawden in 1347: Black Book 54; documents 51, 52. By 1379 the priory held three-quarters of Eachwick: *NCH*, XIII, p. 89.

East Matfen, Northumberland (par. Stamfordham): Black Book, 54 (incomplete). The manor, 6 messuages and 3 carucates were granted by Thomas of Fenwick during Henry III's reign, after 1233. Thomas had inherited the property as a minor before March 1226, and was still a minor in 1233. His grant was confirmed by Robert de Lisle, as superior lord: document 3 (item 51): *NCH*, XII, pp. 350-1, 365. In 1323 the canons were authorized to acquire 3 acres of meadow from Henry Derlyng: document 51. Besides 4 tenements in East Matfen, the canons had a cottage and a croft at West Matfen at the Dissolution: document 4. In 1246 the priory was given the garb tithes of the township or hamlet of East Matfen by Nicholas Farnham, bishop of Durham, in part settlement of a dispute over the church of Stamfordham (q.v.): documents 3 (item 60), 47.

East Newton, [Cleveland and Yorkshire] (par. Stonegrave): no Black Book reference. The priory had 30 bovates, granted as part of the prebend of Salton (q.v.), by Archbishop Thurstan of York, 1114 x 1140: document 71 (item 6). By the later twelfth century six of these bovates were subinfeudated, and are later recorded with the name Scarlet: documents 60, 71 (item 6). See also document 69. Newton was still listed as a component of the prebend of Salton in a survey dated by Raine to the late fifteenth century: *PH*, II, p. 155. Possibly it is absent from the surviving text of the Black Book because of damage to the end of the manuscript.

East Swinburn, see Little Swinburn

Edstone, Cleveland and Yorkshire (par. Great Edstone): Black Book 80. The Black Book records a single small freeholding, 8 acres of demesne meadow, 9 cottages, and 40 bovates leased to tenants. Although adjacent to Salton, the priory's property in Edstone was not part of the prebend. The church with 5 bovates, and an additional toft, 2 carucates of land in Edstone and Holme, and 6s. rent were granted by Hugh of *Twithe*, c.1162 x 1174 (perhaps by 1162 x 1164), and soon afterwards leased it for life to William, count of Aumale: documents 62-4. Their right was confirmed in the king's court in 1209: document 65.

Ellenborough, Cumbria (par. Dearham): with Black Book, 6. The Black Book records a croft and toft with 20 acres of arable and pasture in the town field. The location of Ellenborough near the coast makes it possible that this represents the 4 bovates of land and the house for a herring-fishery in *Eltadala* that were given by Waltheof and his son Alan, sometime before 1167: document 1C. This identification depends upon Raine's identification of *Eltadala* with Allerdale, but it is encouraging that the first element in the two names Ellenborough and Allerdale are both taken from the River Ellen.

Elrington, liberty of Tynedale with Priorsdale and Alston Moor (par. Warden): Black Book 7. The Black Book records a rent as 13s. 4d. from Elrington Mill by gift of Nicholas de Vieuxpont. This was granted by Ivo de Vieuxpont, probably in the earlier thirteenth century: document 3 (item 42). For the dating, see Alston and Garrigill.

Errington, liberty of Hexham (par. St John Lee): no Black Book reference. The Dissolution survey shows that the priory owned the garb tithes: document 4A.

Eshells, liberty of Hexham (par. Hexham): no Black Book reference. The whole township was granted by Thomas of Dilston, 1203 x 1212, but subsequently exchanged with Walter de Gray, archbishop of York, in 1216 x 1226: documents 7, 8. Eshells is therefore recorded in neither the *inspeximus* of 1298 (document 3) nor the Black Book. However, the people of Eshells owed suit to a mill (perhaps Whitley Mill) that the archbishop granted the priory in 1226: document 9.

Featherstone, township, barony of Langley (par. Haltwhistle): with Black Book 19. Rights of pasture in the fee of Featherstone, described in the Black Book as on Featherstone Common, were granted by Adam de Tindale I, baron of Langley, *c.*1165 x 1188: document 20. The Black Book also records rights of there on land formerly belonging to the Lucy family, presumably granted by one of the Lucy barons of Langley, before the main line failed in 1368, though no record of the grant appears to have survived. In 1296, the priory was assessed as having £10 13s. 9d. of taxable goods at Wydon, in the barony of Featherstone, which suggests they had a grange there at that time: *Northumberland Lay Subsidy Roll*, p. xviii, and no. 26, p. 10.

Flaganclough (unidentified), liberty of Tynedale with Priorsdale and Alston (par. Hatwhistle?): Black Book 10. The Black Book records 1½ acres of arable 'at the foot of Flaghonburne'.

Flaxton, Cleveland and Yorkshire (par. Bossall): Black Book 84. The Black Book records a free bovate and 5 customary bovates. Six bovates of land were granted as part of the prebend of Salton (q.v.) by Archbishop Thurstan of York, 1114 x 1140: document 71 (item 7). The canons' title to a messuage and two of these bovates was confirmed by a final concord of 1266: document 70.

Garrigill, liberty of Tynedale with Priorsdale and Alston Moor (par. Alston): Black Book 16. The Black Book records a toft called 'Thruswell' and rights of pasture. It was given to them by Ivo de Vieuxpont before 1232: document 2 (item 7). The chapel, with the advowson of Alston church, was granted to the priory by Ivo de Vieuxpont in the early thirteenth century: document 2 (item 8), and see under Alston.

Givendale in the Hole: see Great Givendale

Great Barugh, Cleveland and Yorkshire (par. Kirby Misperton): Black Book 82. The Black Book records 24 bovates, leased to tenants. This land was granted, as part of the prebend of Salton (q.v.), by Archbishop Thurstan of York, 1114 x 1140. The survey of the prebend of Salton from c. 1294-5 records only 23 bovates: document 71 (item 4).

Great Broughton, Cleveland and Yorkshire (par. Kirkby in Cleveland): Black Book 75. The Black Book records a messuage, 3½ bovates and 14 acres of arable land, all very dispersed, and 4¾ acres of meadow, of which 2 acres was in a croft. There were also 3 cottages with a croft and 3½ acres of land. These probably represent lands given by William de Mowbray 'in Broughton' in the later twelfth century, though it is not possible to identify them closely from the charters: documents 67, 68.

Great Givendale, Cleveland and Yorkshire (par. Great Givendale): Black Book 86. The Black Book records a toft, a garden, and 4 bovates. The 4 bovates were given by William son of Ulf in about 1125, apparently as an attachment to the prebend of Salton, though

Great Givendale, in the East Riding like Millington (q.v.), is some distance away from the other lands of the prebend: documents 1C, 61. These were four of the six bovates ascribed to Millington (q.v.) in *c*.1294-5: document 71 (item 8).

Great Stainton, bishopric of Durham (par. Great Stainton): Black Book 71. The Black Book records 3 tofts, 4 bovates of dispersed demesne arable, and 3 acres of demesne meadow. The origins of the priory's title seem not to be recorded.

Great (West) Swinburn, Northumberland (par. Chollerton): with Black Book 40. The Black Book records an acre in the field there. This was given by John of Worcester, *c*.1240 x *c*.1257: document 3 (item 31).

Greencroft, bishopric of Durham (par. Lanchester): Black Book 68. The Black Book records a property called the Fenhall, of unspecified size, with defined boundaries. The origins of the priory's title seem not to be recorded. It seems likely to have been a gift in free alms by a bishop of Durham as lord of Greencroft: cf. *Boldon Buke: A Survey of the Possessions of the See of Durham*, ed. W. Greenwell, Surtees Society (Durham, 1852), p. 31.

Grindon, Liberty of Tynedale with Priorsdale and Aston Moor (par. Haydon Bridge), with Black Book 8. The Black Book records a rood of land in a demesne toft.

Grottington, liberty of Hexham (par. St John Lee): with Bingfield, Black Book 4. The Black Book records a single 'holding' of Grottington, with stated bounds. Two Grottingtons were granted, with Dotland, by Archbishop Thurstan of York, 1114 x 1140: document 1B, 3 (item 3), 16 (item 4). The smaller of these, Little Grottington, became known as Todridge, as stated in the Black Book, where it is recorded as a 'piece of arable' with defined bounds: Black Book 4. The only indication of size is the Dissolution survey, where a tenure called Grottington is described as containing a tenement, 10 acres of meadow and 30 acres of arable, with common rights: document 4A.

Gunnerton, Northumberland (par. Chollerton): Black Book 34. The Black Book records a tenement, garden croft, 2 husbandlands,

1½ acres of meadow and a tithe barn. Gunnerton chapel was granted to the priory as a dependency of Chollerton (q.v.) by by Odinel I or Odinel II de Umfraville, barons of Prudhoe, before 1182. The Dissolution survey confirms that the canons had the garb tithes there: document 4A. Ralph of Gunnerton and Thurkill of *Cadeiou* granted three tofts and a tithe barn there, together with 2 bovates and 12 acres of land sometime 'time out of mind' before 1298: document 3 (item 25). For Ralph of Gunnerton, see under Chesterhope. Rights of common on Gunnerton moor for 100 cattle coming from Cowden shieling, also granted by Ralph of Gunnerton, are ascribed in the Black Book to the priory's property at Cowden: Black Book 37; document 3 (items 18). The priory's property at Stelden also had pasture on Gunnerton moor: Black Book 38; document 35, 45.

Hallington, liberty of Hexham (par. St John Lee). The Black Book records a tithe barn and an adjacent garden: Black Book 5. The canons were given a rood of land for a tithe barn by archbishops Walter de Gray (1216-55) and Walter Giffard (1266-79): document 3 (item 7).

Hamburn, liberty of Hexham (par. Hexham): no Black Book reference. The mill of Hamburn, together with a Newbiggin Mill and some land, were granted by Archbishop Walter Gray of York, 1216 x 1255. Hamburn is described in Edward I's confirmation charter as a township: Document 3 (item 6). Other early references are simply to the 'mill of Hamburn': Documents 16 (item 8), 17 (item 9), and see *PH*, II, p. 105. Ham Burn is the name of a burn feeding into Rowley Burn (NY 904585), but Hamburn Hall (NY 907584) is recorded in a charter of 1229; *NCH*, IV, p. 59. The mill does not seem to have survived to 1379.

Harlow, Northumberland (par. Heddon on the Wall): with Black Book 54. The Black Book records the process by which the priory acquired a rent of £2 6s. 8d. in Harlow and Whitchester (q.v.) from John of Fawdon, who also granted them the reversion of the tenements and land from which the rent was due through the agency of two trustees, Gilbert of Minsteracres, chaplain, and Thomas of Rainton: Black Book 54. These two acquired a licence to alienate these lands to the priory in mortmain in 1347: document 52; *NCH*, XIII, p. 88. However, the Black Book states that the donor's intentions had not yet been fulfilled by 1379 for want of a licence to enter from Gilbert de Umfraville, earl of Angus, as lord of the barony of Prudhoe.

Hartlepool, bishopric of Durham (par. Hart): Black Book 72. The Black Book records 2 tenements and an (uncollectable) rent of 5s. The origins of their title are apparently unrecorded.

Hawkwell, Northumberland (par. Stamfordham): Black Book 58. The Black Book records an acre of land in the fields of Hawkwell. This is perhaps related to the priory's acquisition of the garb tithes of Hawkwell in 1246 by grant of Nicholas Farnham, bishop of Durham, in part settlement of a dispute over the church of Stamfordham (q.v.): documents 3 (item 60), 47. These tithes are not independently valued in the Dissolution survey: document 4A.

Haydon, Northumberland (par. Warden): Black Book 21. The Black Book records a tithe barn, 7½ acres of land, and stinted common pasture for 30 working beasts and 120 sheep. A messuage, 7 acres of land, and rights of pasture for 300 sheep, had been granted by either Adam de Tindale I (died 1188) or Adam de Tindale II (died 1233), barons of Langley, and the same lords also granted the chapel, described as a dependency of the church at Warden, with the garb tithes: document 3 (items 8, 30). The Dissolution survey suggests that these tithes were particularly valuable: document 4A.

Hazeldean, liberty of Hexham (par. St John Lee): no Black Book reference. This property, whose character is unknown, was granted as a dependency of Dotland by Archbishop Thurstan of York, 1114 x 1140: documents 3 (item 3), 16 (item 4). For the probable identity of Hazeldean with the *Knitelhesell* of the records, see *NCH*, IV, p. 196.

Healeyfield, bishopric of Durham (par. Muggleswick): Black Book 67. The Black Book records a toft and croft, an acre of woody land and 20 acres of arable and meadow in two blocks. The origins of the priory's title seem not to be recorded. It seems likely to have been a gift in free alms by a bishop of Durham at a time when Muggleswick was an area of agrarian expansion: cf. G. V. Scammell, *Hugh du Puiset, Bishop of Durham* (Cambridge, 1956), pp. 206, 209. The greater part of Muggleswick had been given to Durham Priory by 1183: *Boldon Buke: A Survey of the Posessions of the See of Durham*, ed. W. Greenwell, Surtees Society (Durham, 1852), p. 32.

Henshaw, liberty of Tynedale, with Priorsdale and Alston Moor (par. Haltwhistle), with Black Book 8. The Black Book records land in Henshaw called *Ryscheles,* within defined bounds but of unstated size. This corresponds to the carucate of the same name granted by Richard Comyn, 1139 x c.1179: document 3 (item 36). For the dating, see the note to document 19. The Black Book also records that a compact property in Henshaw called *Hamysyde*, containing 9½ acres of arable and an acre of meadow within defined bounds, was joined to *Ryscheles*. Comyn's grant included rights of pasture in Henshaw, and about the same time his knight Aguilf granted half a carucate of land there: document 19. These properties are not separately identifiable in the Black Book.

Heugh, Northumberland (par. Stamfordham): Black Book 56. The Black Book records 169½ acres of demesne arable and meadow, a compact farm of 30 acres, 7 husbandlands, 2 cottages, and an unspecified area of pasture. This probably corresponds to the toft and two carucates of land in the township of Stamfordham given by John de Normanville in the time of prior Bernard, *c.*1226 x *c.*1246: documents 2 (item 3), 3 (item 58), 47; *Heads of Religious Houses 940-1216,* p. 390.

Hexham, liberty of Hexham (par. Hexham): Black Book 1. The Black Book records tenements in the town, a small demesne, and a mill. Various properties were granted by Archbishop Thomas II of York, 1108 x 1114; documents 3 (item 2). At a later date the lands in the town centre were specified as the street called Cockshaw, 24 messuages in Priestpopple, 14 messuages in Market Street and 16 messuages in Hencotes: documents 3 (item 3), 16 (item 4). Archbishop Thurstan gave them 'a piece of land on which their men dwelt' and 'another piece of land there to expand their own house, and land where a hospital is built', 1114 v 1140 : documents 1B, 2 (item 2). The hospital in question, not mentioned in the Black Book, is described elsewhere as a pilgrim hospital (*hospitale peregrinorum*), and was not the same as the hospital of St Giles: document 16 (item 4), and see *PH*, II, p. 134n. Until 1377 the

Properties of Hexham Priory 255

hospital of St Giles, though it adjoined the monastery, was nevertheless independently managed by a warden, under the supervision of the archbishops of York. In that year, however, it was made over to the custody of the priory by Archbishop Neville of York, together with the endowment from which it was maintained, but it is not mentioned in the Black Book: *PH*, II, pp. 145-7. In the Dissolution survey the hospital's lands are described as comprising a messuage, a close containing 2 acres of pasture; and 30 acres of arable scattered in the fields of Hexham: document 4A, cf. *PH*, II, no. 59, p. 157. Hexham church with the tithes arising within the liberty of Hexham were granted by Thomas II, archbishop of York, 1108 x 1114, but there is no independent valuation of the tithes of Hexham itself in the Dissolution survey: documents 2 (item 2), 3 (item 1), 4A.

Ilkley, [West Riding] (par. Ilkley): no Black Book reference. The priory was licensed to acquire the advowson of the church in mortmain in 1378, by gift of Gilbert de Umfraville, earl of Angus, through the agency of Henry Percy, earl of Northumberland: document 55. The rectory is listed as one of the priory's assets in the Dissolution survey: document 4A.

Ingleby, Cleveland and Yorkshire (par. Ingleby Greenhow): Black Book 76. The Black Book records a toft, croft, and single dispersed bovate, and a cottage with 2½ acres of land. The origins of the priory's title are seemingly unrecorded.

Isel, Cumbria (par. Isel): Black Book 6. The Black Book records the church, 6 smallholdings totalling 16 acres, three fields of unspecified size, some woodland, a park, a turbary, a peatery, and common pasture on the wastes and pastures there. These details are added to the Black Book, Raine notes, 'in a more recent hand', suggesting that the priory may have acquired them after 1379: *PH*, p. 13. However, the priory had successfully established its title to the advowson of Isel church before the king's justices in 1292: *PQW*, p. 120. The Dissolution survey records the Isel tithes as the priory's only tithes in Cumbria: document 4A.

Keepwick (lost), liberty of Hexham (par. St John Lee): with Black Book 5. The Black Book records a tithe barn and garden. The canons were given a rood of land for a tithe barn by archbishops

Walter de Gray (1216-55) and Walter Giffard (1266-79): document 3 (item 7). The Dissolution survey confirms that the priory owned the garb tithes: document 4A.

Kimblesworth, bishopric of Durham (par. Kimblesworth): Black Book 70. The Black Book records a toft, croft and orchard, 4 acres of arable, 2 acres of meadow and common pasture for a plough team and 260 sheep. The origins of the priory's title seem not to be recorded.

Kirkby (in Cleveland), Cleveland and Yorkshire (par. Kirkby in Cleveland): Black Book 77. The Black Book records a tenement with a garden, croft, a bovate of land and 3 roods of meadow together with an additional cottage and croft. It seems not to be recorded how it was acquired, but is likely to be related to the nearby grant of scattered properties in Broughton by William de Mowbray: documents 67, 68. The vicar of Kirkby had tenements and 28 acres of land in Little Broughton: Black Book 74.

Kirkheaton, Northumberland (par. Chollerton): Black Book 41. The Black Book records the lordship of Kirkheaton and Coldstrother, containing no demesne lands but some substantial freeholdings, 33 husbandlands and 8 cottages. Kirkheaton chapel was granted to the priory as a dependency of Chollerton (q.v.) by by Odinel I or Odinel II de Umfraville, barons of Prudhoe, before 1182. The manor of Kirkheaton and Coldstrother (q.v.) was subsequently granted by Aline of Bolam, together with James of Cauz and his wife Alice, sometime before 1235. They also granted the homage of John of Cambo for his lands in Kirkheaton and Coldstrother: documents 3 (item 23, 67), 37. John of Cambo's holding occurs in 1235 as large holding of 7 carucates and 31½ acres held by Robert of Cambo as a sixth of a knight's fee: document 38. This was subsequently acquired by the priory from a later John of Cambo. The necessary licence from the crown, obtained in 1314, describes the Cambo property as half the manor of Kirkheaton: document 49. Smaller items of land in the manor were acquired by the canons in accordance with a licence of 1323: document 51.

Knarsdale, liberty of Tynedale (par. Knarsdale): Black Book 12. The Black Book records a territory with fixed bounds 'in the township of Knarsdale'. The nature of the boundaries implies rough pasture. This is likely to have been the gift of one of the barons of Langley, who were major benefactors of the priory: documents 3 (items 8, 11, 30, 69, 70), 20. It may be related to the pasture rights attached to the property at Byers (q.v.), but the details of that gift are not recoverable from the available documentation.

Knitelhesell, see Hazeldean

Lanchester, bishopric of Durham (par. Lanchester): Black Book 69. The Black Book records a farm called *Maydenstanhall* within defined bounds. This was presumably the messuage with 60 acres of arable, 4 acres of meadow and 16 acres of woodland that the priory was licensed in 1347 to acquire from Adam of Bowes: documents 58. The Hatfield Survey of Durham bishopric estates describes the property as in Witton Gilbert: document 59.

Langdene (lost), barony of Langley (Featherstone or Haltwhistle parish): Black Book 19. The Black Book records a property of unstated size within defined bounds. The priory's possession was perhaps consequent upon the gift of Byers (q.v.).

Langley, barony of Langley (par. Warden): no Black Book reference. Either Adam de Tindale I (died 1188) or Adam de Tindale II (died 1233), barons of Langley, granted the chapel, described as a dependency of the church at Warden: document 3 (item 8). The garb tithes seem, from the Dissolution survey, to have been leased with those from Haydon: document 4A.

Little Barugh, Cleveland and Yorkshire (par. Kirby Misperton): Black Book, 83. The Black Book records 4 bovates, 1 free and 3 customary. The priory had lands described *c*.1294-5 as 2 bovates and the tenements of 2 *gresmanni*, granted, as part of the prebend of Salton (q.v.) by Archbishop Thurstan of York, 1114 x 1140: document 71 (item 5).

Little Bavington, Northumberland (par. Thockrington): Black Book, 42. The Black Book records 2 tofts, a garden, 9½ acres of land and common pasture for 15 working beasts and 60 sheep and for 2 horses. At the time of the 1298 *inspeximus*, the priory had had 'from time out of mind' a toft and 6 acres of land there by gift of

Stephen Bataill, and a further 2 tofts and 3½ acres, with common rights as recorded in the Black Book, by gift of Gilbert of Worcester: document 3 (item 24). William of Shaftoe, who occupied the lands in 1379, was descended from the Bataill family: *NCH*, IV, pp. 411-12, 417.

Little Broughton, Cleveland and Yorkshire (par. Kirkby in Cleveland): Black Book 74. The Black Book records the manor, with demesne, an orchard, husbandlands, cottages and a mill. These represent lands given by William de Mowbray in the later twelfth century: documents 67, 68. It is presumably this land that *Abstract,* no. 29 describes as Mowbray's ' demesne messuage with four bovates, and all his other lands, a mill, &c.', suggesting that the priory's possessions in Little and Great Broughton (q.v.) were of approximately equal extent: document 68 note.

Little Owmers, Northumberland (par. Warden): see Owmers

Little (East) Swinburn, Northumberland (par. Chollerton): Black Book 39. The Black Book records the site of a tithe barn that was no longer standing. Little Swinburn chapel was granted to the priory as a dependency of Chollerton (q.v.) by by Odinel I or Odinel II de Umfraville, barons of Prudhoe, before 1182., and a tithe barn, with a garden was later granted by Hugh de Balliol, 1193 x 1205: document 3 (items 14, 75). The Dissolution survey does not give the tithes a separate valuation: document 4A.

Milbourne Grange, Northumberland (par. Ponteland): Black Book 51, 52. The Black Book records a grange, enclosed within defined bounds and incorporating a field called *Byresfeld*, with rights of pasture on *Craklaw* Moor and licence to build a mill. It was granted them as the manor of North Milbourn by Sir Thomas of Dilston, *c.*1285: documents 3 (item 32), 46. This property was held as a knight's fee, and was taxed as such for the aid of 1346: *Inquisitions and Assessments Relating to Feudal Aids with Other Analogous Documents Preserved in the Public Record Office, A.D. 1284-1431*, 6 vols (London, 1899-1920), IV, p. 64. Most of Hexham's lands were held 'in free, unconditional and perpetual alms', and so were not eligible for the payment, but by the time Milbourne was granted to the priory there were increasing restrictions on the granting of land on such generous terms.

Millington, Cleveland and Yorkshire (par. Millington): Black Book 85. The Black Book records 2 bovates lying dispersed in township lands. They represent the 2 bovates granted by Forne and his son Ivo, 1113 x 30: document 1C. In the thirteenth century this land became attached to the prebend of Salton, though Millington, in the East Riding like Great Givendale (q.v.), is some distance away from the other lands of the prebend. They are two of the six bovates 'in the township of Millington', c.1294-5, the other four being at Great Givendale: document 71 (item 8).

Nafferton, Northumberland (par. Ovingham): with Black Book, 62. The Black Book records a mill and miller's cottage. The origin of this right is apparently unrecorded.

Nesbit (lost), Northumberland (par. Stamfordham): Black Book 61. The Black Book records the whole township as belonging to the priory, comprising 6 acres of demesne land, a freehold of 12 acres, 19 husbandlands, 4 cottages and a garden. The manor was granted, with Cheeseburn, by John de Normanvill, 1221 x 1243, probably 1228 x 1243: documents 3 (item 59). A royal confirmation of 1255 associates Robert de Lisle with the gift: document 42. The priory's rights to parts of the property were confirmed by final concords in 1255: documents 43, 44. In 1323 the priory was authorized to acquire 2 tofts and 55 acres of land there from William of Shaftoe, presumably land formerly held from the manor as a freehold: document 51. In 1246 the priory was given the garb tithes of the township or hamlet of Nesbit by Nicholas Farnham, bishop of Durham, in part settlement of a dispute over the church of Stamfordham (q.v.), but there is no independent valuation of these tithes in the Dissolution survey: documents 3 (item 60), 4A, 47.

Newbiggin, liberty of Hexham (par. Hexham): with Black Book 5. The Black Book records a waste watermill at Newbiggin in *Neulandes*. It had been granted, together with Hamburn Mill and 24 acres of land, by Walter Gray, archbishop of York, 1216 x 1255: documents 3 (item 6), 16 (item 8), 17 (item 9). Newbiggin is referred to as a township in documents 3 (item 6), and also occurs as such in a charter of 1355: *NCH*, IV, p. 34. The mill was later known as Linnels Mill: *Ibid.*, IV, p. 32.

Newbiggin by the Sea, Northumberland (par. Woodhorn): Black Book 46. The Black Book records 2 burgage tenements containing 2 acres between them. These represent the toft and 2 acres of land granted by either Bernard de Balliol I (died c. 1150) or Bernard de Balliol II (died 1186-7), barons of Bywell: document 3 (item 61); Sanders, p. 25. Newbiggin had acquired a market in 1204 and its burghal status was recognized by 1307: *Rotuli Chartarum*, ed. T. D. Hardy, Record Commission (London, 1837), p. 119b; M. Beresford and H. P. R. Finberg, *English Medieval Boroughs: a Handlist* (Newton Abbot, 1973), p. 144.

Newburn (on Tyne), Northumberland (par. Newburn): Black Book 64. The Black Book records two fisheries on the Tyne called *Fuyle* and *Drypintille* and half an acre of meadow. The fisheries were granted under the same names by Roger Bertram sometime 'time out of mind' before 1298: document 3 (item 57). A parallel grant by Roger Bertram to William Briton of the fishery called Crook can be dated to 1229 x 1235: *NCH*, XIII, p.152.

Newcastle upon Tyne, Northumberland: Black Book 66. The Black Book records 8 burgage tenures in different parts of the town and a rent from 'the stone house in Westgate', but they had lost track of both one of the burgages and of the stone house, whose location they no longer knew. The remaining rents, from 7 burgages, totalled £2 9s. 6d. Their charters, all before 1298, gave them title to rents of £2 3s. 4d. from 8 messuages by various gifts: document 3 (item 28).

Newton, East, see East Newton

Newton in Coquetdale, in Peels township, Northumberland (par. Alwinton): Black Book, 43. The Black Book records a toft and croft with a compact carucate with defined bounds. This was given to the priory by Walter de Lisle, who had land there in the late twelfth century or early thirteenth: document 3 (item 21); *NCH*, XV, p. 445.

Ninebanks, liberty of Hexham (par. Allendale): with Black Book 5. The Black Book records a plot of land for a tithe barn. The canons were given a rood of land for a tithe barn by archbishops Walter de Gray (1216-55) and Walter Giffard (1266-79): document 3 (item 7).

North Seaton, Northumberland (par. Woodhorn): Black Book 49. The Black Book records a rent of £2 from the township. This was granted by either Bernard de Balliol I (died c. 1150) or Bernard de Balliol II (died 1186-7), barons of Bywell: document 3 (item 62); Sanders, p. 25

Ouston, Northumberland (par. Stamfordham): Black Book 59. The Black Book records an acre of land in the town field and 4 acres of peatery. The origin of their title to this property is unrecorded, but may be connected with their possession of the garb tithes of Ouston by grant of Nicholas Farnham, bishop of Durham in 1246, in part settlement of a dispute over the church of Stamfordham (q.v.): documents 3 (item 60), 47.

Ovingham, Northumberland (par. Ovingham), with Black Book 29. The Black Book records a fishery there. The origin of the priory's title seems not to be recorded. The priory was licensed to acquire the advowson of the church in mortmain in 1378, by gift of Gilbert de Umframville, earl of Angus, through the agency of Henry Percy, earl of Northumberland: document 55. The Dissolution survey implies both that the tithes of Ovingham were exceptionally valuable and that that the priory had accumulated property there since 1379: document 4B.

Owmers (lost), in Allerwash township, Northumberland (par. Warden): Black Book 23, 24. The Black Book records a compact holding of unstated size within defined bounds called *Olmers*, and a further compact holding, presumably smaller, called Little *Olmers*. They correspond to the gift of a carucate in Allerwash 'in a place called *Oulemers*' made by Richard, a former bailiff of Hexham, sometime 'time out of mind' before 1298: document 3, (item 13). This was perhaps Richard son of Alexander, who witnessed documents 32 and 33 in 1239, and who occurs as bailiff of Hexham in 1235, but Richards also served as bailiffs of Hexham in 1252 and 1268: *NCH*, III, p.64.

Plumland, Cumbria (par. Plumland): Black Book 6. The Black Book records that the priory had a quarter share of the mill. The origin of this right is apparently unrecorded.

Priorsdale, liberty of Tynedale with Priorsdale and Alston Moor (par. Alston): Black Book 17. The Black Book records extensive rough pasture within defined bounds. This was granted by Ivo de Vieuxpont before 1232, but perhaps not long before: documents 2 (item 7), 3 (item 39), and cf. document 28. Priorsdale had been granted along with the manor of Alston to the donor's father by William I of Scotland in 1165 x 1170: *RRS II*, pp. 181-2; *HHN*, IV [part 2, vol. 3], p. 43.

Prudhoe, Northumberland (par. Ovingham): Black Book 29. The Black Book records a croft and lands in the town field together totalling 8 acres and half a rood. This was the toft and 8 acres of land granted by Richard de Umfraville, as lord of Prudhoe, c.1192 x 1226: document 3 (item 64); Sanders, p. 73.

Renwick, Cumbria (par. Renwick): Black Book 6. The Black Book records the rectory buildings and the glebe, comprising 13 acres of arable dispersed in the town field and 1½ acres of meadow. The church was granted and appropriated at some point before 5 April, 1359, when the bishop of Carlisle confirmed all of the priory's ecclesiastical possessions in his diocese; *PH*, II, pp. 142-3.

Riplington, Northumberland (par. Whalton): with Black Book 45. A rent of 8s. was granted by Walter son of William, lord of Whalton (q.v.), and Isabella, his wife, sometime 'from time out of mind' before 1298: document 3 (item 56). This is perhaps the 8s. rent 'in the township of Whalton' recorded in the Black Book account of Whalton.

Ryscheles, see Henshaw.

Rowley (lost), liberty of Hexham (par. Hexham): with Black Book 5. The Black Book records a husbandland, a tithe barn and garden. Rowley was reckoned a township in 1226: document 9. The canons were given a rood of land for a tithe barn by archbishops Walter de Gray (1216-55) and Walter Giffard (1266-79): document 3 (item 7).

St John Lee, liberty of Hexham (par. St John Lee): with Black Book, 3. The Black Book implies that the canons had the chapel there. The origins of the priory's title seem to be unrecorded.

Properties of Hexham Priory 263

Salton, Cleveland and Yorkshire (par. Salton): Black Book 78. The Black Book seems to record, beside the the hall and chapel, demesne land comprising 31 bovates of arable, 20½ acres of meadow, and 2½ acres of woodland, together with 60½ bovates of tenant land, 39 cottages, a mill, and a few other minor plots of land (but see the note to Black Book 78). This property, held *ex officio* by the prior of Hexham by virtue of his office as a canon of York Minster, was granted as part of the prebend of Salton by Archbishop Thurstan of York, 1114 x 1140: documents 1B, 2 (item 2), 71 (item 2). Besides the possessions in Salton the prebend included lands in the townships of Brawby, Great Barugh, Little Barugh, East Newton and Flaxton in 'Cleveland', to which were added gifts of land in Great Givendale and Millington in the East Riding: document 71.

Sandhoe, liberty of Hexham (par. St John Lee): Black Book 3. The Black Book records a small demesne of 42 acres, together with 13 husbandlands, 12 cottages and 11 acres of glebe land. The township was granted, with those of Anick and Yarrridge, by Archbishop Thomas II of York, 1108 x 1114: documents 1A, 2 (item 1), 3 (item 2), 16 (item 2). The Dissolution survey confirms that the priory owned the garb tithes: document 4A.

Scales, Cumbria (par. Kirkoswald): Black Book 6. The Black Book records a toft containing an acre and 10 acres of land in dispersed parcels. The origins of the priory's title seem to be unrecorded, but may be associated with its acquisition of the nearby rectory of Renwick (q.v.).

Seaton, see North Seaton

Settlingstones, liberty of Tynedale with Priorsdale and Alston Moor (par. Warden): Black Book 7. The Black Book records two tofts, one with 1½ acres of arable and 3 acres of meadow, the other with 20 acres of arable, 4 acres of meadow and pasture rights. This was property given by Adam of Settlingstones sometime 'time out of mind' before 1298: document 3 (item 9).

Silksworth, bishopric of Durham (par. Bishop Wearmouth): Black Book, 73. The Black Book records Farringdon Grange, with 4 husbandlands and other lands. The priory acquired it before 1312 when Richard son of John Fitz Marmaduke quitclaimed his right to properties in Silksworth held by the priory by gift of his ancestors: *PH,* II, p. xiv (note). The land was apparently held from from Thomas, earl of Lancaster. When Lancaster's estates escheated to the crown, following his execution in 1322, the canons petitioned the king to regrant them their Silksworth property, evidently successfully: document 57.

Slaley, Northumberland (par. Slaley): Black Book 27. The Black Book records 'various tenements' in Slaley, half a carucate of land and other acres, together with the sheepfolds of Slaley and Steel. The land was fragmented into small irregular tenures, and the only husbandland there was partly waste. They had this, together with the church, by gift of Gilbert of Slaley, 1216 x 1272: document 3 (item 26). The donation of the church is discussed in *NCH*, VI, pp. 348-9. The priory's possession of the chapel and garb tithes is confirmed by the Dissolution survey: document 4A.

Stainton, see Great Stainton

Stamfordham, Northumberland (par. Stamfordham): with Black Book 56. The Black Book records a toft and a croft held in Stamfordham in its account of Heugh (q.v.). The church was given by John de Normanville, along with a toft and two carucates of land in Stamfordham (for which see Heugh) in the time of prior Bernard, c.1226 x c.1246: documents 2 (item 3), 3 (item 58), 47; *Heads of Religious Houses 940-1216*, p. 390. Bishop Nicholas of Farnham disputed the priory's right to the avowson, but in 1246 granted it the garb tithes of the 5 townships of East Matfen, Nesbit, Ouston, Hawkwell and Bitchfield, out of the income of Stamfordham church: documents 3 (item 60), 47. The priory eventually secured the advowson of the church by royal grant in 1305 and Bishop Anthony Bek licensed its appropriation in 1307: documents 47, 48.

Stannington, Northumberland (par. Stannington): Black Book 47. The Black Book records a toft, with a garden, and a single husbandland. This corresponds to the grant of a toft and 2 bovates of land in Stannington, by gift of Roger de Merlay I, lord of Morpeth, who died in 1188: document 3 (item 52); *HHN*, IV [part 2, vol. 3], p. 282; Sanders, p. 65. Ralph de Merlay had earlier granted 10s. a year to the canons, 'until he should settle lands on them': document 1C. Roger's grant was presumably in fulfilment of this commitment. It is not known when he succeeded to the barony of Morpeth, but his gift was probably made after the writing of Prior Richard's *History*, which does not mention it. The priory's charters also included the grant by Roger de Merlay of a rent of 1s. 6d. in Stannington that is not identifiable from the Black Book account: document 3 (item 53).

Steel in Slaley township, Northumberland (par. Slaley): with Black Book 27. The Black Book records a sheepfold with an adjoining garden and common pasture for 300 sheep. They had this by gift of Gilbert of Slaley, 1216 x 1272: document 3 (item 26). Little is known of medieval Steel apart from these references: *NCH*, VI, p. 373.

Stelden in Great Swinburn township (lost), Northumberland (par. Chollerton), Black Book 38. The Black Book records 'all Stelden' as subinfeudated, except for a toft, croft, a sheepfold and rights of common on Gunnerton Moor. This was property granted by the abbot of the Cistercian Abbey of Newminster, near Morpeth, probably in the earlier thirteenth century: documents 3 (item 33), 35. The bulk of the property was subinfeudated to John, son of Richard of Little Swinburn *c*.1250 x 1269: document 45.

Stelling, Northumberland (par. Bywell St Peter): Black Book 62. The Black Book records a manor with defined bounds, but of unstated size, and rights common pasture throughout the barony of Bywell. The manor was granted by either Bernard de Balliol I (died c. 1150) or Bernard de Balliol II (died 1186-7), barons of Bywell: document 3 (item 61); Sanders, p. 25. The canons of Hexham managed this property as a grange *Northumberland Lay Subsidy Roll*, no. 92, p. 34.

Stocksfield, Northumberland (par. Bywell St Andrew): Black Book 28. The Black Book records 'all Stocksfield' as subinfeudated for 13s. 4d. a year, of which 1s. was for castle guard. This corresponds approximately to the 13s. 8d from the township of Stocksfield, out of which they were to pay 7s. per year for castle guard, given by William son of Boso sometime 'time out of mind' before 1298: document 3 (item 46). The castle guard was in respect of the royal castle of Newcastle: *NCH*, VI, pp. 255-6. The priory had another charter of William son of Boso granting them the annual rent of 13s. 8d. with the homage of John de Normanville 'for the land of Stocksfield and Apperley': document 3 (item 71). By a later gift by John son of Elias of Stocksfied, the canons also had a rent of 3s. in the township of Stocksfield, 1216 x 1272, but it is unclear how this relates to the property described in the Black Book: document 3 (item 47).

Stonecroft, Northumberland (par. Warden): Black Book 7. The Black Book records this as a toft and 20 acres of land within defined bounds. This corresponds, if imperfectly, to the toft and 30 acres of land; granted by Richard Comyn, 1139 x c.1179: document 3 (item 37). The chapel was granted as a dependency of Warden by either Adam de Tindale I (died 1188) or Adam de Tindale II (died 1233), lords of Langley: document 3 (item 8).

Swinburn, see Little Swinburn, West Swinburn.

Tecket in Simonburn township, liberty of Tynedale with Priorsdale and Alston Moor (par. Simonburn). The Black Book records a toft, croft and 10 acres of arable with defined bounds: Black Book 8. This perhaps relates to the rent of 8s. from Tecket, received by gift of Laurence of Tecket sometime 'time out of mind' before 1298: document 3 (item 41).

Temple Thornton, Northumberland (par. Stannington): Black Book 44. The Black Book records 5 tofts and gardens, 3 crofts, 91¾ acres of land dispersed in the town field and 3 acres of meadow. The lands were divided into 5 husbandlands (corresponding to the 5 tofts and gardens). These were the 5 tofts, 10 bovates of land and 3 acres of meadow in Thornton, granted by William de Lisle and confirmed by Walter de Bolbec as superior lord: document 3 (item 48). The grant must date before Walter's death in 1187: *NCH*, VI, p. 250.

Thirlwall, liberty of Tynedale with Priorsdale and Alston Moor (par. Haltwhistle): Black Book 9. The Black Book records two compact properties of unstated size, Wardrew and *Croymagh* or *Coomhoue*, with a meadow and various other small properties. These presumably correspond to the 6 tofts and carucate of land in Thirlwall given by Brice of Thirlwall and Roger his son sometime

'time out of mind' before 1298: document 3 (item 38). The rights of common pasture included in Brice's grant are recorded with Black Book 11. There is no independent evidence of the priory tenants' freedom to mill at Thirlwall Mill referred to in the Black Book as having been conferred by charter, presumably by grant of the Thirlwall family as lords of the manor. For this family, and Thirlwall Castle, mentioned in the Black Book text, see See A. Rushworth and R. Carlton, 'Thirlwall Castle: a Gentry Residence in Medieval Tynedale', in P. Frodsham, ed., *Archaeology in the Northumberland National Park* (York, 2004), pp. 272-94.

Throckley, Northumberland (par. Newburn): Black Book 63. The Black Book records a toft, croft, 51 acres 2½ roods of arable, and meadows of unstated extent. The relationship between this and the charter evidence is opaque. It probably represents the lands in Throckley of Robert of Throckley whose homage was given to the priory by Robert of Iveston and Christine of Throckley sometime 'time out of mind' before 1298: document 3 (item 74). This grant is likely to be no later than the early thirteenth century, since Christine was the daughter and heiress of Aylmer of Throckley, who was living in 1177: *NCH*, XIII, p. 158. However, the land was no longer subinfeudated in 1379, so the evidence for the priory's title is incomplete. The same donors also gave 2 acres of land and rent of 16s. in Throckley: document 3 (item 50).

Todridge, see Grottington.

Ulpham, barony of Langley (par. Featherstone): with Black Book 18, 19. The Black Book records Ulpham as a property of unspecified size comprising arable and pasture within defined bounds, adjoining Byers and Langdene. There seems to be no record of how the priory acquired it, but it was perhaps consequent upon the gift of Byers (q.v.)

Wall, liberty of Hexham (par. St John Lee). The Black Book records a tithe barn and garden: Black Book 5. The canons were given a rood of land for a tithe barn by archbishops Walter de Gray (1216-55) and Walter Giffard (1266-79): document 3 (item 7). The Dissolution survey confirms that the priory owned the garb tithes: document 4A.

Walwick, barony of Langley (par. Warden): Black Book 26. The Black Book records common pasture for 240 sheep, 16 oxen and 10 cows out of Warden, by grant of Richard Comyn, 1139 x c.1179. There is no independent charter evidence of this grant. Richard Comyn and his wife Hextilda had rights in Walwick that had previously belonged to Hextilda's father: document 19 and note.

Warden, barony of Langley (par. Warden): Black Book 25. The Black Book records the manor with defined bounds, including a park, and beyond these bounds 15 acres of land, an unspecified number of cottages and a ferry boat. The manor was the gift of Adam de Tindale I (died 1188) or Adam de Tindale II (died 1233), lords of Langley, who also granted the church with the dependent chapels of Haydon, Langley and Stonecroft: document 3 (item 8); Sanders, p. 127.

Wardoughan, liberty of Tynedale with Priorsdale and Alston: Black Book 11. The Black Book records a toft to which belonged a quarter share of Wardoughan, including a quarter share of Clesket. The origins of the priory's title seem to be unrecorded.

West Swinburn, *see Great Swinburn*

Whalton, Northumberland (par. Whalton): Black Book 45. The Black Book records a toft, croft and garden, half a carucate (52½ acres) of land in the town field, 2½ acres of meadow, and common pasture for 360 sheep. This corresponds, with inexplicable discrepancies, to the grant of a toft, croft, and 42½ acres of land, with rights of pasture for 480 sheep by Walter, son of William, and Isabella, his wife: document 3 (item 55). The donor occurs as lord of Whalton in 1166 and died before 1188: Sanders, p. 150.

Whetewang (unidentified), seemingly in the liberty of Hexham: no Black Book reference. This property was granted the priory by one of the archbishops of York for a rent of 3s. a year, but surrendered to Archbishop William Melton, c.1328, because it was no longer profitable: document 16 (item 13).

Whinnetley, barony of Langley (par. Warden): Black Book, 20. The Black Book records a tenement and lands of unspecified size with definite bounds, together with two free tenements and stinted

Properties of Hexham Priory 269

rights of common pasture. These probably correspond to the 2 messuages, 40 acres of land and 10s. of rent in Whinnetley given by Adam of Thorngrafton sometime 'time out of mind' before 1298: document 3 (item 10). An Adam of Thorngrafton was a witness of document 20 (c.1165 x 1188)

Whitchester, see Harlow.

Whitfield, liberty of Tynedale with Priorsdale and Alston Moor (par. Whitfield): Black Book 14. The Black Book records 'all Whitfield' as subinfeudated for 16s. 8d. a year. The priory had this by grant of Countess Ada, mother of William I of Scots, confirmed by her son, 1166 x 1178: documents 3 (item 34), 21, 23. It was already subinfeudated, to the countess's chaplain, Robert, at the time they received it, and was subsequently inherited by his son, Matthew of Whitfield: documents 3 (item 73), 22, 24, 25, 27. For the interest of William, king of Scots, in Whitfield, see documents 23-4, 27. Matthew of Whitfield was a witness to documents 7 and 20.

Whitley Mill, liberty of Hexham: with Black Book 5. The Black Book records this as a watermill in *Neulandes*; the 10 husbandlands of Dotland, and all the tenants of *Neulandes* ground their grain there: Black Book 5. It seems likely that this was the mill newly built 'on the large burn between Dotland and the township of Rowley' that Archbishop Walter de Grey granted the priory in 1226: document 9.

Whitlow, liberty of Tynedale with Priorsdale and Alston Moor (par. Kirkhaugh): Black Book 13. The Black Book records 'all Whitlow' as subinfeudated for 4s. a year. This property, already subinfeudated to Adam of Whitlow, was the gift of Adam de Tindale I, lord of Langley, c.1165 x 1188: documents 3 (item 69), 20. The original grant records rights of pasture throughout the fee of Featherstone (q.v.); these are separately recorded at Black Book 19.

Witton Gilbert, bishopric of Durham. See Lanchester.

Yarridge, liberty of Hexham: with Black Book 5. The Black Book records 6 husbandlands. The township was granted, with those of

Anick and Sandhoe, by Archbishop Thomas II of York, 1108 x 1114: documents 1A, 2 (item 1), 3 (item 2), 16 (item 2).

York, Yorkshire: no Black Book reference. A house was granted by Sunnulfus the priest, before 1167 (i.e. before the death of Prior Richard who wrote the *History of the Church of Hexham*): documents, 1C. This is presumably the messuage in Goodramgate granted to the archbishop's chaplain and his heirs in 1191 x 1194: document 66. This or another property in the same part of York was held by John of Cottingham, rector of the church of North Cave, in 1366, as appropriated to the prebend of Salton: document 73.

6. GLOSSARY OF ENGLISH WORDS IN THE THE BLACK BOOK

abbay	abbey
alegraves	ale officers (ale+graves)
balk(e)	baulk
bank	bank, hill
be(e)ngarth	enclosure planted with beans (bean+garth)
bog(g)	bog
bradetofte	broad toft
brokes	lands broken up for cultivation
burne	burn, stream
buttes	irregularly shaped or sized rigs (q.v.)
castel	castle
cheregarth	cherry orchard (cherry+garth)
connyngarth	an enclosed rabbit warren (conning+garth)
corner	corner
cote	cottage
cotgarth	cottage yard or garden (cot+garth)
croftes	crofts
croftesendes	croft ends
crosse	cross
crossstandanestan	cross standing stone, perhaps a standing stone with a cross
deene	a narrow (usually wooded) vale
dik(e), dyke	ditch
eschape	escape, escaping, running loose
est	east
estemer	eastern boundary (east+mere)
estend	east end
estheued	east end (east+head)
estsyde	east side
feld	field, cultivated land
flatt(e)	furlong, a section of an open field with parallel strips or rigs.
flok	flock, herd
ford	ford
for(e)land	land in front, perhaps land beside the street, in front of dwellings

fote	foot, bottom
furlang	furlong, see *flatte*
-garth	enclosed yard, garden or paddock
gate	road
gatehous	gatehouse
gesthall	guest hall
girsgarth	enclosure under grass (grass+garth)
hac	hedge
hegegarth	hedge(d) garth (hedge+garth)
hegeyard	hedge(d) yard (hedge+yard)
heued(e)	head, top, end
heuedlandes	the part of a furlong, or flat, where the plough turns at the end of a selion, or rig (head+lands)
heuedyard(e)	head+yard (significance uncertain)
horsepoile	pool for watering or washing horses (horse+pool)
hotte for *holte?*	a small wood or copse
houghes	hillocks, knolls. *The Houghes* should perhaps be treated as a place-name.
husband	a customary tenant
husbanddales	allotments of meadow to husbandlands
husbandlandes	the standard holding of a customary tenant, traditionally two bovates
karre	rock
kylngarth	kiln yard (kiln+garth)
kyrkway	church road (kirk+way)
law	hill
lech(e)	ditch with running water
lidyete, ludyet	lidgate, gate to stop cattle straying (but see n. 68)
lonyng	lane
lonyngheuede	top of the lane, lane end (loaning+head)
louthre	louvre, an aperture in the roof
marlpottes	marl pits
mason	stonemason
mayndyk	demesne (boundary) ditch (main+dike)
maynes	demesne lands
medow(e)	meadow
mer(e)s,	boundaries

Glossary

merlpottes	see *marlpottes*
milndore	mill door
milndamhede	head of the mill dam (mill+dam+head).
milne	mill
milnfleme mylnefleme	millstream (mill+fleam)
milnpost	post for a post mill
milnsyd	side of the mill
modirdame	principal dam? (mother+dam)
more	moor
moss	bog, peat-bog
multirgrafe	multure officer (multure+grave)
mylndame	mill dam
mylnefleme	see *milnfleme*
mylnraw	mill + row (apparently meaning mill dam)
myre	mire, bog, swamp
northend(e)	north end
northest	north-east
northestcorner	north-east corner
northwest	north-west
overnoke	top corner (over+ nook)
owtgang	road out
oxenpasture	pasture for oxen
park	park
pengarth	an enclosed yard serving as a pen (pen+garth)
peth	path
petmyre	peat bog (peat+mire)
pole	pool
post	post, for a post mill (see also *milnpost*)
pottes	pits (cf. *marlpottes*)
rawe	row (of dwellings)
redcrosse	red cross
reygne	baulk
rigges	selions, strips of arable running parallel across a flat, or furlong.
rode	road
rud	rood
salgh	willow
schaw	small wood, thicket
schipcote, schepcott	sheep cote. A building for sheltering sheep

sclak	*meaning uncertain*
siket	siket, a rivulet, a small watercourse (cf. *syk*)
smythous	smith's house, smithy
southcorner	south corner
southend	south end
southest	south-east
southwestend	south-west end
stable	stable for horses
stanbrig	stone bridge
standandstanes	standing stones
stanegate	stone road
strothre	marsh
syd	side
syk	watercourse
thorne	thorn (bush)
Wall	(Hadrian's) Wall
wateregraves	water officers (water+graves)
waye	way, road
well	spring
westkyrkstyle	western church stile (west+kirk+stile)
westrecorner	western corner (wester+corner)
wildirland	uncultivated land (wildern+land)
wodlibusk	thicket (woody?+bush)
wythebusk	willow bush, perhaps an osier (withy+bush)

7. GAZETTEER OF THE BLACK BOOK

Acome, Akome, Acomb (NY 932664)
Akwod, Oakwood (NY 950647)
Aldeneston, Alston (NY 716465)
Alden(n)estonmore, Alston Moor (NY 735440)
Alle(r)wass(c)he, Allerwash (NY 870670)
Allerwesscheles, Allerwash *scheles* (lost, presumably about NY 865675)
Alne (rivulus de), River Ellen (NY 050369)
Alneburgh, Ellenborough (NY 045355)
Alwenton, Allendale Town (NY 838558)
Alwenton, Alwinton (NT 922064)
Auk(e)landgate (in Great Stainton), the road to Bishop Auckland (NZ 330224)
Aynwyk, Anick (NY 955655)
Babynton (Parva), (Little) Bavington (NY 988787)
Barousford, Barassfurd, Barrasford (NY 916734)
Be(a)ufront, Beuanfront (parcum de), Beaufront Park (NY 967658)
Beaumond, Beaumont (NY 756729)
Belacys, Bellasis Farm (NZ 194781)
Benwell, Benwell (NZ 205645)
Bergh (Magna), Great Barugh (SE 749790)
Bergh, Lytill, Little Barugh (SE 761797)
Birkburne, Birkey Burn (NY 950661)
Bisschopton, Bishopton (NZ 365213)
Blenkhowe, Blencow (NY 456325)
Boclive, Boclyve, Beukley (NY 983709)
Brauby, Brawby, Brawby (SE 738782)
Brenklawe, Brenkley (NZ 217751)
Broghton (Magna), Great Broughton (NZ 547063)
Broghton (Parva), Lytilbroghton, Little Broughton (NZ 559068)
Bro(u)ne (rivulus de), River Browney (NZ 180463)
Burnhopheuyde, Burnhope Head (NY 791382)
Buroudon, Burradon (NT 981062)
Byngfeld(e), Bingfield (NY 978726)
Byres (Le), cf. Byers Hall (NY 652599) and Byers Fell (NY 660577)
Byrtelye, Birtley (NY 880782)
Bywell, Bywell (NZ 048614)

Cadden, Catton (NY 828578)
Caldcotes, Coldcoats (about NZ 144748)
Carraw, Carraw (NY 850711)
Catrawe, Catraw (NZ 201795)
Ches(e)burgh(e), Cheeseburn (NZ 094713)
Chestrehope in Redesdale, Chesterhope (NY 900852)
Chipches, Chipchase (NY 883757)
Chollirton, Chollerton (NY 931719)
Cleveland, Cleveland
Clifton, Clifton (NZ 203827)
Cocelye, Coastley (NY 904658)
Coksyd(e), Consett (NZ 100500)
Colden, Cowden (NY 917793)
Coldenburne, Cowden Burn (NY 908794)
Coldenkyrk, Cowden Kirk (NY 920786)
Collewelle, Colwell (NY 953755)
Cookdale, Coquetdale, see *Neuton in Cookdale*
Corbrig(g), Corbryg, Corbridge (NY 987644)
Crokitburn(e), Crook Burn (NY 781353)
Crokytburnheued, Crook Burn Head (about NY 792368)
Dalton, Dalton (NZ 112720)
Dalton (in Hexhamshire), (NY 919582)
Daltonway, the road to Dalton from Cheeseburn Grange (NZ 095718)
Daventre, Daventry (SP 572623)
Der(e)strete, Dere Street (NY 964729. NY 970722)
Derlyngtonway (in Great Stainton), the road to Darlington (NZ 337210)
Derwent (aqua de), River Derwent (NY 150338)
Deulawrige; cf Dewley (NZ 163678)
Dipden (in Hexhamshire), lost, but see Diptonmill (NY 929610)
Dissington, Dissyngton(e), Dysyngton, Dissington (NZ 117718)
Donnismore, Duns Moor (NY 995728)
Dotland, Dotland (NY 923595)
Doufe (ripae de), River Dove (SE 700835)
Dunley, cf. Dinley Hill (NY 886774)
Durhamgate (in Great Stainton), the road to Durham (NZ 350215)
Ech(e)wyk, Eachwick (NZ 117711)
Edestan, Dead Stones ? (NY 794399)
Edeston, Edstone (SE 706840)

Elleryngton, Elrington (NY 861635)
Elstobbe, Elstob (NZ 340238)
Elstobrode (in Great Stainton), Elstob Lane (NZ 335230)
Ereanbrig , *Eriane (pons de)*, Erring Bridge (NY 964729)
Ereane, Eriane, Eryane (aqua de, rivulus de), Erring Burn (NY 950725; NY 970733)
Erlehouse, Earl's House (NZ 251451)
Eryngton, Errington (NY 959716)
Esbymarche (in Ingleby Greenhow), the township boundary of Easby
Esbywaye (in Ingleby Greenhow), the road to Easby
Esgylheued, Eskgillheuede, Ash Gill Head (about NY 782416)
Eskgilfote, Ash Gill Foot (NY 754403)
Eskgille, Ash Gill (NY 767408)
Esschelez, cf. High Eshells (NY 897578) and Low Eshells (NY 899576)
Falofeld, Fallowfield (NY 929685)
Farendongrange, Farondongrange, cf. Farringdon (NZ 371535)
Faudon, Fawdon (NZ 225695)
Fenwyk, Fenwick (NZ 057729)
Fenwikburn. Fenwykburne, cf. Fenwickfield (NY 852737)
Ferlyngton, Farlington (SE 614675)
Fethirstanhalgh, cf. Featherstone Castle (NY 673610) and Featherstone Common (NY 660625)
Flaxton, Flaxton (SE 678623)
Gerardgill, Garrigill (NY 745415)
Geveldale in le Hole, Great Givendale (SE 813539)
Gillisland, Gilsland (NY 631665)
Glendue, Glendue Fell (NY 640550)
Glendeuburn, Glendue Burn (NY 665565)
Gofden, Gofton (NY 833756)
Gonwarton, Gunwardton, Gunnerton (NY 905750). Gunnerton Moor is probably around Gunnerton Fell (NY 906772)
Grencroft(e), Greencroft (NZ 159494)
Grendon, Grindon (NY 821695)
Grendenmore, cf. High Grindon (NZ 324241)
Grendonrode, cf. Grindon (NZ 360550)
Gren Heley, see *Heley*
Grosgilheued, Crossgill Head (NY 729355)
Grotyngton, cf. Grottington Farm (NY 976700)

Gunwardton, see *Gonwarton*
Gryndstanlaw, Grindstone Law (NZ 003734)
Haliden(e), Hallington (NY 985758)
Haltwesyle, Haltwhistle (NY 710642)
Hamstell, cf. Hamsteels Hall (NZ 175449), West Hamsteels (NZ 171450)
Harbotell, Hirbotle, Harbottle (NT 935046)
Hartburn, Hart Burn (NZ 100853)
Hartelyburne, Hartley Burn (NY 666604)
Haukwell, Hawkwell (NZ 077717)
Hayden, Haydon (NY 843654)
Haynyngcrofte (in Hexham), Haining Croft, map of c. 1844 (NY 935637)
Heddirslawmedow, in Heatherslaw (NZ 081743)
Heddon, Black Heddon (NZ 079760)
Heley, Healeyfield (NZ 070482)
Hencotis (in Hexham), Hencotes (NY 933639)
Henneshalgh, Hennishalgh, Henshaw (NY 765645)
Herryngton, East Middle or West Herrington (NZ 3453-3653)
Hertburn, Hartburn (NZ 090860)
Hertilpole, Hertyllpull, Hartlepool (NZ 528337)
Hesilden, Monk Hesleden (NZ 4537)
Hexham, Hextildesham, Hexham (NY 935641)
Hexhamshyre, Hextildeshamschyre, Hexhamshire
Hildreton, Ilderton (NU 017218)
Hirlaw, Harlow Hill (NZ 079683)
Hogh(e), Heugh (NZ 083732)
Hoghton, Houghton-le-Spring (NZ 343499)
Holmishalhraw, Humshaugh (NY 920715)
Ingleby, Ingleby Greenhow (NZ 581063)
Isale, Isall,, Isel (NY 158338)
Karleol, Karleon, Carlisle (NY 398559)
Kellauburne, Kellah Burn (NY 612611)
Kellaw, Kelloue, Kellow, Kellah (NY 660612)
Kepewyk, Keepwick (NY 951714)
Knaresdale, Knarsdale (NY 678538)
Kyme(le)sworthe, Kimblesworth (NZ 260475)
Kirkbe, Kyrkbe in Cleveland, Kirkby (NZ 539060)
Kyrkheton, Kirkheaton (NZ 018773)
Lambleye, Lambley (NY 672586)

Lan(g)chestre, Lanchester (NZ 167474)
Langdene, name lost (probably NY 660606)
Langlye, Langley (NY 828612)
Lanhope, Langhope (NY 882644)
Linburn(e), Linn Burn (NY 984727)
Lindeslawe, Linnlaw (NZ 126817)
Litilblakburne, cf. Black Burn (NY 660582)
Lytilbroghton, see *Broghton (Parva)*
Lytill Bergh, see *Bergh, Lytill*
Malteby, Maltby (NZ 466133)
Matfen, Matfen (NZ 030718)
Matfen Est, East Matfen (NZ 040712)
Maydengate, Maiden Way (NY 666625, NY 670568)
Maydenstanhall, Manor House (NZ 179472)
Mikleblakburne, cf. Black Burn (NY 660582)
Milkrigeburn, Melkridge + burn (NY 738639)
Mil(l)ington, Millington (SE 830519)
Milnburn(e), Milbourne (NZ 117754)
Milnburne (burne de), Mill Burn (NZ 115753)
Milnburn, North, see *Northmilnburn(e)*
Minstreacres, Minsteracres (NZ 025555)
Morpethway (in Temple Thornton), the road to Morpeth (NZ 100858)
Mugilsworth (sic), Muggleswick (NZ 044501)
Naffirton, Nafferton (NZ 056654)
Natresgille, Natrass Gill (NY 726448)
Nesbit(te), cf. Nesbit Hill Head (NZ 075695)
Nethreton, Netherton (NT 989077)
Neubigyng (in Hexhamshire), Newbiggin (NY 946607)
Neuburgh, Newbrough (NY 875678)
Neutonhall, Newton Hall (NZ 037653)
Neuton in Cookdale, Newton (NT 945070)
Newbiggyng, *Newbiggyng super Mare*, Newbiggin by the Sea (NZ 310876)
Newburne, Newburn (NZ 165655)
Ninistanes, Noonstones (Hill) (NY 748380)
Nobbokscheles, cf. Nubbock Fell (NY 870620)
Northmilnburn(e), Milbourne Grange (NZ 119753)
Nynbenkys, Ninebanks (NY 783533)
Ogle, Ogle (NZ 140790)

Ottrington, North or South Otterington (SE 363897, SE 371875)
Ovyngeham, Ovingham (NZ 085637)
Ovyrwardon, High Warden (NY 910671)
Penreth, Penrith (NY 515302)
Plumland, Plumland (NY 150390)
Poltreskburn, Poltross Burn (NY 620645)
Pont (burn called), River Pont (NZ 055714)
Ponteland, Ponteland (NZ 165729)
Prestpofyll (in Hexham), Priestpopple (NY 939640)
Pr(i)esdale, Priorsdale (NY 780411)
Proudehowe, Prudhoe (NZ 095629)
Ratonraw, Rattenraw (NY 830644)
Ravenwyk(e), Renwick (NY 597435)
Redesdale, Redesdale (NY 900852)
Riell, Ryal (NZ 013743)
Rokehope, Rookhope (NY 939429)
Roulyburn, Rowley Burn (NY 913578)
Roulye, Rowley, cf. Rowley Wood (NY 890557), Rowley Head (NY 907561)
Ryvaux, Rievaulx Abbey (SE 576850)
Sadlyngstanes, Settlingstones (NY 843683)
Salton, Salton (SE 717799)
Sandhill, Sandhill (NZ 252639)
Sandow, Sandhoe (NY 969662)
Sant John Le, St John Lee, church of (NY 933657)
Sant Maregate (in Corbridge), cf. St. Mary's Chare (NY 989643)
Scales, Scales (NY 571431)
Schaftow, cf. East Shaftoe (NZ 060817) and West Shaftor (NZ 044815)
Scheldeschaw, cf. Shield Hall (NY 954587), Shieldhall Wood (950588), and Shieldhall Fell (NY 956589)
Schellawe, Schellez, Schellis, cf. Shellbraes (NZ 001719)
Sclavelye, Slaley (NY 973577)
Seton, Seton Wodhorn, North Seaton (NZ 296866)
Sewyngscheles, Sewyngshelez, Sewing Shields (NY 810703)
Silkisworth, Silkysworth, Silksworth (NZ 376529)
Smalhopburne, Smallhopeburn (NZ 160482)
Sondreland, Sunderland, (NY 180356)
Stancroft, Stonecroft (NY 864683)
Stanfordham, Stamfordham (NZ 080719)

Gazetteer of the Black Book   281

Stanyngton, Stannington (NZ 213794)
Staynton in Strata, Great Stainton (NZ 337220)
Stelden(e), in Great Swinburn, lost.
Stele (Le), Steel Hall (NY 936566)
Stellyng, Stelling (NZ 050657)
Stillyngtongate (in Great Stainton), the road to Stillington (NZ 350223)
Stobflatte, cf. Stob Hill (NZ 088703)
Stokesfelde, Stokysfeld, Stocksfield (NZ 054613)
Stokeslay, Stokesley (NZ 526085)
Swynburn (West), Great Swinburn (NY 935755)
Swynburn Est, Little Swinburn (NY 949776)
Teket, Tecket (NY 865729)
Temelhope, Temple Heap (NY 641675)
Temple Thornton, Temple Thornton (NZ 104857)
Tepermore, cf. High Teppermore (NY 863715), Teppermoor Hill (NY 868722), Low Teppermoor (NY 877720)
Thrilwall, Thirlwall (deserted), cf. Thirlwall Castle (NY 660662).
Throkelaw, Throckley (NZ 158668)
Todryge, Todridge (NY 992718)
Tunstale, Tunstall (NZ 388534)
Tyndale, Tynedale
Ulgham, Ulgheham, Ulpham, otherwise known as Ulwham (NY 655607)
Ulkeston, Ouston (NZ 073706)
Wall, Wall (NY 917690)
Walwyk(e), Walwick (NY 903705)
Walwykwaye (in Warden), Homers Lane (NY 912670)
Wardoghall, Wardoughan, (NY 632652)
Wardoghalschaw, cf. Shawfield (NY 625649)
Wardon, Warden (NY 913665)
Wardrew, Wardrew Farm (NY 641683)
Wermouth, Bishop Wearmouth (NZ 390572)
Westgate, Westgate Road (NZ 247640)
Westheryngton, West Herrington (NZ 347531)
Whalton, Whalton (NZ 131814)
Wharnelye, cf. East Wharmley (NY 886667), West Wharmley (NY 881667)
Whitchestre, Whytchestre, Whitchester (NZ 099683)
Whynetle, Whynetleye, Whinnetley (NY 816650)

Whytfeld, Whitfield (NY 778585)
Whytlaw, Whitlow (NY 698484)
Whytley, Whytlye (molendinum de), Whitley Mill (NY 925582)
Whyttingeham, Whittingham (NU 066120)
Widryngton, Widdrington (NZ 253955)
Wodburne, Woodburn (NY 893868)
Wyndmylnstob (in Hexham), perhaps Windmill Hill (NY 932644)
Yarowryge, High Yarridge (NY 917624)
Yngowlande, cf. Ingoe (NZ 038748)
Yngowlech, cf. Ingoe (NZ 038748)
Yrthin water, River Irthing (NY 637676)

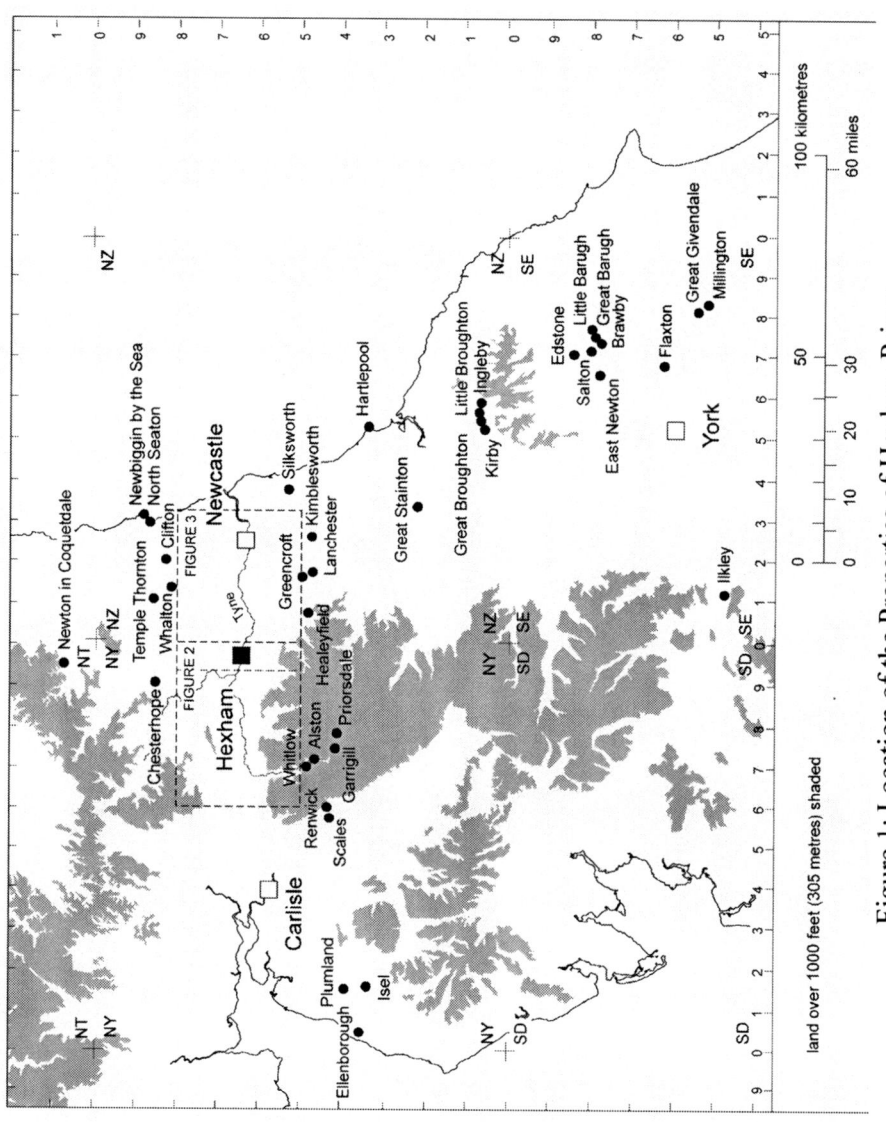

Figure 1: Location of the Properties of Hexham Priory

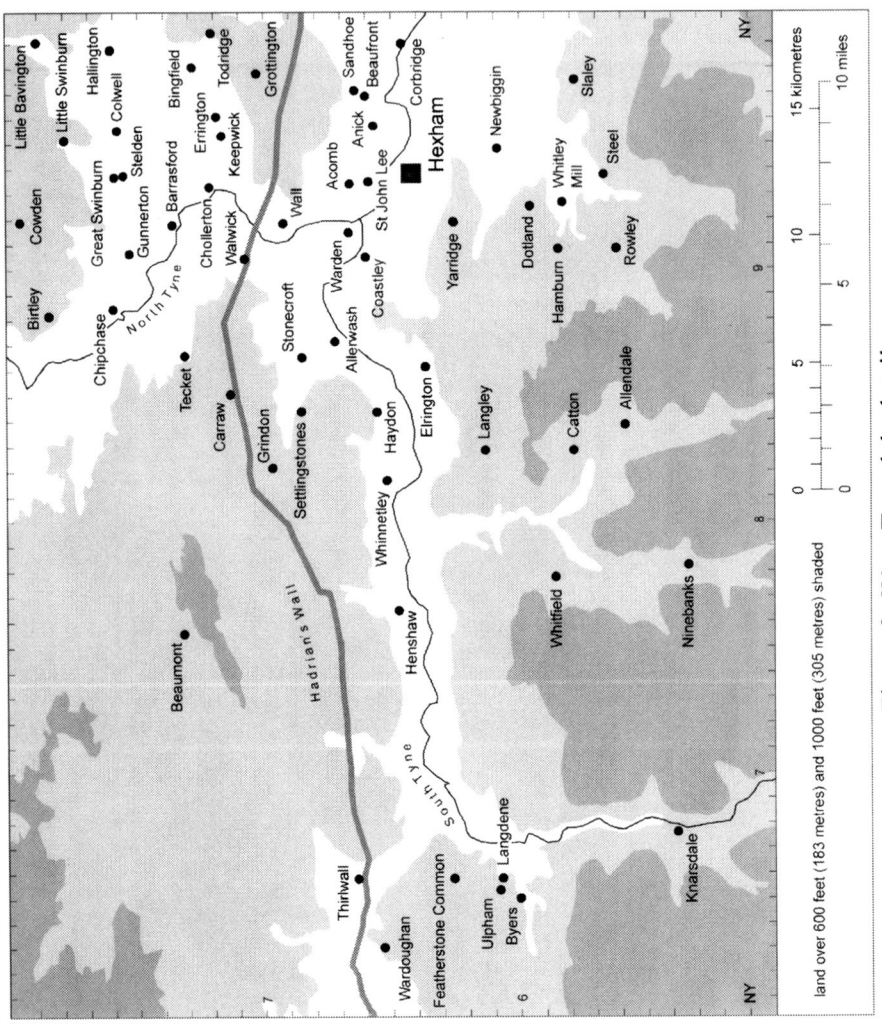

Figure 2: West Tynedale detail

INDEX

Acomb, 29, 40, 50, 87, 153, 180, 239; mill, 189, 196, 206; tithe barn, 19, 50, 156, 239
Ada, countess, 201-5, 269
Adam, Thomas son of, 215
advowsons, 18-19, 153, 217-19, 223-5, 240, 250, 255, 261, 264
Aguilf, knight, 200, 254; Nicholas, brother of Aguilf, 200
aid, common, 140, 147
Alan, Richard son of, 154
Aldesheles by Tecket, 57, 160, 239
Allendale, 1, 180, 189, 239; church or chapel, 186, 188, 193, 239
Allerdale, 151-2, 239, 249
Allerwash, 15, 156, 181, 239-40, 261; mill, 16-17, 28, 69-70, 156, 239; Uchtred of, 156, 239
Allerwasseschelez, 69, 71
Alston, 15, 17, 62-4, 153, 159, 205-6, 240, 262; church, 18-19, 153, 181-2, 224-5, 240, 250; mill, 63
Alston Moor, 3, 63, 172, 181, 240
Alwinton, 29, 50; church, 50, 89; glebe of, 19, 50; Diana, daughter of Roger of, 214;
Angus, earl of, 88-9, 101, 253, 255, 261; *and see* Umfra-ville
Anick, 1, 7, 9-12, 37-40, 42, 98, 150, 153, 155, 169-70, 179, 185, 188, 194, 196, 198, 222-3, 240-1, 246, 263, 270; brewery, 40; church, 185; court, 59, 62, 110; grange, 11, 37, 240; mill, 10, 16, 39-41, 240
Apperley, 163, 241, 266

Appleton, Robert of, 221, 246
arable land, compact or enclosed, 6, 3, 44, 71, 107, 144, 234, 260; dispersed, 4, 6, 13-14, 27, 43, 51-3, 55, 60-1, 74, 79-81, 88, 90, 93-4, 97-8, 101, 104-5, 125, 128-9, 131-3, 145-8, 165, 192, 245, 250, 255, 262-3, 266; *and see* closes
Ash Gill (*Eskgille*), 15, 63-4
assarts, 60, 155, 189-92, 196, 247
assize of bread and ale, 1, 51, 155, 194
Athol, Sir Aymer of, 26, 112
Augmentations, Court of, 182, 185
Aumale, William (le Gros), count of, 228-9, 248
Aukelandgate, 119
bakery (*pistrinum*), common, 140; *and see* oven
Balliol, Bernard I or Bernard II de, 94, 162, 260-1, 265; Hugh de, 162-3, 258; John de, 161, 215
Barnard Castle, 224
Barrasford, 17, 81-2, 85, 157, 181, 241; mill, 82; tithe barn, 19, 82, 239
Barugh, Great, 144, 235, 250, 263
Barugh, Little, 145, 235, 257, 263
Bataill, Stephen, 157; Theophania, 163; William, 155
Bavington, 87; Gilbert of, 221
Bavington, Little, 4, 88, 157, 257
Beauchamp, Walter de, king's steward, 163
Beaufront, 171, 241; park, 37

Beaumont, 15, 28, 77-8, 153, 157, 241
Beaumont, W. B., 25
Bek, Anthony, bishop of Durham, 218-9, 264
Bellasis, 93
Bellingham, William of, 221, 247
Belsay, Robert of, 234
Benedict, canon of Hexham, 227
Benwell, 2, 114, 160, 241-2
Bernard, prior of Hexham, 94, 152, 191, 211-14, 217-18, 228, 245, 254, 264
Bertram, Robert (1) and Mabel his wife, 231; Robert (2), 222; Roger, 161, 203, 260
Beukley (*Boclive, Boclyve*), 44, 47
Beverley, 188
Bingfield, 1, 4-5, 7, 9, 11-12, 21-2, 26, 42-6, 85, 155, 164, 171, 180, 196, 198, 242; church or chapel, 180, 183, 194; common brewery, 46; grange, 8, 44; mill, 16, 46; tithe barn, 19
Birkey Burn, 38, 188-9, 196, 240
Birtley, 17, 83, 156, 176, 181, 242; chapel, 20, 156, 242, 245; mill, 83
Bishopton, 120
Bitchfield, 161, 218, 242, 264
Black Book of Hexham, its appearance and make-up, 25, 28; its character and content, 26-7; damage to, 249; date and context, 20-2, 26; state of the text, 27-30;
title, 26; translation, 30-2
Black Burn (*Blakeburne, Mikleblakburne*), 66, 209
Black Burn, Little, 65-6

Black Death, 21-2
Blanchland Abbey, 182
Blencow, 77
Blenkinsopp, castle, 60
Bolam, barony of, 212; Aline of, 154, 157, 162, 212, 256; James of, 212
Bolbec, Sir Walter de, 160, 266
Boltby, Adam de, 68
bondsmen and bondlands, 7-9, 11, 99, 134-7, 140, 144-5, 242; size of bondlands, 9-10, 99; *and see* husbands and husbandlands
Borgoyne, William de, 94
Boso, William son of, 160, 163, 265-6
boundary stones, 56, 68, 70-1, 78, 89, 109, 112, 209, 233
bounds of property, 15, 44, 47, 49, 54, 56-68, 70-2, 77-8, 83, 89, 96, 103, 108, 112, 114, 116, 118, 121, 153, 156, 159, 188-9, 192, 196, 202, 205-7, 209, 211, 222, 233, 240-1, 243-4, 246, 251, 254, 256-8, 260-2, 265-8; of townships, 202; perambu-lation of, 222-3
boroughs, *see* burgage plots
bovates, 5, 9, 20, 64, 119-20, 126-8, 131-7, 139-47, 152, 156, 158, 161-2, 185, 227-9, 233-5, 240, 242, 244-5, 248, 250-1, 256-7, 259, 263, 266; size of, 9, 119, 126, 128, 131-4, 140, 142, 145, 147-8
Bowes, Adam of, 226, 257
Bradford, Everard of, 212
Brawby, 9, 17, 21, 140-2, 184, 236, 242, 263; mill (inoperative), 140, 142
Brenkley, 95, 98-100, 242-3; mill, 95, 161, 242; brewing, 40, 46, 53, 100, 124, 139, 142

breweries (*bracine*) and brewing (*bracinagium*), 40, 46, 53, 100, 124, 133, 139; *and see* assize of bread and ale
bridges, 53, 62-3, 71, 76-8, 104, 193, 205-6
Bridlington, *see* Peter
Broughton, Great, 6, 31, 128-30, 232-3, 250; grange, 129
Broughton, Little, 6, 9, 124-8, 130, 179, 232-3, 258; mill, 16, 124-8, 232-3, 258
Browney, River, 117
bullocks, 107
bulls, 4, 45, 85, 139, 245
burgage plots, 76-7, 92, 114-15, 246, 260
Burnhope Head, 15, 64
Burnton, William of, 94, 220
Burradon, 15, 89
Buteland, Richard of, 155
Byers, 4, 28-9, 65-8, 156, 209, 243, 257, 267; court, 15; park, 15, 65-6, 178, 243
Bywell, 41; barony of, 112, 260-1, 265, *and see* Balliol; John of, 212-14
Bywell St Andrew, 222
Cadeiou, Thurkill of, 158, 252
Calin, Robert, 153, 247
calves, 183
Cambo, John (1) of, 162, 213, 256; John (2) of, 219, 256; Robert of, 213, 220, 256; Robert, son of Hugh of, 221
Carlisle (*Karleol, Karleon*), 54, 58, 151, 243; diocese and bishop of, 182, 262; Caldewgate, 54; Dow-beck, 54
Carnaby, Sir Reginald, 181
Carraw, 15, 28, 30, 55-6, 159, 200, 243; mill, 16, 56;
Carraw Side, 159, 243

carucates, 9, 74, 89, 91, 153, 156-9, 161, 185, 200, 213-14, 220, 228-30, 234, 240, 245, 247-8, 254, 256, 260-1, 264, 266, 268
Carvoran, 61
castle guard, 76, 265
Catraw, 93
Catton, 29, 50, 187, 207, 244; tithe barn, 19, 50, 156, 244
Cauz, James de, and Alice his wife, 153, 157, 162, 212, 256; John de, 153, 212; Aline, wife of, *see* Aline of Bolam
chapels, *see* churches and chapels
Charron, Guiscard de, 154
charters cited in the Black Book, 45, 59, 68-9, 73-4, 84-5, 88, 95, 99, 101, 124, 145, 165; loss of, 155, 165, 198
Cheeseburn, 6, 17, 28, 39, 108-10, 161, 244, 259; chapel, 108, 244; grange, 14, 109, 174, 244
Chesterhope, 29, 31, 64-5, 157, 244
Chipchase, 82-3, 158, 181, 244; chapel, 20, 156, 244-5; tithe barn, 19, 83, 244
Chollerton, 5, 15, 77-9, 86, 153, 178, 181, 244-5, 241; church, 20, 156, 182, 244-6, 251, 256, 258; tithe barn, 19, 78
Christmas, renders due at, 11, 39, 41, 47, 137, 220, 235
churches and chapels, 18-20, 228; *and see* advowsons, Alston, Bingfield, Choller-ton, Garrigill, Haydon, Hexham, Ilkley, Langley, Ovingham, priests, St John Lee, Slaley, Stamfordham, Stonecroft, tithes and tithe barns, Warden

Clera, Ralph de, 230
Cleveland,
Clifton, 94, 245
closes, 36, 58, 116, 133, 165, 167-9, 172, 174, 176-7, 234, 255
coals, 56
Coastley, 50, 72, 180, 245
Coldcoats, 96
Coldstrother, 2, 7-9, 28, 86-8, 153, 157, 162, 164, 212-13, 220, 245, 256
Colwell, 4, 8, 45, 158, 164, 181, 245-6; chapel, 20, 86, 156, 245; tithe barn, 19, 85-6, 245
common aid, *see* aid
common pasture, *see* pasture
Comyn, Richard, 160, 200, 202, 243, 254, 266, 268
Conrad, archdeacon, 230
Consett (*Coksyd*), 118
Coquetdale (*Cookdale*), see Newton
Corbet, Walter, 157
Corbridge, 7, 13, 26, 37, 74, 76-7, 158, 222-3, 240, 246; the *Bisshopprek*, 37, 240, 246; Saint Mary Gate, 76
cottagers and cottages, 3, 7. 11-12, 21, 39, 46-8, 63, 68, 72-3, 79-80, 87, 98-100, 103, 106-7, 111, 123, 127, 130-2, 137-9, 141-3, 165-8, 175-6, 240, 242, 248, 250, 254, 256, 258-9, 263, 268; waste, 21, 46, 87, 106-7, 111-12, 124, 137, 142-3
Cottingham, John of, vicar of North Cave, 237, 270
courts, 51, 124, 126; *and see* Anick, Byers, Kirkheaton, Priorsfield, Salton, Silksworth

Cowden, 4, 83-4, 157, 166, 181, 246, 252
Cowden Burn, 83
Cowden Kirk, 83
cows, 4, 45, 55, 63, 69, 73, 84-5, 107, 139, 153, 157, 203, 205, 211, 245, 252, 268
Craklaw Moor, 4, 95, 158, 258
Craven, 135-6
crofts, nature of, 3
Crokedayk, Adam of, 154
Crook Burn, 15, 57, 64
Crook Head, 64
crosses, 52, 54, 79-80, 86, 105, 107, 130, 206; 'cross standing stone', 57-8
Crossgill Head, 15, 64
customary rights, 6
customary tenures, 10-11; *and see* bondlands, husband-lands, labour services
Dacre, William Lord, 178
Dalton, near Stamfordham, 7, 9-10, 22, 101-3, 108, 162, 173, 221-2; mill, 16-17, 102-4, 110-11, 173, 246; William of, 162, 246
Dalton (in Hexhamshire), 9, 49
Daltonway (in Cheeseburn), 109
David I, king of Scots, 151, 200, 243
Dead Stones ? (*Edestan*), 64
Delaval, Hugh, 161, 241; Richalda mother of Robert, 151, 160, 247; Robert son of Hubert, 151, 247; Thomas of, 160, 247; Sir William, 114
demesne land, 44, 56, 61-71, 74, 77-8, 83, 95-6, 108-9, 112, 114, 115-18, 121-2, 135-7, 140; arable, 6, 36-8, 40, 42-3, 44-5, 48-9, 51-3, 54-5, 57-63, 71-2, 76, 81-3, 88-91, 93-4,

97-8, 101, 103-5, 108-10, 111, 113, 118-20, 125, 128-134, 147-8, 165, 171, 192-3, 234, 240, 242, 254, 263; meadow, 37-8, 43, 49, 55, 59, 87-8, 91, 94, 98, 101, 103-6, 113, 118, 120, 124-5, 130-3, 143, 146, 193, 234, 240, 251, 254, 263; *and see* pasture
depopulation, 21
Dere Street, 40, 43, 47, 77, 83
Derlyng, Henry, 221, 248
Derlyngtonway (in Great Stainton), 120
Derwent, River, 52
Deulawrige; 113
Dewley, *see Deulawrige*
Dilston, 202; Thomas of, 187, 249; Sir Thomas of, 158, 217, 258
Dinley (lost), 83
Dipton (lost), 48
Dissington, 42, 96-7, 247; mill. 96-7, 99, 247
Dotland, 1, 9, 11-12, 16, 29-30, 47-9, 150, 153, 155, 171, 188-92, 194, 196, 198, 247, 253, 269; moor, 49; park, 14, 47, 49, 165, 195, 198-9, 247
Dove, River, 137, 140
Duns Moor, 44
Durham, 186; archdeaconry, 185; bishops and bishopric, 117, 156, 158, 178-9, 182, 186, 239, 253, *and see* Anthony Bek, Nicholas of Farnham, Thomas Hatfield, Hugh du Puiset; priory, 27, 115, 162, 184, 254, *and see* Hatfield Survey
Durhamgat (in Great Stainton), 119
Eachwick, 4, 6,8-10, 12, 31, 96-100, 108, 151, 153, 160, 174-5, 221-2, 247; brewing, 100; Thomas of, 160; William of, 154
Earl's House, 118
Easby, *see Esbymarche, Esbywaye*
Edstone, 134, 142-4, 184, 228-31, 248; church, 228-9, 248
Edward I, king of England, 154, 163-4, 217-9, 224-5, 240
Edward II, king of England, 219-21, 224-5, 240, 246
Edward III, king of England, 221-2, 225
eels, 150, 188
Eilaf I and II, priests, 185
Elias, John son of, of Stocksfield, 160, 266
Ellen, River (*Alne*), 53, 249
Ellenborough (*Alneburgh*), 53, 152, 248
Elrington, 28, 54, 207, 249; mill, 54, 160, 249
Elstob, 119
Elstob Lane, 119
Erring Bridge, 43, 77-8
Erring Burn, 43, 45, 78-9
Errington, 44, 181, 249
Errington, Ralph, 25
Esbymarche, Esbywaye, 131
Eshells, 87, 187-9, 249
estovers, 64, 118, 192
Eure, Sir Ralph de, 26, 96, 118
exchequer land, 48, 247
Fallowfield, 104
Farlington, Henry of, 95, 161, 243
farms, compact, 15; *and see* bounds
Farnham, Nicholas of, bishop of Durham, 161-2, 218-9, 242, 248, 253, 259, 261, 264
Farringdon Grange, 121-2, 178, 263v

Fawdon, John of, 99-101, 247, 252; Peter of, 160, 247
Featherstone and Featherstonehaugh (lost), 4, 68, 201, 207-8, 249, 269; Elias of, 207; Thomas of, 154, 208; Thomas son of, 154
Fenhall in Greencroft, 15, 116, 251
Fenwick, 22, 106-7; Thomas of, 161, 247
Fenwick Burn, 57
Fethreshaue (in Carraw, 15, 55, 243
fields, *see* arable lands, closes, demesne arable
final concords, 149, 211-14, 230-1, 234, 250
Fisher, Jon, 221, 246
fisheries, 76, 113-14, 151, 161, 176, 260-1
Fitz Mamaduke, Richard son of John, 264
Flaganclough, 60, 250
flats, definition of, 4-5
Flaxton, 5, 9, 124, 145-7, 234-5, 250, 263; Nicholas of, and Emma his wife, 234
foresters, 193
Forister, John, 7
Forne, *see* Sigulf
Fourstones, 181
freeholders and free tenements, 7, 68-9, 74, 98, 102, 110, 116, 121, 126, 144-5, 246-8, 256-7, 259
Garrigill (*Gerardgill*), 63, 153, 250; chapel, 1543 240, 250
geese, 183
Geoffrey, archbishop of York, 194, 231
Germund, 155, 194, 242

Giffard, Walter, archbishop of York, 156, 239, 244, 255, 260, 262, 267
Gilsland, lordship of, 15, 61, 66-7
Givendale, Great, 147-8, 151-2, 227, 250, 259, 263; mill dam at, 148; Gilbert of, 235
glebe land, 18-19, 42, 50, 52, 239, 262-3
Glendue, 61, 209
Glendue Burn, 15, 61, 66
Glendue Fell, 15
goats, 61, 159
Gofton, 56
Graham, Sir Henry de, 57, 160, 239
granges, 14, 129-30, *and see* Anick, Bingfield, Cheeseburn, Farringdon, North Milbourne, Stelling
Gray, Walter de, archbishop of York, 155-6, 187-94, 196, 239-40, 244, 247, 249, 255, 259-60, 262, 267, 269
Greencroft, 15, 116, 251
Greenfield, William, archbishop of York, 229
Greenhead, 60
Grendenmore (in Great Stainton), 119
Grendonrode, 121
Greystoke, barony of, 147
Grindon, near Settlingstones, 57, 251
Grindstone Law, 44
Grottington, 8, 26, 44, 47, 151, 155, 172, 194, 247, 251
Grottington, Little, *see* Todridge
Guisborough, *see* Richard
Gunnerton (*Gonwarton, Gunwardton*), 5, 32, 42, 50, 82-3, 158, 177, 181, 211, 244, 251-2; chapel, 20, 82, 156,

245, 252; moor, 84, 157, 216, 246, 251, 265; Peter of, 211; Ralph of, 157-8, 162, 246, 252; tithe barn, 19, 82, 158, 252

Hache, Eustace of, 163

Hadrian's Wall, 1, 15, 56, 60-1, 113, 200, 243-4

Hallington, 29, 50, 252; tithe barn, 19, 50, 156, 252

Halton, William of, 154, 187

Haltwhistle, 57-8

Hamburn, 252; mill, 155, 195, 198, 252, 259

Hamsteels, 117

Harbottle, 88-9

Harhaugh (*Hardhalgh*), 72

Harlow, 100, 222

Hart Burn, 91

Hartlepool, 119-20, 253

Hartley Burn, 15, 66

Hatfield, Thomas of, bishop of Durham, 226

Hatfield Survey of Durham bishopric estates, 25, 226, 257

Hawkwell, 108-9, 161, 218, 253, 264

hay, 7, 116, 119, 124, 126, 145, 183, 193, 207, 236, 242

Haydon, 4, 57, 69, 158, 164, 181, 253; chapel, 20, 156, 253, 268; tithes and tithe barn, 19, 69, 253

Haydon Bridge, 15, 57

Hazeldean, 155, 194, 247, 253

Healeyfield, 8, 115-16, 253; mill, 116

Heatherslaw Meadow, 103

Heaton, Little, 213

Heavenfield, church at, 19, 42

Heddon, 201

Heddon, Black, 103

Henry II, king of England, 152, 228

Henry III, king of England, 152-4, 155, 215, 240

Henry, earl of Northumber-land, son of David I of Scotland, 151, 200-2, 243

hens, 3, 11, 39, 41-2, 47-8, 137, 141, 183

Henshaw, 28, 57, 159, 200, 243, 254

Heron, Sir William, 26, 57, 77

Herrington, 121

Herrington, West, 7

Hesleden, Monk, 120

Hetson, William, 220

Heugh, 5-6, 31, 103-5, 254, 264

Hexham (*Hextildesham*), 8, 13, 35-7, 150-1, 153, 165-8, 194, 196, 198, 254; church or chapel and parish, 182, 185-6, 255; Cockshaw, 194, 254; Haining Croft, 36, 192, 198; Hencotes, 36, 155, 194, 198, 254; Market Street, 155, 194, 254; mill, 16-17, 37, 254; pilgrim hospital, 194, 254; Priest-popple, 13, 35-6, 155, 192, 194, 254; Pudding Row, 13, 36; Richard, bailiff of, 156, 261; St Giles hospital, 165, 254; St Giles Street, 198; the *Sele,* 187, 194-5, 197; *Westemoore,* 167-8; *Wyndmylnstob,* 36

Hexham Priory, 6, 155, 164-5 and *passim*; almoner, 55, 77, 88, 199; bursar, 82; cellarer, 16, 49, 53, 62, 73, 92, 94-5, 120-1; groceries (*species*), 117; income of, 2, 19-20, 166-86; jurisdiction of, 1, 51, 97, 155, *and see* courts; kitchen, 53, 62, 73, 92, 216; prior, personal requirements of, 66, 97, 116, 119, 126, 140-1, 147, *and see*, Bernard, John, Richard, Robert, William; sacrist, 62, 92, 114-16, 198; terrar, 105, 116, 119, 126

Hexhamshire, 1-2, 16, 35-51, 155, 180, 191, 207

Hextilda, wife of Richard Comyn, 200, 268

Hodgson, John, 25, 28-9, 56

Holme, 228-9, 231

homage and fealty, 7, 59, 62, 75, 84-6, 126, 162-3, 194

Homers Lane (*Walwykwaye*) in Warden,

horses,, 55, 61, 63, 69, 88, 107, 112, 116, 119-20, 126, 134, 139-40, 145, 153, 157, 159, 205, 211, 257; *and see* working beasts

Houghton-le-Spring, 123

Humshaugh (*Holmishalhraw*), 57

Huntercombe, Walter of, 163

husbands and husbandlands, 3, 5-8-9, 11-12, 16, 20, 39-41, 44-7, 49-50, 64, 68, 74-5, 80, 82, 87, 91, 93-4, 98-9, 102-3, 106, 110, 126, 132, 148, 234, 240, 242, 244-5, 247, 251, 254, 256, 258-9, 262-4, 267, 269; size of husbandlands, 9-10, 39, 41, 45, 47, 64, 87, 99, 102, 110, 122-3

Ilderton, Sir Thomas of, 7, 26, 86

Ilkley church and rectory, 19, 179, 223-4, 255

indentures, 77, 84, 118, 171, 174, 178-9

Ingleby Greenhow, 31, 131, 232-3, 255

Ingoe, mill, 175

Ingoe Land, 106

Ingoe Letch, 105

Irthing, River, 58

Isel, 22, 52-3, 255; common brewing, 53; church and glebe, 19, 255; park, 14, 52-3, 255; tithes, 20, 182

Iveston, Robert of, 160, 163, 267

John, king of England, 225

John, prior of Hexham, *see* John of Lasenby

Kearsley, 178

Keepwick, 29, 50, 180, 255; tithe barn, 19, 50, 156, 255

Kellah, 66-7

Kellah Burn, 67

Kimblesworth, 4, 118-19, 256

Kirkby (in Cleveland), 5-6, 28, 31, 128, 131-2

Kirkheaton, 2, 7-9, 12, 21, 26, 28, 86-8, 153, 157, 162, 164, 172, 212-13, 219-21, 245, 256, 245; chapel, 20, 156, 256; court, 86

Knarsdale, 2, 15, 28-30, 210, 256

labour services, 10, 39, 41, 45, 126-7, 134-5, 137-42, 145, 234-5

Lambley, 66, 210; priory, 65-6, 209-10, 243

Lancaster, Thomas, earl of, 225, 264

Lanchester, 117, 179, 226, 257 *Maydenstanhall* in, 15, 117, 179, 226, 257

Lanercost Prriory, 225

Langdene, 4, 15, 28, 67, 164, 267

Langhope, 50, 207

Langley, barony, 65-73, 181, 208, 243, 249, 257, 253, 257, *and see* Tindale; chapel, 20, 156, 257, 268

Langton, Walter, bishop of Coventry and Lichfield, 163

Lasenby, John of, prior of Hexham, 204, 216, 230, 234
lessees and leases, 7-8, 26, 44, 47, 52, 54-5, 60, 64-5, 73-4, 78, 116, 130, 192-3, 204-5, 229-30
Lewyn, John, 26, 117-18
Lincoln, dean and chapter, 224
Linn Burn, 43
Linnels Mill, 259, *and see* Newbiggin
Linnlaw, 91
Lisle, Robert de, 158, 161, 208, 215, 217, 244, 248, 259; Walter de, 157, 260; William de, 160, 267
long hundred, 45
Lovell, Richard, and Isabel his wife, 218
Lucy family, 4, 68, 249; Thomas de, 68
Maiden Way, 15, 61, 66, 209
Maltby, 135
manors and townships, 3
market towns, 13, *and see* burgage plots
marl pits, 79, 81, 95
Marton, Ernisius, prior of Marton, 227
Matfen, 7, 12, 22, 31, 41-2
Matfen, East, 21-2, 106-8, 161, 176, 218, 221, 247-8, 264
Matfen, West, 176, 248
Maungevillein, Robert, 154-5
Maydenstanhall in Lanchester, *see* Lanchester
meadow, nature of, 6-7
Meaux, Philip abbot of, 229
Melkridge 57; Burn, 58
Melton, William, archbishop of York, 197, 268
Merk, John of, 163

Merlay, family chantry, 245; Ralph de, 151; Robert de, 245; Roger de, 152, 161, 264-5
Middleton, John of, 7, 84
Milbourne, 95; Burn, 95-6; *Byresfeld*, 28, 96; Grange, 28, 95-6, 158, 164, 172, 217, 258
Millington, 147, 152, 228, 235, 251, 258-9, 263
mills, 16-17, 50, 54, 82-3, 95-7, 116, 129, 148, 150, 153, 155, 160, 175, 189, 192, 201, 206, 211, 245, 258; and see Allerwash, Anick, Bingfield, Little Broughton, Carraw, Dalton, Hamburn, Hexham, Nafferton, New-biggin, Plumbland, Salton, Silksworth, Whitley,
Minsteracres, Gilbert of, chaplain, 100, 221-2, 252
mortmain, grants in, 99, 101, 158-9, 215, 217, 219-22, 224-6, 246-7, 252, 255, 261
Mowbray, William de, 232, 250, 256, 258; William, son of William,. 232
Muggleswick, 115, 253-4
Nafferton, 97, 260; mill, 16, 112, 259
Natrass Gill, 62, 205
neifs, 12-13, 39-42, 45, 48, 87, 99
Nenthead, 15
Nesbit (lost), 9, 17, 21, 108-11, 161, 173-4, 215-16, 218, 221, 244, 259, 264; Walter, son of Walter of, 215
Netherton, 89
Neville, Alexander, archbishop of York, 255
Newbiggin, in Hexhamshire, 260; mill, 16, 49, 155, 195, 198, 259

Newbiggin by the Sea, 13, 92-4, 162, 259-60
Newbrough, 55, 181
Newburn, 113-14, 161, 176, 260
Newcastle upon Tyne, 13, 114-15, 154, 158, 163, 175, 260; castle guard at, 265; leper hospital of St Mary Magdalene, 113; Sandhill, 114; Westgate, 115, 260
Newlands, in Hexhamshire, 49, 269
Newminster Abbey, 85, 159, 211, 216, 265
Newton, in Coquetdale, 9, 15, 88-9, 157, 214, 260
Newton, in Givendale, 234
Newton, East, 227, 235, 248, 263
Newton, John of, 234; William of, 235
Newton Hall, 112
Ninebanks, 29, 50, 260; tithe barn, 19, 50, 156, 260
Noonstones, 15, 64
Normanby church, 236
Normanville, family, 221; John de, 153, 161, 163, 215, 218, 244, 254, 259, 264, 266
Northnewton, 15
Nubbock (Shields), 49
Oakwood, 28, 188, 192, 194, 196, 198
oats, 193
Ogle, Robert of, 26, 50, 55, 94, 102
orchards, 36, 118, 125, 133, 165, 256, 258
osier beds. 140
Otterington, North or South, 136
Ouston (*Ulkeston*), 2, 31, 108-9, 161, 218, 261, 264
oven (*furnum*), common, 124, 139; *and see* bakery

Ovingham, 183, 261; church, 19, 182, 223-4; fishery, 76, 261; tithe barn, 183
Owmers, 15, 28, 70, 156, 261
Owmers, Little, 15, 71, 261
oxen, 4, 45, 69, 73, 84-5, 107, 109, 118, 120, 122, 157, 192, 211, 245, 268; *and see* working beasts
Oxford, Balliol College, 103
oxgangs, *see* bovates
palfrey, prior's, 140-1, 147
pannage, 40, 42, 83, 151, 153
parks, 14-15, *and see* Byers, Dotland, Isell, Sewing Shields, Warden
pasture, common, 3-4, 6, 20, 38, 45, 48-9, 52, 56, 60-1, 63-5, 68-9, 73, 75, 78, 85, 88-9, 91-2, 95, 100, 107-8, 112, 116-18, 153, 156-9, 161, 165-78, 188, 190, 192, 196, 200-1, 205-6, 209, 211, 213, 239-41, 243, 246, 249, 251-3, 255-8, 265, 267-9; several, 15, 38, 43-4, 66-7, 70, 105, 122, 138, 240, 243
peateries and peats, 49, 53, 75, 108, 195, 198, 211, 255, 261
Penrith, 115
Percy, lordship, 222; Henry, earl of Northumberland, 19, 223, 255, 261
Peter, brother of the prior of Bridlington, 186
pigs, 61, 69, 107, 159, 194; *and see* pannage
ploughland, *see* arable land, bovate, carucate
Plumbland, 53; mill, 16-17, 53, 261
Poltross Burn, 61
Pont l'Évêque, Roger de, archbishop of York, 187, 230

Pont, River, 47, 109-10
Ponteland, 96
priests, 42, 50, 72-3, 94, 100, 114, 128, 131, 137-8, 143-4, 173, 177-8, 185, 203-4, 218, 223, 228, 236-7
Priorsdale (*Presdale*), 9, 15, 29, 63-4, 153, 159, 240, 261-2; court, 63
Prudhoe, 76, 89, 162, 175, 262, 241-2, 252-3, 256, 258, 262; *and see* Umfraville
Puiset, Hugh de, bishop of Durham, 187
Raine, James, 25, 27-31
Rainton, Thomas of, 100
Ralph, son of Ralph, 228
Rattenraw, 69
rectories, 18-19, 51-2, 179, 184, 225, 237, 255, 262-3; *and see* tithe and tithe barns
Redbourne, William of, 229
Redesdale, 29, 64, 89, 111
Renwick (*Ravenwyk*), 51-2, 262-3
Ribil, Robert of, 163
Richard, John son of, of Little Swinburn, 216-17, 265
Richard II, king of England, 223-4
Richard, prior of Guisborough, 186
Richard, prior of Hexham, 150, 152, 185-6, 227, 265, 270
Riddlesdale, 88
Rievaulx Abbey, 129-30, 232-3
rigs, defined, 5, 44
Riplington, 161, 262
Rither, William of, 163
Robert, chaplain of Countess Ada, 201-4, 269; Matthew his son, *see* Matthew of Whitfield
Robert (of Whelpington), prior of Hexham, 236

Romeyn, John le, archbishop of York, 195
Rookhope, 46
Rowley (lost), 9, 29, 50, 55, 189, 262, 269; tithe barn, 19, 50, 156, 262
Rowley Burn, 49
Ryal, 43
rye, 192
Ryscheles in Henshaw, 28, 57-8, 159, 243, 254
St John Lee, church or chapel of, 19, 42, 180, 183, 262
salmon, 183
Salton, 7, 9, 11, 21, 28, 32, 133-41, 143, 182, 184, 235, 262-3; brewing, 133, 139; chapel and rectory, 184, 234, 236, 263; court, 134-5, 140, 146-7, 235; mill, 11, 16, 134-5, 137, 139-40, 144-5, 234-5, 263; manorial officers, 135; prebend of, 2, 151-2, 154, 182, 227-8, 234-7, 242, 248, 250, 257, 259, 263, 270
Sandhoe, 1, 6, 9, 11-12, 22, 40-2, 45-6, 150, 153, 155, 169, 179, 189, 194, 196, 240-1, 263, 270
Scales, 52, 263
Scheldeschaw, 74-5
Scots, 194; invasions by, 21, 153, 164, 197, 224-5
Scrope, Henry, 92
Seaton, Adam of, 94; Helen of, 94; Robert (1) of, 120, 151-2; Richalda, mother of, 151; Robert (2) of, 220
Seaton, North (*Seton Wodhorn*), 94-5, 162, 164, 220, 260-1
Settlingstones, 28, 55, 156, 263; Adam of, 156, 263
Sewing Shields, park, 15, 55

Shaftoe, 87-8; William of, 221, 258-9
sheep and wool, 4, 45, 55, 63, 69, 73-5, 84, 88, 91, 118, 153, 157-8, 161, 180, 183-4, 205, 211, 216-17, 236, 240, 242, 245, 253, 256-7, 265, 268
sheepcotes and sheepfolds, 37-8, 40, 43, 48, 75, 84, 96, 107, 134, 140, 196, 216, 264-5
Sigulf, Forne son of, and Ivo his son, 151-2, 259
Silksworth, 5, 9, 14, 121-4, 164, 225, 263-4; common brewing, 124; court, 124; mill, 16-17, 122-3
Simonburn, 239
Skipton, Robert of, 155, 242
Slaley, 4-5, 7, 9, 45, 74-5, 164, 176, 181, 211-12, 264-5; church or chapel, 158, 181-3, 264; Gilbert of, 158, 264
Smallhopeburn, 116-17
Stainton, Great, 6, 119-21, 179, 251
Stamfordham, 103-4, 161, 254, 259, 261, 264; church, 18, 153, 161, 217-9, 242, 253-4
Stanbridge, Hugh of, 218
standing stones, 67, 83, 104; *and see* boundary stones
Stannington, 5-6, 9, 20, 31-2, 93-4, 152, 161, 177, 264-5; church, 94, 245
Steel, 4, 45, 75, 158, 264-5
Stelden (lost), in Great Swinburn, 7, 84-5, 159, 216-17, 251, 155, 194, 265
Stelling, 41-2, 112, 162, 174, 213, 265
Stephen, king of England, 151
Stillyngtongate, 119
Stirling, Sir John of, 7-8, 26, 86, 116

Stobflatte, 108
Stocksfield, 7, 75-6, 160, 163, 176, 265-6
Stokesley, 132
Stonecroft, 28, 54, 159, 200, 244, 266; chapel, 20, 156, 266, 268
Stonecroft Burn, 54
Stonegrave, 227; Sir J. of, 235; William of, 227
Sunderland (in Cumbria), 52-3
Sunnulfus, priest, 152, 270
Sweethope, William of, 154
Swinburn, Great (West), 78-80, 84-6, 158, 211, 268; castle, 86; chantry chapel, 162; Nicholas of, 162; *and see Stelden.*
Swinburn, Little (East), 84-5, 162-3, 216, 258, 265; chapel, 20, 156, 245, 258; synodal dues, 184, 230; tithe barn, 19, 85, 163, 258; John of, 162
Tecket, 57, 160, 266; Laurence of, 160, 266
Tees, River, 15, 64
Templars, 130
Temple Heap, 58
tenements, waste, 36, 50, 52, 54, 92, 94, 147; *and see* cottages, tofts, waste land
Teppermoor, 56
Teye, Walter of, 64
Thirlwall, 15, 17, 28, 58-60, 159, 162, 164, 266-7; castle, 59, 267; mill, 59, 267; Brice of, and Roger his son, 159, 162, 266-7; Richard, 162; Richard, son of Brice of, 163; Roger, son of Brice, 159, 162; Thomas, son of Richard son of Brice, 163

Thomas II, archbishop of York, 20, 153, 155, 191, 194, 230, 239-40, 254-5, 263, 270
Thoresby, John, archbishop of York, 199
Thorngrafton, Adam of, 156, 201, 269
Thornton, Thomas son of Robert of, 214
Thornton in Tynedale, 200, 214
Thornton, Temple, 4, 6, 21, 28, 30-1, 89-91, 160, 178, 266
Throckley, 27, 113, 160, 163, 267; Aylmer of, 267; Christine of, 160, 163, 267; Robert of, 163, 267
Thurstan, archbishop of York, 150, 153, 155, 194, 230, 242, 247, 250-1, 253, 263
Thwing, John of, vicar of Salton, 236
Tindale, Adam I of, 162, 200-1, 209, 269; Adam II of, 188, 208; Adam I or Adam II of, 20, 156, 158, 243, 253, 257, 266, 268
Tipalt Burn, 60
tithes and tithe barns, 18-20, 43, 53, 69, 78, 82-3, 85-6, 125, 134, 155, 158, 161, 163, 179-84, 191, 196, 200, 207, 225, 234, 236, 239-42, 244-6, 248-9, 252-3, 255-62, 264, 267
Todridge, 43-4. 151, 155, 194, 251; *and see* Grottington
tofts, nature of, 3; waste, 21, 53, 74, 88-9, 91, 93, 98-9, 103, 111
township (*villa*), characteristics of, 2-3; common lands of, 4; fields of, 14
Tregoz, John 163
Tunstall, 123

turbaries and turfs, 53, 56, 75, 100, 105, 255
Turpin, Richard. 154
Twithe, Hugh of, 228, 230, 248
Tyne, River, 15, 36-7, 62-4, 71-2, 77, 82, 113-14, 150-1, 153, 161, 189, 192, 194, 205-6
Tynedale, 200; barony of, 1, 208; William of, 154; *and see* barony of Langley
Ulf, William son of, 151, 227-8, 250
Ulpham, or Ulwham, 4, 15, 28, 66-8, 267
Umfraville, Gilbert de, 85, 89, 153, 157, 163, 200, 202, 223, 241, 244, 253, 255, 261; Margery de, 157, 241; Odinel I and Odinel II, barons of Prudhoe, 20, 156, 200, 244-6, 252, 256, 258; Richard de, 157, 162, 187, 242, 246, 262
Vaux, Peter de, 188-9, 191, 196
Vieuxpont, Ivo de, 54, 62, 153, 159-60, 205-6, 225, 240, 249-50, 262; Nicholas de, 54, 249; William de, 225
Wall, 29, 50, 180, 267; tithe barn, 19, 50, 156, 267
Waltheof and Alan his son, 151, 249
Waltheof, Uhtred son of, 200
Walwick, 4, 28, 71, 73-4, 164, 200, 268
Warden, 28, 71-3, 156, 177, 268; boat, 73, 269; church, 20, 156, 182, 253, 257, 266, 268; park, 15, 71-2, 268
Warden, High, 71-2
Wardoughan, (*Wardoghall*), 3, 60-1, 268
Wardrew, 15, 58, 266
waste land, 21-2, 40, 42, 44, 52-3, 59-61, 64, 74-5, 88, 94, 99,

102, 106, 110, 121, 125, 140, 142, 145, 147, 195-6, 198, 201-2, 255, 264; *and see* cottages, tenements, tofts
Waukelin, William son of, 211
Wearmouth, Bishop, 122
West Riding, archdeaconry, 150-1, 230
Whalton, 4, 9, 91-2, 161, 175, 262, 268
Wharmley, 72
wheat, 192-3
Whetewang, 195, 269
Whinnetley, 68-9, 156, 269
Whitchester, 4, 100, 111, 222
Whitfield, 7, 62, 159, 173, 201-5, 269; mill, 201-2; Matthew of, 173, 187, 201, 203-5, 269
Whitfield, Matthew, 7
Whitley, 1; mill, 16-17, 47-9, 189, 198, 249, 269
Whitlow, 28, 62, 200-1, 269-70; Adam of, 163, 269; William of,
Whittingham, 41
Widdrington, Roger of, 26, 44, 85-6; Sir John, 181
William, Walter son of, and Isabel his wife, 161, 262, 268
William I, king of Scots, 159, 163, 201-3, 205-6, 243, 262, 269
William, chaplain of Geoffrey archbishop of York, 231
William, prior of Hexham, 188, 230
windmill, 122
Woodburn, John of, 94
woods, 48, 52, 64-5, 70, 71, 114-16, 133, 199, 204, 206, 226, 247, 253, 257, 263
Worcester, Gilbert of, 158, 258; John of, 158, 162

working beasts (*averia*), 55, 61, 64-5, 69, 78, 84, 89, 100, 157, 159, 210, 246, 253, 257
Wydon, 249
Yarridge, 9, 49, 150, 153, 155, 170, 188, 194, 240, 263, 270
Yetholm, Nicholas of, 154
Ylving, Patrick son of, 211
York, 218, 231, 235, 237, 270; archbishops of, 1, 20, 35, 165, 190, 193-9, 228, 247, 255, 268, 270, *and see* Geoffrey, Walter Giffard, Walter de Gray, William Greenfield, William Melton, Alexander Neville, Roger de Pont l'Évêque, John le Romeyn, Thomas, John Thoresby, Thurstan; cathedral and chapter, 150, 155, 182, 195, 227-8, 237, 263; Goodramgate, 231, 270; Ogleforth, 235; Robert, dean of, 227; vicars choral, 237; Alan of, smith,and Alice his wife, 213

Lightning Source UK Ltd.
Milton Keynes UK
UKOW01f0421130117
292001UK00001B/34/P

9 780956 507839